Forensic Identification and Criminal Justice

Forensic Identification and Criminal Justice
Forensic science, justice and risk

Carole McCartney

WILLAN
PUBLISHING

Published by

Willan Publishing
Culmcott House
Mill Street, Uffculme
Cullompton, Devon
EX15 3AT, UK
Tel: +44(0)1884 840337
Fax: +44(0)1884 840251
e-mail: info@willanpublishing.co.uk
website: www.willanpublishing.co.uk

Published simultaneously in the USA and Canada by

Willan Publishing
c/o ISBS, 920 NE 58th Ave, Suite 300
Portland, Oregon 97213-3786, USA
Tel: +001(0)503 287 3093
Fax: +001(0)503 280 8832
e-mail: info@isbs.com
website: www.isbs.com

Hardback
ISBN-10: 1-84392-184-7
ISBN-13: 978-1-84392-184-4

British Library Cataloguing-in-Publication Data

A catalogue record for this book is available from the British Library

Project management by Deer Park Productions, Tavistock, Devon
Typeset by GCS, Leighton Buzzard, Beds
Printed and bound by T.J. International, Padstow, Cornwall

Contents

Acknowledgements

The research for this book involved holding in-depth interviews with 14 respondents, chosen for their intimate involvement with both the criminal justice system, policy developments, and fingerprinting and DNA analysis. The data gathered from these individuals has informed the following chapters, with direct quotes (always reproduced anonymously). Their co-operation was invaluable and their views and insights represented faithfully.

This research would not have been possible without financial support from the Brian Hogan Scholarship (2001–2004) at the School of Law, University of Leeds, and an ESRC Post-Doctoral Fellowship (2004–2005). I was also in receipt of invaluable support from colleagues, in particular, Prof. Clive Walker. However, it would not have come to fruition had I not married an unrivalled husband and father, and had two beautiful daughters, who provide all the motivation and encouragement one could wish for.

Introduction

Forensic science and forensic identification technologies

Although considered largely a twentieth-century innovation, the use of medical evidence in courts, usually furnished by ill-prepared surgeons testifying to the cause of death, dates back to the Middle Ages (Forbes 1985), with foundations laid by scientists such as Edmund Locard (1877–1966) whose 'Principle of Exchange' (that every contact leaves a trace) paved the way for forensic science. The American-favoured term 'criminalistics', as the science dealing with the recognition, collection, identification, individualisation and interpretation of physical evidence, and the application of the natural sciences to law-science matters, originated in the book *Handbuch fur Untersuchungsrichter als System der Kriminalististik* (3rd edn, 1898) by Hans Gross (NIJ 2004: 2). From these beginnings, as understanding of the true extent of the unreliability of human memory has grown, at the same time as scientific and technological power and knowledge have increased, scientific methods of criminal detection have been developed, until the contribution of science to the detection of both major and volume crime is now lauded as 'clear and substantial' (Blakey 2002: vi).

Forensic science can be considered broadly as the application of natural and physical sciences to the resolution of legal conflicts (not limited to the criminal courts, but increasingly used in civil litigation and other regulatory matters), with the House of Lords Select Committee on Science and Technology outlining the task of forensic science as 'to serve the interests of justice by providing scientifically based evidence relating to criminal activity'.[1] The Forensic Science Service (FSS), the primary provider of forensic science services in England and Wales, considers itself an integral part of the criminal justice system, with its mission 'to provide forensic science information and expertise to support the investigation and detection of crimes and the prosecution of offenders, and to contribute to the prevention, deterrence and reduction of crime' (FSS 2001: xi). They also state that their vision is 'to realise the full potential of forensic science to contribute to a safer and more just society', thus giving themselves a much larger potential sphere of influence (an influence yet to be fully explored and examined).

Scientific detection methods originate in a variety of scientific disciplines and have included the analysis of an almost infinite variety of 'exhibits', including the 'numerical, descriptive and photographic recording of bodily characteristics …' of suspects, victims and witnesses (Valier 2001: 247). There is potentially no limit to the scope of physical evidence (or 'trace' evidence) that can be utilised by forensic scientists, from the smallest fragment of glass, to the most obscured fingerprint, to the tiniest swab of human tissue, to the entire scene of a major explosion or the realms of cyberspace. In addition, there are no exclusions which curtail the number of disciplines that may be utilised in a forensic investigation. Most often, forensic science is a sub-discipline of a larger scientific body such as pathology, odontology, toxicology, serology or genetics. There are also 'experts' who may be called upon to testify on matters at hand (such as forged documents, firearms, etc.), each being a 'forensic specialist' for the purposes of a criminal trial. Indeed, the list of potential 'experts' is almost boundless, with even estate agents having testified as 'forensic housing experts'.[2] Many are able to apply for registration with the Council for Registration of Forensic Practitioners (CRFP), which has deliberately been left open 'to all types of forensic practitioner who give expert evidence anywhere in the UK', with a view to producing an 'inclusive register'.[3]

---

1   See House of Lords Select Committee on Science and Technology (session 1992–93) 5th Report: *Forensic Science*. [HL 24, 24-I & 24-II] para. 1.5.
2   Example used by Justice Hooper (2002) 'Expert Witnesses – a view from the judiciary', paper presented to the conference *The Challenge of the Auld Report: Expert Witnesses Under Review*, London, April.
3   Council for the Registration of Forensic Practitioners (2001) *Introductory booklet*: 2.

The variety of methods employed in forensic investigation and the number of specialities involved have tended to obscure the reality that the most commonly used forensic scientific evidence takes the form of bodily samples such as fingerprints, urine, hair samples, mouth swabs, and breath or blood samples. Significant developments in the identification of individuals since the advent of fingerprinting, and the resulting legal reforms enacted in the wake of DNA testing in particular, make the critical assessment of the use of such technologies and their evidential impact essential. This book then focuses upon the forensic identification technologies of fingerprinting and DNA typing as the two identification technologies most often relied upon in criminal investigations. With emergent identification technologies (often referred to as 'biometrics') such as iris identification, facial 'mapping', or voice recognition – yet to be proven reliable – their use is consequently restricted at present, though pilots and security upgrades are increasingly utilising such biometric technologies (Aas 2004). In contrast, the use of fingerprinting by Scotland Yard dates back to 1902, and its use has been widely accepted for decades, their reliability, and trusted status, just like that of forensic science in general, remaining intact in the face of recent scrutiny:

> Stories, both fictional and factual, detailing the use of science to catch criminals flood our television screens, showing the public's endless fascination with forensic science. This fascination seems to go hand in hand with faith in its reliability. However mundane and 'unscientific' it really is, fingerprinting appears to benefit from this faith. Just as the criminal justice system managed to continue its day to day functioning unperturbed in the wake of widespread media coverage given to miscarriages of justice in the early 1990s, so the skeletons in the fingerprinting's closet seem unlikely to make much difference to its successful deployment. (Redmayne 2002b: 150)

Whilst DNA is hailed as the 'holy grail' of identification techniques, the more humble fingerprint retains its status as the most commonly utilised method of forensic identification and despite controversy over the standard required before a 'match' can be declared, it remains unassailable in the criminal courts as a unique identifier, although methods of collection or negligent interpretation means that it has given rise to appeals, particularly in the US. Domestically, the fingerprint 16-point standard also gave rise to challenges, resulting in *R* v. *Buckley*,[4] which removed the numerical standard.

The perception of DNA evidence as infallible now also pervades popular culture and has permeated the criminal process. Portrayals of DNA being able to solve crimes almost instantaneously, beyond any doubt (even from 'beyond the grave'), are increasingly common. The very same evidence that can remove a suspect from an inquiry, or prove persuasive at appeal, is also an almost insurmountable hurdle when presented as evidence of guilt. In tandem, legislative reform and case law since the advent of criminal DNA profiling in the late 1980s, and the inception of the England and Wales National DNA Database (NDNAD) in 1995, has: repeatedly expanded the list of those from whom DNA samples may be taken; downgraded the authority required to sanction and perform sampling; increased access to the database; as well as permitting samples (in addition to the resulting profile) to be retained indefinitely. Provisions in the *Criminal Justice Act* 2003 permitting the taking and retention of fingerprints and DNA samples from all arrestees, then came as little surprise.

Portrayals of the infallibility of DNA and its unrivalled ability to 'solve' crime have led to determined effort and financial investment to significantly increase the use of DNA evidence in court and as a tool of detection through the NDNAD. Indeed, the 'Forensic Integration Strategy' from the Home Office Science Policy Unit (2004: 18) aims to 'achieve a step change in the impact of forensic science on police performance in order to make major contributions to crime reduction and closing the justice gap'. This book therefore traces the advent of forensic identification technologies in the criminal justice system, elucidating the uses of forensic identification technologies, their proliferation, and increased utilisation. It will detail the legal developments relating to, and in consequence of, the growing deployment of forensic identification technologies. Overarching the book is the critical analysis of the wholesale adoption of forensic identification technologies, their shortcomings and fallibilities as well as ethical issues, highlighting their potential for creating injustice in contrast to their stated rationale and beliefs in their infallibility.

For a while the 'revolution' of DNA typing at first appeared to offer an end to queried identifications in criminal investigations, parental disputes, and immigration cases (where it originated). However,

---

4   *R* v. *Buckley* (1999) 143 SJ LB 159.

the use of DNA profiles had an uncertain start and, while now more sophisticated, still retains features which render its reliability less than 100 per cent. Despite this, DNA typing has captured the public imagination as a way of convicting serious offenders, while the Forensic Science Service (FSS) and Her Majesty's Inspectorate of Constabulary (HMIC) recommend its increased use in clearing up 'volume crime'.[5] In line with this confidence, the Prime Minister announced in September 1999 that an extra £109 million would be provided for the 'DNA Expansion Programme' to be commenced in April 2000, committing the government to an expenditure of £182.6 million to increase the collection of DNA samples and to build up the NDNAD. This money was in addition to £19 million per annum from individual police forces. The 'aim' of the programme was to input 3 million samples onto the NDNAD by April 2004, or 'a DNA profile for all known active suspect offenders'.[6] Until then, the cost of processing samples had limited the tests to only those suspected of serious crimes. The total value of government investment in the programme to March 2005 was £240.8 million, with polices forces adding £90 million from their own budgets (FSS 2004). Monetary support, coupled with legislative reform permitting the taking of samples from a broader spectrum of suspects, and their retention, has enabled exponential growth of the NDNAD.

Whilst this book considers both fingerprints and DNA profiles together, they remain qualitatively different, with DNA possessing properties that raise ethical and social concerns not readily applicable to fingerprints. DNA can indicate sensitive information, such as propensity to disease, hereditary markers, and familial relations, with such information able to be derived from minute quantities of human tissue, shed involuntarily by everyone. Racial and ethnic categories can also be determined from DNA profiles, as well as other information, such as skin tone and hair and eye colour. Additionally, DNA is durable, retaining its informational content for long periods (Kimmelman 2000: 209). Such distinctions do militate against direct comparison with fingerprints, but this book concentrates upon the wider societal and legal context of forensic identification evidence and its use in criminal justice processes, along with its ability to be

---

5 See FSS (2001) *Annual Report* (http://www.forensic.gov.uk/forensic_t/ inside/about/docs/00-01.pdf); HMIC (2002).

6 Caroline Flint, Ministerial Written Answers, Hansard, HC (series 5), vol. 426, col. 298W (3 November 2004).

databased, rather than the finer detail of the technologies. This is not to deny the specific problems of DNA over and above those of fingerprints, and these shall be considered where relevant, but the focus shall be on its wider implications rather than individual instances where DNA and fingerprints differ. Similarly, there are different DNA profiling technologies in use, and emergent technologies (such as Single Nucleotide Polymorphisms, or 'SNPs' technology), which will not be considered in great detail but their potential will be explored in brief in the concluding chapter.

Forensic identification in the risk society

The rapid expansion of the National Fingerprint Identification System (now known as IDENT1) and the NDNAD, and the significant public expenditure and rhetoric concerning their utility is best understood within the theoretical tenets of the 'risk society'. Legal and social control developments have been fostered by advances in forensic science, and surveillance and databasing technologies, which are altering system priorities where 'risk society promises a world in which fail-safe risk technologies rather than fallible people rule' (Ericson and Haggerty 1997: 53). Such developments downplay or deny the applicability of the problems of 'scientism'[7] to forensic science. Scientism, representing a belief that science is the only reliable path to truth, has gained a foothold in the criminal justice system as in wider society, with reliance upon 'scientific' methods to detect crime, monitor offenders and 'predict' dangerousness and risk. This 'blinding by science' of criminal justice professionals and the public (including juries) has reduced public resistance to reforms aimed at introducing inquisitorial processes and has ensured widespread acceptance of the explicit justifications for the NDNAD, which may ultimately lead to the creation of a compulsory and comprehensive national DNA database.

Thus, to present a coherent understanding of the role of forensic identification technologies in the modern criminal process without discerning wider trends in that process, and observing social as well as legal developments, would be perfunctory at best and misleading at worst: 'the incorporation of this scientific technique

---

7 The inappropriate transfer of methods from the natural to the social sciences.

into the evidentiary network must be set within the context of wider developments within the criminal law ...' (Redmayne 2001: 209). As Johnson *et al.* (2003: 26) stress:

> any effort to understand the trajectory of the technical application and operational implementation of the set of scientific innovations that constitute DNA profiling and databasing in the UK requires a dense – and sociologically sensitive – account. This account needs to attend to the interwoven series of technical, legislative, and organisational changes which have underpinned its development.

Social structures traditionally providing meaning from uncertainty and reassurance in confusion (i.e. the church), have been losing popular support in recent decades, while societal dependence on science has increased:

> modern societies rely on scientific knowledge and concepts for their stability in a way which previous societies depended on religion, or political and social tradition ... There is a real social need and desire for certainty and security of the kind that traditional sources of religious and political authority used to provide. (Ashworth 1997a: 1)

The vision of science as a positive force shaping the future of society, as outlined in Daniel Bell's *The Coming of the Post-Industrial Society* (1973), assumed the continuing increase of demand for scientific knowledge, leading ultimately to more rational political planning and the mitigation of social inequalities, such was the optimism of the 1970s (Krucken 2002: 125). The turn to science was coupled with growing deference paid to science because of its presumed 'neutrality' and 'objectivity': as Dreyfuss and Nelkin assert, 'science is considered uncontaminated with political values and therefore an objective arbiter of truth'. This neutrality meant that governments could increasingly utilise it: 'science has been a political resource – a way to define and legitimise governmental actions as impersonal, rational and value-free' (Dreyfuss and Nelkin 1992: 339).

Scientific knowledge does now penetrate all spheres of life, with society 'permeated by science' (Nowotny *et al.* 2002: 3). However, dependence upon science to provide certainty misunderstands the nature of science. Science does no more than produce evidence to support or disprove hypotheses, and this evidence is open to constant revision: in the words of Giddens (2003: 23) 'science is built on shifting sands'. A realistic appraisal of science should lead to a healthy public scepticism concerning claims of certainty, as Karl Popper (1992: 4) explains: 'since we can never know anything for sure, it is simply not worth searching for certainty; but it is well worth searching for the truth; and we can do this chiefly by searching for mistakes so that we can correct them'. (Although postmodernism stresses the relativity of 'truth', making any truth claims hollow also.) Despite this, risk society continues in its search for greater certainty, or, at least more detailed information with which to better calculate risk and take precautions. However, even when such risk information is available and widely disseminated (e.g. that air travel is safer than travel in motor vehicles) 'public perception of the relative magnitude of different risks does not necessarily coincide with scientific estimates of relative risk' (Krebs and Kacelnik 1997: 35).

The aura surrounding science then rivals that surrounding the law, with developing technologies presumed to be scientifically legitimate 'justified as valid, objective, neutral, universal, consensual and fair', thus overlooking 'the fact that results are socially interpreted (and thus potentially disputable) and it overlooks the personal interests of control agents and the sectarian, social constructed interests agents may represent' (Marx 2001: 1). The position of science in society however is now undergoing further change (too complex to cover in depth here). In Beck's (1992) 'risk society' science is not the panacea for a society searching for security but a source of further risks. Such a conception of science and technology as perpetrating new risks, is extended by theorists who explain that while scientific and technological knowledge has brought about a transformation of structural social conditions, 'science and technology have not only identified but have created new risks' (Blake 1989: 13). Despite an expectation that science can provide the knowledge whereby society can protect itself from or manage risk, there is a growing cynicism regarding scientists and their objectivity, as well as diminishing faith in the ability of science to solve problems more often than it creates them, a situation capitalised upon by the media:

> Technological advance can make us feel triumphant and terrified, hopeful and alarmed in quick succession. It is perhaps because our lives are so enriched by technology that we worry about becoming dependent upon it, doubt its promises and fear the future it might create for us. Spreading alarm is good business. Fear and terror are as much part of the modern entertainment

industry as excitement and sex. Science provides an obvious villain. [8]

The fallibility of science as focused upon by the media, is now recognised by a public demystified by the Brent Spar debacle, the BSE crisis, the GM food debate and so on, with 'the public image of certain aspects of "policy related" science ... changing from one of reassurance to one of concern' (O'Riordan *et al.* 1997: 13). The recent rejection by many parents of the Measles-Mumps-Rubella vaccine in the UK reveals this increasing unease about the objectivity of scientific – particularly government financed – advice. This apprehension has led to a call to the scientific community to come to terms with the fact that:

> as its special expertise is ever more widely deployed to address questions of interest to society, the unique objectivity claimed by many scientists for their work will be questioned. Scientific truth will be contested and cannot necessarily be accepted as the only, or final, word in many situations. (Ashworth 1997b: 5)

As a result of several public *volte-face*, science has now become, according to Michael (2002: 115), 'a source of comfort and discomfort, the arbiter of truth and the harbinger of uncertainty, it shapes the way we situate ourselves in relation to nature and society, and yet we subject its pronouncements to our keenest scepticism'. Such scepticism may have negative consequences (as in the MMR controversy), and should not 'obscure the importance of engaging in critical debate about the appropriate uses of scientific methods and technology in gaining evidence' (Redmayne 2001: 215). However, scepticism should extend to the realms of forensic science and expert evidence in criminal courtrooms. Indeed, the recent 'cot death' cases,[9] have led to welcome scrutiny of the status of the expert medical evidence presented in such cases. The protections against miscarriages of justice afforded by the adversarial system need supporting by a strong commitment to quality control, regulation, education, and

---

8 Leadbeater, C. (2002) 'We should look forward to the future', *The Observer*, 30 June.

9 See *R* v. *Clark* (2003) EWCA Crim. 1020; *R* v. *Cannings* (Angela) (2004) EWCA Crim 1; *R* v. *Patel* (Trupti) (Unreported, 11 June 2003).

rigorous scrutiny of scientific evidence. Whilst regulation has long been in place for sciences impacting upon public health issues (for food production, engineering work, and so forth), such regulation is itself now proving controversial. While the public raise concerns over precedent and seek long-term considerations of developments, regulatory bodies continue to focus on immediate applications rather than the potential longer-term implications. This has meant that:

> More and more of society's controversies in the domain of science, policy and risk are now potentially of this kind, reflecting tensions between, on the one hand, public unease about physical and social implications of trends and trajectories, and, on the other, official regulatory frameworks that continue to be based more narrowly on individual artefacts and their immediate impacts. (Grove-White 1997: 55)

Whilst forensic scientists are slowly working to ensure proper regulation after scandalous revelations of quality, standardisation, and oversight revealed by high-profile miscarriages of justice, this regulation is limited in its extent to the accreditation of individual scientists, laboratories, or forensic techniques and technologies. The application of technologies, the operational principles of scientists, laboratories, organisations, and companies, etc., remain largely unregulated by law, lacking legal oversight. This book contends that long-term trajectories of developments and the implications of the applications of forensic science also require scrutiny and critical debate.

While technology does not automatically lend itself to undesirable outcomes, it is essential to keep in check the unscrupulous, immoral, or unethical application of such technologies: 'the availability of a certain technology is only a prerequisite but not a reason for the applications that it will find' (Redmayne 2001: 26). Regulatory bodies do a poor job of fulfilling this particular role. Governments are presently legislating to demarcate limits to scientific progress, but these are often neatly sidestepped by private or overseas concerns, with scientific genies very difficult to put back in their bottles. Advances in fingerprinting and DNA profiling are not inherently lent to questionable application, and are often essential tools in crime detection and prosecution, but the applications being found for these technologies and their impact upon criminal process reform is in need of informed debate coupled with vigilant regulation and oversight.

The necessity of research into forensic identification technology

The recent dramatic growth of forensic science provision and utilisation in England and Wales has taken place almost entirely in a vacuum of socio-legal academic interest, with minimal research undertaken on the impacts, and potential implications, of the rapid assimilation of forensic science into the legal system. This is despite significant government investment (both financially and in terms of legal reform) in forensic sciences, increasing reliance placed upon such evidence at both the investigation and trial stages of the criminal process and previous cases of wrongful conviction resting upon forensic science and expert evidence (Mahendra 2004: 269). Critical research into the status and use of forensic identification technology is timely, particularly when the ideology and operation of the criminal justice system has shifted in the late-modern 'risk society'; assisted by advances in forensic science and surveillance technologies, and fuelled by repeated periodic breakdowns in public confidence in the criminal justice system and the apparent continuation and prevalence of miscarriages of justice.

While forensic science is now ubiquitous in the media, with fictitious crime scenes visited by the obligatory 'forensics' and TV detectives regularly consulting 'white coats' in laboratories, it has a blemished history. Many infamous miscarriages of justice of the 1980s had at their heart scientific evidence that was either undisclosed, flawed, or misrepresented in court. The Irish bombing trials used methods of testing for explosives that were invalid, while cases such as that of Kevin Callan (1997) exemplify grave miscarriages caused by flawed scientific evidence. The successful appeal of Sally Clark[10] focused attention again on the non-disclosure by the prosecution of important medical evidence as well as the use of erroneous statistical calculations. Such cases demonstrate that the accuracy and objectivity of forensic science and of expert witnesses can, and should, be called into question. With the justice system increasingly calling upon the expertise of scientists to determine the 'truth' and lend certainty to verdicts, the role of forensic science in late-modern society is in need of review.

---

10 *R* v. *Clark* (2003) EWCA Crim. 1020.

Despite the record of flawed forensic science, the non-disclosure of forensic tests or the misinterpretation of forensic evidence being implicated in miscarriages of justice, commentators continue to make claims for the ability of science to end indeterminancy within criminal justice and other areas of decision-making, with the goal of forensic evidence said to be to improve decision-making with 'verdict accuracy' as its goal (Redmayne 2001: 4). However, miscarriages of justice will flourish in a culture which fails to properly scrutinise and question 'scientific' evidence. As Redmayne (1998: 442) warns: while DNA technology provides substantial benefits, 'these benefits should not, however, blind us to the problematic issues that accompany the technology'.

In a climate where adversarialism is being eroded in criminal trials as well as other quasi-legal arenas, and forensic scientists and expert witnesses gain credibility as guarantors of 'accurate' findings of guilt or innocence, there can be, as Blake (1989: 13) asserts, the creation of a 'technological tyranny'. This increases the risk of miscarriages of justice through error, such conventionally understood miscarriages of justice potentially resulting from mismanaged or erroneous collection, analysis and storage of forensic evidence, as well as misinterpretation and statistical errors arising from probabilistic calculations. This will be particularly so if reform precedes attempts to introduce regulation (albeit self-regulation) and a form of quality assessment with the accreditation regime commenced by the Council for Registration of Forensic Practitioners (CRFP).

Ericson and Shearing (1986: 155) wrote nearly 20 years ago that inquiry into policing needed to expand beyond the sociology of 'law and order', to become a sociology of 'law, science and order', addressing itself 'to the implications of the new laws and technologies of surveillance for the social dimensions of time and space and the related matter of the institution of privacy'. They also presciently warned of an 'amplification effect': 'whereby police find new ideas for law, science and technology in the very process of using them'. It is this very amplification and its attendant socio-political implications, in the 20 years since Ericson and Shearing wrote of the 'scientification of police work', that demands critical scholarly attention. With particular regard to the advent and rapid advance of forensic DNA profiling, critics of scholarship to date, indicate that it is readily apparent that there is a 'dearth of objective, in-depth quantitative assessments of the role of DNA profiling from a criminological perspective' (Briody 2002: 160), while; 'the links between the deployment of DNA technology and broader socio-political trends in the context of criminal justice,' remain missing (Corns 1992: 7).

As Walsh (2004) demonstrates, in a survey of mainstream international forensic journals since 1990, only 0.9 per cent of articles looked at legal issues, and only 0.4 per cent at specific legal issues relating to DNA, indicating the lack of interest in legal issues shown by the forensic science community. However, Walsh suggests that the ideological gap, while vital to forensic scientists, is perhaps best filled by legal and sociological experts. Similarly, Johnson *et al.* argue that we now require 'a nuanced interpretation of the historical development and socio-political context of the NDNAD ... to understand ways in which it now appears as a central scientific policing tool imbued with the rhetorical promise of a "weapon" which can be legitimately deployed to tackle crime' (Johnson *et al.* 2003: 27).

There are significant consequences arising from neglect of the 'subtle, adverse effects of the increasing pervasiveness of science in criminal justice' (Corns 1992: 7). As Corns goes on to explain, one result of the 'theoretical lacuna concerning the science-justice relation,' is that civil liberties have been lost, and police powers increased 'virtually without challenge or question'. He calls for urgent critical recognition, and understanding of the power which science has to alter the fundamental relations between the state and citizen, particularly the consequences arising from the 'scientific appropriation of the criminal process'. As Ericson and Shearing explain, the utilisation of science in the criminal process has particular dangers, as it promises:

> special powers of construing the truth which reduce complexity to statements of authoritative certainty. It also offers the procedural characteristics of being universal, general, uniform, and neutral. It gives the police a general warrant of the type, Because we are doing things the scientific way, we are doing them the right way and you have no legitimate grounds for criticism. (Ericson and Shearing 1986: 133)

Technological advances have historically revolutionised police practices and as Chan posits, there is every reason 'to expect that the latest round of technological change ... would have an equally dramatic impact on policing'.[11] Forensic DNA profiling, like fingerprinting before it,

---

11 See Chan (2001: 140). Chan's research however was limited to the information technology revolution.

has been portrayed and accepted 'as a certain, error-free method of personal identification', which has 'profoundly influenced the degree of trust invested in it, compared with other forms of criminological evidence' (Lynch 2003: 93). The potential for the strengthening of the social control net at the same time as the thinning of the mesh, (see Cohen 1979) and the very real possibility of injustice from mistake, mis-targeting and misinterpretation demand attention be turned to forensic identification technologies. Further, erosions of privacy and extensions of state authority and police powers to obtain and retain personal data such as fingerprints and DNA profiles *en masse* has negative impacts upon civil liberties, and possibly civic participation and compliance. As such, these developments must be widely publicised and accepted by the general public before the negative consequences are entrenched and irredeemable. Such moves must take place within a political and popular culture that has a realistic appreciation 'of what science can and cannot be called upon to do' (Durant 2003: 74).

Chapter 1

Forensic identification: the legal framework

Police investigations and forensic identity evidence

There is no denying the power of fingerprints and forensic DNA evidence to exculpate innocent suspects and incriminate the guilty, potentially assisting with the swift and certain detection of criminal offences. However, these forensic identification techniques may also have undesirable side effects. As risk aversion priorities predominate in late-modern society, precautions are increasingly taken that do not attempt to 'balance' risks, but seek to avoid risks (at the cost of potentially creating other risks). This chapter, in documenting the use of fingerprinting and DNA technology during criminal investigations, considers whether the 'risks' addressed by policing (such as victimisation, criminality, insecurity, etc.) are not averted without the potential for new 'risks' (such as wrongful arrests and miscarriages of justice) being created. Detailing the use of forensic identification techniques in the context of police investigations, the legal provisions, and the potential influence that forensic identification evidence can have on investigations, the chapter considers the protections afforded suspects during investigation in light of forensic identification evidence, including the potential for refusing sampling and consequences flowing from refusal to consent.

The identification and verification of the identity of suspects is not the only purpose for which bodily samples are demanded by law-enforcement authorities. Indeed, fingerprints and buccal swabs (for DNA profiling) are not the only instances where the law provides the police (or others such as immigration officers) with powers to compulsorily demand fingerprints and samples from individuals. Road traffic offences, most obviously drink-driving offences, give rise to a raft of police powers to demand samples of breath, urine or blood from drivers. These however are not for the purposes of identification but for proof of commission of a crime i.e. exceeding the blood alcohol limit whilst driving. Likewise, in connection with drug or other offences they can prove class A drug use; relevant to determine charges, bail conditions, and possible sentence, for example.[1] The provision for the taking of samples in road safety legislation, while highly controversial upon introduction in 1967,[2] now appears accepted as necessary if not desirable (Evans 1973).

The rationale for powers to take samples from drivers differs slightly from that of the law regarding fingerprinting or DNA sampling, both of which remain primarily used to prove identity (although semen stains in rape cases for example can be probative evidence, and a blood-soaked shirt may strongly suggest that the wearer was involved in assault, particularly if it is the victim's blood, etc.). The presence of fingerprints or DNA does not usually constitute proof of guilt for any crime on its own (as yet), though fingerprints have long been used to secure convictions for property crimes where latent prints are found on stolen goods.[3] Bodily samples are increasingly being utilised to evidence guilt however. In the case of *R v. Apicella*,[4] a bodily sample was used by the prosecution to prove that the appellant suffered from the same disease contracted by the victims of sexual assault, a precedent followed where men have been prosecuted for infecting others with HIV.[5]

1 See *PACE* s. 63(b); *Criminal Justice and Court Services Act* 2000 s. 48; *Criminal Justice Act* 2003 s. 161; and *PACE 1984 (modifications to Codes C and D) Order* 2003 s. 17(1) which provides for the testing of persons charged with a 'trigger' offence if it is suspected that misuse of class A drugs caused, or contributed to the offence. Refusal to provide a sample can lead to prosecution (s. 17(4)(c)) and possible imprisonment, although force may not be used to obtain sample (s. 17(11)).

2 Reflected in heated exchanges surrounding the passing of legislation in the House of Commons debates of the time.

3 However, see *R v. Court* [1960] *Criminal Law Review* 631 where evidence of a fingerprint on a stolen car did not prove 'possession' of the car for the purposes of proving the charge of theft.

4 *R v. Apicella* [1986] *Criminal Law Review* 238.

5 Although *R v. Dica* (2004) EWCA Crim. 1103 now appears to reverse the situation, see Warburton, D. (2004) 'A Critical Review of English Law in Respect of Criminalising Blameworthy Behaviour in HIV+ Individuals', *Journal of Criminal Law*, 68(55): 32.

The *Police Reform Act* 2002 s. 56 provides for the taking of blood samples from unconscious drivers, or those medically unable to consent, invoking concerns about issues of consent and the ethical involvement of medical personnel in taking blood from non-consenting adults. Such provisions stretch 'public safety' justifications to their fullest extent, with police powers being extended and drivers increasingly subject to instant penalties, and offences proved by 'objective' evidence, such as bodily samples, or other evidence such as speed or red-light cameras. Whilst perhaps the public attitude towards road safety continues to permit the extension of police powers (though some road safety measures are increasingly questioned), safeguards are likewise being eroded in other areas of the law, with the removal of requirements for consent and the provision for the use of 'reasonable force' by the police to obtain bodily samples. Such changes are taking place in the legal provisions for fingerprinting and DNA sampling.

Fingerprints[6] and DNA sampling: the legal framework

The genesis of the 'science'[7] of dactyloscopy – commonly known as 'fingerprinting', has been well documented.[8] Credit for the work that saw fingerprinting become a universal identification tool for the police and legal system is disputed, remaining shared between three men. Francis Galton undertook in the late 1880s to build upon the work of a civil servant using fingerprints in India; William Herschel, while Henry Faulds, a Scottish physician working as a medical missionary in Japan also 'discovered' fingerprint identification. Edward Henry utilised the work of Galton to establish the first Scotland Yard fingerprint branch in 1901, although it was Henry Faulds who published a 'Guide to finger-print identification' in *Nature* in 1905, and it was his classification system that saw the adoption of fingerprints as the identification evidence of choice for the legal system (Beavan 2003).

Fingerprints serve two purposes within the criminal justice system: to identify individuals before the police for the purpose of matching

---

6 'Fingerprints' in this discussion includes 'palm prints' and other skin impressions.

7 Fingerprinting has been characterised as not an 'exact' science and the debate over whether fingerprint identification is closer to art than science still occupies practitioners, academics, and legal professionals.

8 For example, see Beavan (2003) and Cole (2001).

them with their criminal record, and secondly, to compare with 'latent' prints located at the scene of a crime (Lidstone and Palmer 1996: 461). The impetus for the development of reliable identification systems came from the need to certify the identity of those before the courts and detained in prisons for the determination of sentence (repeat offenders being in receipt of harsher penalties), as it moved away from its origins as a tool in civil disputes and in the correct disbursement of pensions in the British colonies. However, it was their second purpose – the detection of suspects and offenders for the successful prosecution of crime – that later came to prominence, and this remains, in the public imagination, the principal utility of fingerprints. This remains so even though at a typical crime scene, approximately only 10 per cent of latent prints will result in a match.[9]

With the adoption of fingerprinting by the legal system, the law had to set out criteria for when individuals were to be lawfully subject to it. Likewise, after the technique first known as 'genetic fingerprinting' was used in 1985 in a major police investigation (see later, the case of *Pitchfork*), the potential of the technique developed by Prof. Alec Jeffreys (see Jeffreys *et al.* 1985) was realised, and laws enacted to utilise this scientific development.

Fingerprint collection

The *Penal Servitude Act* 1891 first provided for the measuring, photographing and fingerprinting of convicted prisoners.[10] Those on remand could only be fingerprinted pursuant to a warrant issued by a magistrate on the application of a police officer not below the rank of superintendent. In the event of a person being subsequently discharged, their fingerprints were to be destroyed (Leigh 1985: 228). This legal framework remained relatively unchanged for almost half a century, providing the only statutory authority for the compulsory collection of fingerprints. Home Office Circular (481468/34) of January 1926 clarified that the police had no common law power to take the fingerprints of an accused, and that fingerprints may only be taken – should the accused object – after he has been remanded to prison,

---

9 Testimony of Mr Bayle at p. 18, *US* v. *Llera-Plaza* (2002) Cr.No. 98-362-10,11,12.

10 Regulations for the Measuring and Photography of Criminal Prisoners, SR & O 1896/762. This provision being continued by the *Prison Act* 1952 ss. 16 and 54(3).

or an order authorising the taking of fingerprints had been obtained either from the Secretary of State or from a Justice of the Peace.

In Scotland there had been an early series of appeals dealing with the taking of fingerprints. In 1916 in *Adamson* v. *Martin*,[11] Adamson had been taken to a police station (not under arrest) to be fingerprinted against his wishes, and the court ruled that the forcible taking of fingerprints amounted to an assault under common law. In *Adair* v. *McGarry*,[12] the only evidence against the accused was fingerprints on stolen items. However, contrary to the ruling in *Adamson*, it was held that when the identity of the criminal depends upon the identification of the suspect by means which the accused bears about his person, it is:

> beyond all doubt that, provided a person has been legally arrested by the police, they may search him for stolen goods, or weapons, or other real evidence connecting him with the crime, and that neither his consent not a magistrate's warrant is required for that purpose.[13]

The admission of fingerprint evidence taken without consent was justified by reasoning that while every man is entitled to his personal liberty 'he forfeits that right by committing crime', and his liberty will be unavoidably invaded to the extent necessary for police to establish the identity of the accused and his connection with the crime.[14] If the accused is innocent: 'no harm is done in fingerprinting ... If, on the other hand, he is guilty, the process renders it more likely that his guilt may be established'.[15] While the protection of individual liberty was desirable, the taking of fingerprints was considered important:

> Promptitude and facility in the identification of accused persons and the discovery on their person or on their premises of *indicia* either of guilt or innocence are of importance for criminal investigation with a view to the detection of crime. On the other hand, the liberty of the subject must be protected against any undue or unnecessary invasion.[16]

---

11   *Adamson* v. *Martin* (1916) SC 319.
12   *Adair* v. *McGarry* (1933) SLT 482.
13   *Adair* v. *McGarry* (1933) at 486.
14   *Adair* v. *McGarry* (1933) at 482.
15   *Adair* v. *McGarry* (1933) at 488.
16   *Adair* v. *McGarry* (1933) at 492.

In 1944, in *Dumbell* v. *Roberts*, Scott LJ posited that the lack of statutory powers for the police to take fingerprints, without consent, of persons yet to be convicted or committed for trial was because such powers would be: 'inconsistent with our British presumption of innocence until proof of guilt; and it is natural for it to be regarded as a slur on a man's character. Without free consent it involves trespass to the person ...'.[17]

Despite such principled reservations, a call for greater powers to fingerprint suspects was responded to in the *Criminal Justice Bill* of 1948. While the Act was primarily concerned with the death penalty and corporal punishment, Home Secretary Chuter Ede 'took the opportunity to propose a power for the courts to order the fingerprints of any arrested person of whatever age' (Levenson 1980: 704). It met with some resistance in the House of Commons, with condemnation of the provision as 'an infringement of the liberty of the subject',[18] and dissent over who should authorise the taking of fingerprints, as well as who should be included in such provisions. While concerns were expressed about the extension of fingerprinting to those not yet convicted, the act of taking fingerprints itself was deemed 'unobjectionable' with the now common adage 'only the guilty need worry', effectively employed in debate:

> there is a grave danger of abuse of a certain constitutional and individual right of freedoms in that of which we are very proud. On the other hand, there is nothing objectionable in the physical operation of having fingerprints taken ... If fingerprints are to be taken at all then let it be general. Let it not be done through the police court at the whim of a police officer who may have, police being only human, certain reasons for taking the fingerprints of this or that person. The innocent person does not mind his fingerprints being taken. It is the old lag, the expert, who hates the operation and avoids it if at all possible ... There should be no taking of fingerprints before conviction. After conviction is a very different matter. There I think lies the gravamen of the situation.[19]

---

17 *Dumbell* v. *Roberts* [1944] 1 All ER 326, 330.

18 Mr Hector Hughes MP, Hansard, HC (series 5) vol. 444, col. 2276 (28 November 1947).

19 Mr Price-White, Hansard, HC (series 5) vol. 444, cols. 2237, 2238 (27 1947).

The expression of reservations concerning fingerprinting before conviction did not prevent the extension of powers to take fingerprints from suspects, subsequently provided for by s. 40 of the *Criminal Justice Act* 1948, a provision included in the successive *Magistrates' Courts Act* of 1952 and of 1980.

Section 40(1) of the Magistrates' Courts Act 1952 allowed for an order to be made (upon the application of a police officer not below the rank of inspector) for the fingerprinting of any person over 14 years old taken into custody and charged with an offence before a magistrate's court, provided that the court thought it fit. These were to be taken either at the court or where the person was being detained, and reasonable force may be used by a constable if it be necessary for that purpose (s. 40(2)). Section 40(4) continued to require destruction of fingerprint records if the person was subsequently acquitted or not committed for trial. These legal provisions meant that in ordinary circumstances the police did not take fingerprints of persons charged with minor offences and in the absence of a court order, the fingerprints of a person in police custody could only be taken with consent.[20]

The *Criminal Justice Act* 1967 extended these provisions to include persons coming before magistrates in answer to a summons (not already in custody) for any offence punishable by imprisonment (s. 33). The Act also extended 'fingerprinting' to include palm prints (powers that were replicated in s. 49 of the Magistrates' Courts Act of 1980). The case of *Ryser*,[21] ruled that the powers of magistrates to order the taking of fingerprints had to be exercised judicially, with clear grounds upon which an order could properly be made. In this case, the only ground which the magistrate had for giving the order was that the applicant had refused to consent: 'if that were sufficient reason then *ex hypothesi* an order could be made in every case where there was such a refusal'.[22] The law was increasingly criticised however, and police complained of frustration in having to seek the authority of magistrates. In 1978 it was commented that the taking of fingerprints was 'commonplace' and 'a regular and accepted part of police procedure', and it was felt that 'despite obvious interference with the liberty of the subject involved, it is now almost taken for granted by the general public' (Warner 1978: 639). However, opinion

---

20 Hansard, HC (series 5) vol. 570, cols. 1397, 23 May 1957.
21 *R v. Marylebone Magistrates Court and the Commissioner for Police for the Metropolis ex. P. Ryser* [1985] Criminal Law Review 735.
22 As above at 736.

remained divided over compulsory fingerprinting and the law was still criticised:

> there are many shades of opinion between those who regard the taking of any prints as cause for a feeling of unease and those who advocate compulsory fingerprinting of the whole population. The present state of the English law is ..., a typically English compromise with a number of vague and unsatisfactory features and insufficient protection for the person whose fingerprints are sought. (Warner 1978: 640)

The enactment of the *Police and Criminal Evidence Act (PACE)* of 1984, consolidating the powers of the police, repealed s. 49 of the Magistrates' Courts Act 1980, replacing it with provisions under which the police regulate the taking of fingerprints on their own authority. Terrorism, as well as immigration legislation, has also subsequently conferred powers on other authorities to take fingerprints from individuals.[23] Fingerprints will ordinarily be taken with consent, but s. 61 of *PACE* gave police the power to take fingerprints without consent where an officer of at least superintendent rank (subsequently downgraded to inspector by s. 78 of *Criminal Justice and Police Act* 2001) had reasonable grounds for suspecting the involvement of that person in a criminal offence, and the fingerprints tended to prove or disprove his involvement, or facilitated the ascertainment of his identity.[24] They could be taken without consent where the person had been convicted for, or given a warning or reprimand in respect of, a recordable offence, or told that he will be reported for one, provided the reason for their collection was relayed to him and recorded before they were taken. An officer also had to inform the person that their fingerprints would be subject to a speculative search (s. 61(7)(a)).

The *Criminal Justice Act* 2003 extended the powers of police to take fingerprints without consent upon arrest for a recordable offence. Amending s. 61 of *PACE*, s. 9 permits the taking of fingerprints

---

23 See *Terrorism Act* 2000 Schedule 8 Part I s. 10; *Anti-Terrorism, Crime and Security Act* 2001 s. 89 (201); *Asylum and Immigration Appeals Act* 1993 s. 3; *Immigration and Asylum Act* 1999 s. 141.

24 Authorisation can only be given for the purposes of identification if the person refuses to identify themselves or the officer has reasonable grounds to suspect that he is not who he claims to be: s. 61(4)(a). Consent must be given in writing at the police station or can be oral if given elsewhere (s. 61(2)).

without consent upon arrest for, or being informed that the subject shall be reported for, a recordable offence if he has not previously had his fingerprints taken during investigation for that offence. (It remains to be seen whether the limitation that the offence must be 'recordable' will be relaxed in the future, now that – since January 2006 – all offences have become 'arrestable'.) Reasonable force can be used to take fingerprints after arrest or charge, or after conviction (s. 61(3) and s. 61(6)). *PACE* also preserves the power of compulsory fingerprinting contained in immigration and terrorism legislation (s. 61(9)) while s. 27(3) gives the police the power to request someone to attend the police station to be fingerprinted, with a power of arrest for the purpose of taking fingerprints for a recordable offence. The power to take fingerprints without consent applies to a suspect of any age. In view of the high proportion of crime committed by the youngest of offenders, it was considered important to be able to compulsorily fingerprint suspects regardless of their age.[25]

Despite the early controversy noted, the collection of fingerprints from suspects without consent now appears widely accepted. The rationale for the latest reforms to the legal provisions for fingerprinting were based not upon efforts to increase convictions directly, but to tackle the problems created when suspects give the police false details. The previously time-consuming checking of a person's identity has been significantly speeded up with the introduction of LIVESCAN fingerprint database consoles at police stations. LIVESCAN captures fingerprints electronically, by the person placing a hand on a glass platen and sending the 'print' to IDENT1 for comparison, circumventing the problems associated with 'ink and roller' methods.[26] However, LIVESCAN is costly to implement (the machines are about the size of an upright fridge-freezer), meaning that only 175 units have been installed (52 within the Metropolitan Police force area) across the country (from a total of over 518 custody suites), with 16 police forces having no LIVESCAN capability.

The objectives of LIVESCAN include: correctly ascertaining a detainee's identity prior to release (the Metropolitan police have found since installing LIVESCAN that 4 per cent of arrestees have provided false details); establishing innocence as quickly as possible;

---

25 See Session 1983–4, HC Standing Committee E, col. 1465.

26 The *Criminal Justice Act* 2001 requires that all equipment in use by the police be 'type-approved', demanding the testing and certification of technologies and applications, which NAFIS and LIVESCAN have yet to undergo.

identifying outstanding warrants and linking offences to individuals; and identifying people with warning markers (Home Office 2001: 46–7). More than 100,000 records of arrests are made, and 80,000 scenes-of-crime marks are searched each month, with on average 4,000 'identifications' made in an automated process which has dramatically shortened the time taken to perform such tasks.[27] LIVESCAN consoles enable officers to determine the identity of suspects (who have fingerprints stored on the national fingerprint database, IDENT1), circumventing the need to rely upon the suspect's honesty: 'this will ensure that anyone arrested and wanted in connection with previous offences is quickly identified'.[28] It is hard to know exactly how many offenders evade detection by providing false details, thereby not alerting authorities to outstanding warrants and so on, but police officers were clearly frustrated by such instances and lobbied to have their powers extended in order to utilise the new technology available.[29]

Alongside the investment in DNA technology, the government has invested approximately £150 million in IDENT1 since 2000. The increase in attendance at crime scenes, one of the central aims of the DNA Expansion Programme, has led to a 5 per cent increase in fingerprints being yielded from crime scenes (in contrast to a 3 per cent increase in DNA sample yields). However, whilst fingerprints are more readily located at crime scenes, there is a greater 'attrition' rate, whereby the erosion of the potential value of fingerprints is greater, with fewer fingerprint yields resulting in a detection (only about 10 per cent of crime scenes yielding fingerprints result in a fingerprint detection, compared with 20 per cent for DNA samples). While fewer DNA samples are yielded, they are more likely to result in detections, although there still exist great variations between forces in yield rates, as well as in detections resulting from yields. These results have prompted calls for further investment to improve the performance in fingerprint detection rates, which could prove more cost-effective than further investment in DNA technology (Home Office 2005).

So, even with domestic police powers extended, there are still complaints and claims that fingerprint technology could be improved:

---

27 See http://www.pito.org.uk/what_we_do/identification/ident1.htm.
28 Ian Blair, Deputy Commissioner of Metropolitan Police quoted in 'Police DNA Powers to be extended', BBC News, 27 March 2003 (http://news.bbc.co.uk/1/hi/uk_politics/2890047.stm).
29 Interviewee 3/L/P.

'Sometimes the taking of fingerprints can be very slow. In the area of terrorism, on the international front, the process of gathering together of fingerprints is abysmally slow and needs greater international cooperation and coordination'.[30] As well as further investment in LIVESCAN technology, mobile fingerprinting consoles are now being piloted, after successful trials in Project Lantern in a handful of police areas, which permit the instant fingerprinting of suspects at a scene.

The acceptance of large-scale fingerprinting must remain assumed, however. The limited roll-out of mobile fingerprinting means that to date we do not have citizens being regularly fingerprinted in lay-bys and shopping centres. It is unlikely however that such scenes, and the continued growth of IDENT1, will become problematic as what little 'public debate' there is over the sampling of citizens (which has tended to be based upon concerns regarding identity cards) largely focuses upon the collection of DNA samples. While the laws pertaining to the collection of DNA samples and fingerprints are now largely the same, the development of the law with regard to samples requires analysis of its own.

Sample collection for forensic DNA analysis

The Royal Commission on Criminal Procedure 1981 (the Phillips Report) first considered police powers in relation to suspects and detainees stating that 'only people who have raised a reasonable suspicion in the minds of the police should be subject to coercive powers'.[31] The Report rejected non-consensual sampling: 'the use of physical compulsion to obtain intimate bodily fluids..., seems to us to be objectionable, and none of us would recommend that it should be made lawful to obtain such samples in this way'.[32] Since the Phillips Report the law relating to the taking of samples including the need for consent, definitions of 'intimate' and 'non-intimate', when samples can be taken and by whom, and also the retention of sample data, have undergone numerous and significant changes.

Subsequent to the Phillips Report, *PACE* was enacted in 1984, detailing (with additional codes of practice) police powers. *PACE* set out the law concerning the taking of samples for DNA analysis, defining 'intimate' and 'non-intimate' samples (s. 65 and Code D para 5.11), who was authorised to take samples and when consent

---

30 Interviewee 3/L/P.

31 Royal Commission on Criminal Procedure (The Phillips Commission) (1981) Report (Cmnd 8092) London: HMSO, para. 3.128.

was required. In line with the sentiments expressed in the Phillips Report, intimate samples (including dental impressions, samples of blood, semen, saliva or any other tissue fluid, urine, pubic hair and swabs taken from a person's body orifices) could only be taken by consent, by a doctor or dentist. In addition, samples were to be authorised by an officer at least the rank of superintendent.[33] The sample could only be authorised if there were reasonable grounds to suspect that the detainee was involved in a serious arrestable offence and that the sample would confirm or disprove such involvement. Non-intimate samples however (defined to include a sample of hair (other than pubic), a sample taken from under a nail, a footprint or similar impression of a person's body other than their hand), could be taken by a police officer and without consent.[34]

The *Criminal Justice Act* 1988 (s. 149; sch.14) conferred sampling powers available to the police in England and Wales to the Royal Ulster Constabulary (RUC) in Northern Ireland. Whilst the government asserted that it was simply making available to the RUC the same powers enjoyed by domestic forces, there was an important difference to the provision in *PACE*. In the Northern Ireland provisions in schedule 14, the list of items defined as 'non-intimate' included buccal (mouth) swabs, whilst in *PACE* mouth swabs and saliva samples were listed as 'intimate' and therefore only able to be taken with consent. The rationale for this difference was the utility of mouth swabs in DNA profiling and consequently, the identification of terrorists (although use of these powers were not limited to terrorist suspects): 'in the particular circumstances of Northern Ireland..., it seems to us to be entirely reasonable and necessary, in the interests of protecting the law-abiding public, to give the police powers to take a mouth swab, if necessary, without the suspect's consent'.[35] Taking such samples without consent was justified by the argument that terrorists are less likely to consent and more likely to resist usual methods of policing.[36] The distinction did not pass backbenchers unnoticed however:

---

32 As above at para. 3.137.

33 *PACE* s. 62(1).

34 *PACE* s. 63. Later legislation spelt out specific powers in road traffic matters in relation to the taking of blood and urine samples under the *Road Traffic Act* 1988, ss. 4–11.

35 Mr Stanley, Hansard, HC (series 5) vol. 135, col. 650 (16 June 1988).

36 Hansard, HC (series 5) vol. 135, cols. 638–9 (16 June 1988).

a wanted terrorist or suspected drug trafficker could be stopped at Belfast airport and a swab taken ... which could establish that he is the wanted person, or just as importantly, eliminate him from the investigation. But once the same man gets to Heathrow airport the Metropolitan police will not be able to take a swab ...[37]

It was then perhaps inevitable that the reclassification of mouth swabs for the mainland police would not be long in coming.

The Royal Commission on Criminal Justice 1993 (the Runciman Report) revisited police powers and recommended reclassifying offences to widen the definition of 'serious arrestable offence', thereby extending the range of offences for which samples could be demanded from suspects to include assault and burglary.[38] Not surprisingly in light of the Northern Ireland provisions, the Runciman Report recommended the reclassification of mouth swabs and saliva samples to non-intimate samples, permitting their collection without consent. Such recommendations, in common with most of those made in the report, supported the significant extension of police powers without serious consideration of civil liberties issues (Redmayne 1998: 442). The Runciman Commission supported the police assertion that in light of developments in forensic science and the unrivalled power of forensic science to assist in the fight against crime, they should be permitted to forcibly remove samples of hair or saliva, etc. Such powers were justified in the interests of 'justice': 'we recommend that in the interests of justice, power to take a sample of hair should extend to hair that is plucked as much as hair that is cut'.[39] Here 'justice' can be seen to have been equated with the criminal justice system's surveillance needs 'to enhance police power to pluck scientifically useful knowledge from the suspect (Ericson and Haggarty 1997: 65)'. However, there may have been a more pragmatic reason for the change in status:

When legislation was being drafted the scientists were consulted and we asked for blood samples to be provided. This was considered unacceptable as they would have to be something

---

37 Sir Eldon Griffiths, Hansard, HC (series 5) vol. 135, col. 656 (16 June 1988).
38 Royal Commission on Criminal Justice (Runciman Commission) (1993) Report (CM 2263) London: HMSO.
39 Royal Commission on Criminal Justice (1993): 14.

which was less invasive and could be collected by a policeman rather than a medical practitioner. Hair roots or buccal scrapes appeared to be acceptable. As legislation was already framed around intimate and non-intimate samples it was simply a matter of moving samples from one category to another. It might seem common sense to call the mouth an intimate area but legally it becomes non-intimate.[40]

Others suggest that the police asked for the mouth to become 'non-intimate' for a slightly different end: to search for drugs which suspects may have concealed in their mouths.[41]

Implementation of the recommended reforms came in the *Criminal Justice and Public Order Act* 1994 (*CJPOA*), which went even further than the Runciman Commission in extending the new powers to take non-intimate (and therefore potentially non-consensual) samples to an even wider range of offences by replacing the 'serious arrestable offence' criterion with 'recordable offence'. As a result of the *CJPOA*, bodily samples for DNA analysis could be taken in largely the same circumstances as fingerprints, with non-intimate samples taken without consent when authorised by an officer of the rank of at least superintendent, with reasonable grounds for suspecting the involvement of the suspect in a recordable offence when a sample will assist in proving or disproving their involvement. Significantly, the *CJPOA* amended sections 62 and 63 of *PACE* in line with the Runciman recommendations, redefining mouth swabs and saliva samples as non-intimate and thus no longer requiring consent. This was criticised for providing the police with unjustifiable powers as 'the taking of a mouth swab without consent must be considered an invasive procedure' (Steventon 1995: 412).

The power to collect samples was also supported in the *CJPOA* by an arrest sanction; providing that individuals required to provide samples must do so within one month of receipt of seven days' notice, or risk arrest. This power then extended sampling powers to cases where DNA evidence may not have been relevant to proving guilt and suspects may not be in police detention. This was perhaps the first legislative signal that samples were now to be taken, not simply to prove guilt in the present investigation, but to commence the building of a database of DNA samples from a wide range of

---

40 Dr Werrett in 'Summary of the Discussion' (1997) *Forensic Science International*, 88: 104.
41 *Ibid.*

convicted offenders: 'By allowing samples to be taken after a decision to charge has been made, sampling becomes a tool for DNA profiling and intelligence gathering, rather than simply as forensic evidence in establishing guilt or innocence in the immediate case' (Belloni and Hodgson 2000: 36). The *CJPOA* also inserted s. 63(a) to ensure that 'speculative searching' of this growing database was legally provided for so the police could now compare samples with those on the database from other crime scenes (Starmer *et al.* 2001: 85).

It is perhaps at this point in the evolution of the legal framework that concerns over civil liberties came into sharp focus. The debate over the rights and privacy of the individual and the powers required by the police to effectively detect and prevent crime at this time became more pertinent than ever, with commentators noting that favourable reception of the *CJPOA* provisions:

> depends to some extent on what is often seen as the traditional conflict between the rights and privacy of individuals and the necessity to detect and prevent serious offences ... Many of the new provisions can be linked to the desire to obtain DNA evidence, both to aid an ongoing investigation and to enable an extensive investigative DNA database to be established ... In order to justify the taking of samples for this purpose in relation to such a wide variety of offences, the benefits for the detection of crime must be clear. (Steventon 1995: 418–19)

It soon became apparent however that legislation had left a loophole, with offenders convicted before the *CJPOA* came into effect in April 1995 escaping the new sampling regime and inclusion on the DNA database. In order to remedy this supposed failure and plug the apparent hole in the database, the *Criminal Evidence (Amendment) Act 1997* enabled police to take non-intimate samples from individuals convicted of serious offences (listed in schedule 1) if convicted before 10 April 1995 and still serving a prison sentence. The date is significant 'because this was when the powers in *PACE* were modified to enable non-consensual mouth swabbing' (Redmayne 1998: 445). By repealing s. 55(6) of the *CJPOA*, which had ensured the powers were non-retroactive, the *Criminal Evidence (Amendment) Act* permitted samples to be taken from people convicted of serious offences (or detained under the *Mental Health Act* 1993) before the *CJPOA* came into effect, thus extending the scope of the DNA database still further.

Bucke and Brown (1997: ix; 44–46) record that in 1997 non-intimate samples were only taken in a very small proportion of cases – just 7 per cent, although this proportion was higher in the 'targeted' offence groups: 20 per cent in cases of violence against the person; 28 per cent for sexual offences; and 19 per cent for burglary, most of these samples being given with consent. Mouth swabs were the most usual form of sampling, with resort to hair samples only when a suspect's refusal to comply made taking a buccal swab difficult (10 per cent of samples were taken without consent). Intimate samples were rarely taken with only 1 per cent of cases attracting the supply of an intimate sample (usually a blood sample), in cases of murder, rape and robbery. From the 10,496 suspects in the custody-record sample used in the 1997 study, only 40 gave intimate samples (not including the 94 who gave blood or urine under road traffic legislation). Twenty-three of these individuals were given a 's. 62 warning' that adverse inferences could be drawn from their refusal to consent, with three of these suspects still refusing their consent (they had been arrested for robbery). The Home Office research indicated that most samples were taken post-charging to add to police records, with only a small proportion taken to actively assist in determining guilt or innocence in the particular case. Such samples were then taken to add to the NDNAD.

Soon, s. 64 of *PACE* began giving rise to a series of appeals (see *Cooke* and *Nathaniel* detailed in Chapter 3) with more to follow (*R v. Weir*[42]), prompting consideration of further legal changes to the taking and retaining of bodily samples. In July 1999, the Home Office published proposals for revising legislative measures on fingerprints, footprints, and DNA samples, asserting that change was necessary because as well as problems in the appeal courts, in the 14 years since *PACE* had been enacted, technological advances had helped to 'improve the efficiency and effectiveness of fingerprint collection, storage, cross-searching and matching', making it important that the 'relevant legislation keeps *PACE* with these advances in technology'.[43] It went on to explain that while 'safeguards for the individual suspected of an offence must be preserved', at the same time, 'existing and developing fingerprint systems should not be unnecessarily hampered by the legislative framework in which they operate'.[44] The proposals detailed technological developments, including the operationalisation of a National Automated Fingerprint Identification

---

42 *R v. Weir* (2000) *The Times*, 16 June.
43 Home Office (1999) Available at http://www.homeoffice.gov.uk/ppd/finger.htm, para. 1–2.
44 As above at para. 2.

System (NAFIS), capable of supporting a database of over 6 million ten-print sets and over 2 million crime-scene marks (since expanded to a capacity of 8.2 million and updated to provide datasets for other identification technologies including palm prints and shoe prints, and now called IDENT1).

The Home Office proposals of 1999 included legislative changes which would provide for: the taking of fingerprints electronically and without consent at any location; taking a second set of prints if the person's identity is suspected when responding to bail or if an individual disputes the fingerprints; taking fingerprints without consent when a caution is issued or in connection with warnings given for recordable offences; checking of fingerprints and DNA samples against those from outside the jurisdiction; and s. 64 of *PACE* be amended to permit the retention and use of DNA samples.[45] There was also consideration by the House of Lords in 1999 of the use of DNA samples kept in breach of s. 64 of *PACE*, ruling that such evidence was admissible (see Chapter 3 for details).[46]

Subsequently, the *Criminal Justice and Police Act* 2001 enacted most of these recommendations, including speculative searching of databases and the retention and use of fingerprints and DNA samples. Section 81 (amending s. 63(a) of *PACE*) added to the list of databases against which police are able to cross-search fingerprints or DNA samples.[47] More significantly, s. 82 removed the obligation under s. 64 of *PACE* to remove fingerprints and DNA samples when an individual is acquitted or proceedings against them halted. Additionally, as well as being able to retake fingerprints, the police were now permitted to take fingerprints from those whose cases were disposed of by way of caution, warning or reprimand (which under s. 82 could be kept indefinitely). The Act also downgraded the level

---

45   *Ibid*. Other provisions included the retaking of fingerprints if there have been errors in capture or fingerprints were of poor quality or insufficient, and also for a better quality to improve the database, and also if they only posses an elimination or incomplete set; retaking of DNA samples should scientific failure inhibit the production of a profile or where the sample has been destroyed prior to analysis; with footprints to be subject to the same provisions as fingerprints.

46   *Attorney General's Reference (No 3 of 1999)* [2001] 2 WLR 56.

47   These were extended to non-mainland police forces by the *Criminal Procedures and Investigations Act* 1996 s. 64, but were now to include foreign police forces, the Ministry of Defence and the armed forces police.

of authority required for the taking of samples without consent, with a superintendent being replaced with an inspector. Whilst challenged by the opposition, the government asserted that this was reflective of the 'flexible restructuring of the police force that is currently taking place'.[48] Finally, the taking of non-intimate samples which previously had to be carried out by a doctor could now be carried out by a nurse.

The legislative developments concerning fingerprints and DNA sampling have all been in a similar vein; extending the circumstances in which samples may be taken and the type of samples able to be taken without consent, relaxing restrictions on who can authorise sample collection and who can take the samples, as well as authorising the retention of samples in all circumstances, for the purposes of building national databases for use in speculative searches. For example, the Anti-Terrorism and Security Act 2001 s. 36, amended s. 143 of the *Immigration and Asylum Act* 1999, removing the requirement that fingerprint records of asylum seekers be destroyed on the resolution of their asylum or immigration applications. The *Police Reform Act* 2002 also authorised other health-care professionals to take intimate samples from individuals rather than doctors and registered nurses.

Most recently the *Criminal Justice Act* 2003, ss. 9 and 10 (amending s. 63 of *PACE*), permits the taking of fingerprints and non-intimate samples without consent upon arrest for a recordable offence providing they have not already been supplied as part of that investigation. This enables police to take fingerprints and samples from almost all arrestees, and pre-empts technological advances which are expected to see mobile fingerprint and DNA-testing kits more widely used in the coming years (by omitting the words 'in police detention'). It also means that fingerprints and samples can be taken upon 'reasonable suspicion' for an offence, regardless of whether they will indicate guilt or innocence, or even whether they have any possibility of use during the investigation. The law is now explicit that anyone who comes under police suspicion is liable to have fingerprints and/or a DNA sample taken and compared with IDENT1 and the NDNAD. The course that an investigation takes, or if a prosecution even proceeds, are of little or no significance.

With arrest now sufficient for taking fingerprints and DNA and running speculative searches, it is widely expected that there will be an increase in the number of samples taken from arrestees. The

---

48   Mr Clarke, Hansard, HC (series 5) vol. 364, col. 598 (8 March 2001).

growth of the NDNAD certainly indicates that samples are already being taken on a scale quite different from that indicated by the 1997 Home Office study. The government 'targets' to expand the NDNAD, and police targets to take samples from suspects in particular types of offence (i.e. the recent focus on DNA in volume crimes), mean that one can safely assume that sample taking is becoming a routine element of police detention procedure. Indeed, Chief Constable Mike Baxter of the Association of Chief Police Officers (ACPO) stated that by spring 2005 all people entering police stations would have their fingerprints and DNA samples taken as a matter of course.[49] However, specific data on the taking of samples is not available to the public, so we can only surmise this from the growth of the database (detailed in Chapter 4). Working on this assumption, an interviewee commented that: 'the chances of your entering a police station and leaving again without having had your DNA and fingerprints taken are getting slimmer by the day'.[50]

The compatibility of a sampling regime with human rights legislation depends upon any invasion of bodily integrity being necessary in a democratic society for the prevention of crime or protection of rights and freedoms of others (Article 8 (2)). Protection against torture, inhuman or degrading treatment or punishment (Article 3) may prevent the use of force when taking a non-consensual sample; the European Court ruling in *Ribitsch* v. *Austria* that the use of physical force against an individual which is not strictly necessary for the detention of the individual will be contrary to Article 3.[51] However, the effects of the force used must be sufficiently serious to give rise to a violation of Article 3. For example, handcuffing in *Raninen* v. *Finland*[52] was unnecessary but the effects not serious enough to violate Article 3, just as the solitary confinement of a prisoner for over four months in a cold and cockroach-infested cell for 23 hours a day was not severe enough to amount to inhuman and degrading treatment in *Delazarus* v. *UK*.[53] It is unlikely then that the forced plucking of a hair or a physically compelled mouth swab will attract censure by Europe.

---

49 Paper presented at Forensic Science Society Annual Conference, Wyboston, 5–7 November 2004.
50 Interviewee 1/P/C.
51 (1995) 21 EHRR 573 para. 38.
52 (1997) 26 EHRR 563 paras 56–57.
53 (1993) Application no.17525/90.

In *X* v. *Netherlands*,[54] and *Peters* v. *Netherlands*,[55] the European Commission of Human Rights held that compulsory sampling was contrary to Article 8. In these cases (involving the taking of a blood sample from a driver and urine sample from a prisoner respectively) the applicant's personal conduct did not merit the demand, as both were part of random sampling regime. However, in *Peters* v. *Netherlands*, the compulsory taking of a urine sample for drug testing was 'necessary' in regard of the ordinary and reasonable requirements of imprisonment, the interference for the 'prevention of crime or disorder' justified in the case of a prisoner. Similarly, in *X* v. *Germany*, the right to physical integrity was justified in terms of crime prevention, and the applicant required to undergo psychiatric assessment during investigations for the purposes of crime prevention, even if 'the investigated facts of the accused person's life are not in themselves criminally relevant'.[56] So in order to comply with human rights obligations, the sampling laws must be justifiable by reference to Article 8 (2); being necessary in the interests of national security, public safety and the prevention of crime or disorder, or protection of freedoms of others, necessitating assessment of the use of fingerprints and DNA by the police and authorities.

Police powers to take fingerprints and bodily samples have been extended through a series of criminal justice acts. Whilst related, the retention of samples and DNA profiles as computerised digital records has become less controversial, with legislation empowering authorities to retain fingerprints and DNA samples for forensic purposes, particularly since the advent of forensic identity databasing. While the retention of computerised records attracts apparent public approval, the retention of DNA samples remains more controversial, requiring legal justification by the courts in recent cases.

Retention of fingerprints and DNA samples

R v. *Cooke*[57] first raised the issue of retained DNA profiles that was to trouble the courts and prompt legislative change. Whilst there was never a statutory requirement to destroy DNA records of persons detained under the *Prevention of Terrorism Act* 1989 (the Home Office

---

54 (Application no. 5239/78) 16 DR 184.
55 (Application no. 21132/93) 77-A DR 75.
56 (Application no. 8334/78) 24 DR 103 para. 38.
57 *R* v. *Cooke* (1995) 1 Cr.App.R 318; J of CL (1995) 59 (4) 354 and Crim LR [1995] 497.

advising that profiles from terrorist suspects should be 'retained in a searchable form on the DNA database irrespective of the outcome of detention' (Wrench 1995: para. 20), the same was not true for non-terrorist offences. *PACE* s. 64 demanded the destruction of DNA samples taken from suspects who had no action taken against them or were acquitted. In a series of cases DNA profiles used at trial, or instrumental in the bringing of charges against an accused, had been unlawfully retained in contravention of s. 64 of *PACE*. In *Cooke*, a sample given during an investigation for a rape for which Cooke was acquitted had then been matched to another rape scene, leading to his re-arrest whereupon three police officers entered his cell adorned with riot headgear, proclaiming that force would be used to obtain a hair sample. The trial judge ruled inadmissible the evidence from the first rape trial but permitted the DNA evidence from the subsequent arrest prior to the second rape trial. The DNA was the only evidence produced by the Crown against Cooke, who then appealed. The appeal court upheld the trial judge's ruling, holding that even if DNA evidence had been obtained improperly, the accuracy and strength of the evidence remained unaffected, thereby not impacting upon the fairness of proceedings within s. 78 of *PACE*.

R v. Nathaniel[58] again raised the issue of admissibility of DNA evidence kept after an acquittal, even in the absence of bad faith on the part of the police. The appeal, on the grounds that the DNA evidence was wrongly admitted, was successful, because when gaining consent to a blood sample the accused had been assured by police that the sample was only for use in the investigation of a rape (of which he was acquitted) and would then be destroyed. So, not only had s. 64 been breached, but the accused had been misled, and had also been warned that a jury would be asked to draw inferences from his refusal to consent to a sample. The Court of Appeal concluded that to permit this evidence to be used four years later in a totally unrelated trial would have an adverse effect on the fairness of the trial. This case gave the first indication that the requirement to destroy DNA profiles under s. 64 was going to become problematic, as Kennedy LJ stated:

> The police must act in good faith, but the public interest would not be served if a sample lawfully obtained in connection with an investigation could not be compared with blood left at the

---

58 *R v. Nathaniel* [1995] 2 Cr.App.R.565; J.of CL (1995) 59(4) 378.

scene of another serious crime. If a serial rapist were to be arrested and were to give a sample in the course of the inquiry into an offence which he did not commit, it can hardly have been the intention of Parliament that the sample which he gave could not then be compared with a whole series of specimens obtained from rapes which he had committed.[59]

The order to destroy fingerprints and DNA samples was then amended by s. 82 of *Criminal Justice and Police Act* 2001, allowing for their retention after they have fulfilled the purposes for which they were taken. They can be used for the prevention and detection of crime, the investigation of an offence or the conduct of a prosecution and consent to their retention cannot be withdrawn. Fingerprints and DNA samples, and the profiles derived from them, may be accessed only by relevant law-enforcement authorities listed in s. 63(a) of the 1984 Act. Likewise, s. 36 (1) of the *Anti-Terrorism, Crime and Security Act* 2001 nullified the requirement to destroy fingerprints upon the resolution of asylum and immigration cases under s. 143 (3–8) of the *Immigration and Asylum Act* 1999. Such changes were controversial inasmuch as they legislated for prior illegal practice with an HMIC report in July 2000 announcing that s. 64 was 'honoured in the breach', and an audit of police databases revealing the potential for over 50,000 records to be on file illegally. As Lord Phillips of Sudbury proclaimed in the House of Lords:

> it seems an extraordinary response to the fact that this crucially sensitive state instrument – the collection of citizen information – should have been so cavalierly misused. Yet the Government do not respond by saying, 'This is dreadful. We'll put this right and it won't happen again'; they seek to make a norm of the present illegality.[60]

Further to such objection, the amendments rendered the treatment of those convicted and those acquitted, or not even tried, the same. Lord Phillips again took exception to this:

> It would treat those acquitted of a crime and those never prosecuted for a crime in the same way as if they were convicted criminals. Merely to state that proposition invites a great deal

---

59   *R* v. *Kelt* [1994] 2 All ER 780.
60   Lord Phillips of Sudbury Hansard, HC (series 5), col. 960 (8 May 2001).

of inquiry as to what could justify such an extraordinary state of affairs. To create this new category, as it would be, is wholly without precedent, wholly adventitious and truly unprincipled.[61]

This legislative development was inevitable however, in light of *R v. B, the Attorney General's Reference No 3 of 1999*[62] in which Steyn LJ ruled that the use of DNA evidence which had been kept in breach of s. 64 did not automatically render the evidence inadmissible but that admissibility would be left to the trial judge's discretion. The *Criminal Justice and Police Act* 2001 made such discretionary decisions by judges unnecessary, as now all fingerprints and samples taken can be, at the discretion of the Chief Constable, kept indefinitely (normally until the death of the individual), regardless of whether the individual was actually proceeded against or acquitted for the charge for which the sample was collected. Indeed, the Attorney General justified the changes to legislation by reference to the anomaly *R v. B* had created:

The Joint Committee on Human Rights ... commented: 'This [ruling in *R v. B*] has the curious result that the police are under a legal duty to destroy material, but are able to use it as evidence if they breach their duty by keeping it'. The Bill's proposals ... seek to put right that anomaly. The ruling of the Judicial Committee of the House of Lords allows the court a discretion to use the information, but that only affects cases where by chance, inadvertence or inefficiency the samples have been kept ... The Government's view is that the evidence should not be discarded and that the police should be able to make use of that valuable and objective evidence. In my view, once it is acceptable that prints and samples should be able to be retained and properly used in the defence of individual liberty, which has been attacked by criminals if they are proved to be such, it is a proportionate use of the power of society to enforce the protection of the individuals who compose it.[63]

---

61 *Ibid.*
62 *R v. B, the Attorney General's Reference No 3 of 1999* [2001] 2 A.C. 91.
63 The Attorney-General (Lord Williams of Mostyn), Hansard, HC (series 5) vol. 625, col. 1042 (9 May 2001).

The legislation boosted the number of samples that could be kept on forensic identification databases. Additionally, those samples given voluntarily for elimination purposes could now be retained and subsequently used, or be subject to a speculative search, providing the volunteer gave written consent (which once obtained cannot be withdrawn, although Home Office circular 25/2001 stresses that 'it is important to ensure that consent is both fully informed and voluntary'[64]). Such a move was deemed reasonable in response to a professed problem with volunteers being approached on more than one occasion to proffer a sample during mass DNA screenings. During such screenings, volunteers had purportedly inquired as to why initial samples could not be reused (this being of apparently increasing concern to police, fearing that volunteers would refuse to keep submitting samples). Thus, the retention of DNA samples of volunteers was claimed to be 'mutually beneficial'.

The reasoning behind the need for retention was deemed to be made obvious by cases where serious offenders had been fortuitously caught by samples taken in connection with other offences. There were, as was expected, differing views of the validity or necessity of retention however, with one officer stating that:

> The retention of records really is the power behind the technology. People who have a criminal career at 16 or 17, may commit a crime later in life, then they will be caught. They'll make mistakes when they're young and get on the database, then if they get into more serious crime when they are older, we can catch them.[65]

In addition to such benefits, there was a more pragmatic reason for retention of samples in addition to data profiles:

> The reason for keeping the sample, is to do with the changing technology. We've had four or five generations of DNA technology. The next one coming, SNIPS, is not compatible with the current technology. If SNIPS allows us to test DNA in minutes and the cost is significantly lower, then even if it is a massive matter of converting the database, it's got the benefits that probably outweigh the costs of doing it. We do need to

---

64   Home Office Circular 25/2001, 11.
65   Interviewee 1/L/P.

retain samples because we might find technology allows us to do testing much easier, quicker and cheaper in the future. That's the sole reason for keeping the sample – a back-up sample.[66]

Views expressed by non-law-enforcement interviewees focused on the civil rights and legal implications of the retention of samples: 'I have some civil liberties reservations about the retention of samples that were taken for a particular purpose which no longer exists'.[67] Another interviewee made clear that retention of samples required serious consideration for a number of reasons, independent from debate over the actual taking of samples:

> Taking DNA from people is one thing, but the retention of that is another matter. There is little objection to retaining DNA records of people being prosecuted or those convicted, but then it should be destroyed after proceedings if there is no conviction.[68]

Indeed, a Council of Europe Recommendation in 1992 on the use of DNA in criminal justice stated that: 'Samples or other body tissues taken from individuals for DNA analysis should not be kept after the rendering of the final decision in the case for which they were used, unless it is necessary for purposes directly linked to those for which they were collected'.[69] Further, the Council stated that since the aim of collecting samples is the 'identification of offenders and the exoneration of suspected persons, the data should be deleted once persons have been cleared of suspicion'.[70] However, they did consider that there may be a need to set up databases in 'certain cases for specific categories of offences which could be considered to constitute circumstances warranting another solution, because of the seriousness of the offences'.[71] Such offences, decided upon by individual states, should be those committed against the life, integrity and security of a person.

In X v. *Federal Republic of Germany*, the European Commission of Human Rights stated that: '[T]he keeping of records, including

---

66 Interviewee 1/L/P.
67 Interviewee 3/L/P.
68 Interviewee 2/P/C.
69 Council of Europe Recommendation No. R (92) 1: 8.
70 As above at p. 31.
71 *Ibid.*

documents, photographs and fingerprints, relating to criminal cases of the past is necessary in a modern democratic society for the prevention of crime and is therefore in the interests of public safety'.[72] Similarly, in *McVeigh, O'Neill and Evans* v. *UK*,[73] the Commission considered the retention of records and fingerprints legitimate. The applicants, detained upon arrival in Liverpool from Ireland under anti-terrorism legislation, were searched, questioned, and their fingerprints and photographs taken to ascertain their identities. It was held that their right to privacy had been interfered with, but this was justified under Article 8(2) as necessary for the prevention of crime, though it was 'open to question' whether the retention of fingerprints amounted to interference with the right to private life at all.[74] In *Kinnunen* v. *Finland*, the applicant complained that his rights under Article 6(2) were infringed by the retention of his fingerprints and photographs on a police file despite his acquittal on all charges.[75] The Commission considered that the retention of his details did fall under Article 8 (but not Article 6) of the convention.[76]

Subsequently, in *Leander* v. *Sweden*,[77] the European Court of Human Rights held that the storage of personal information in a secret police register and its release, coupled with a refusal to allow an opportunity to refute it, were an interference with the right to respect for private life. Similarly, in *Rotaru* v. *Romania*, the ECtHR held that Article 8 is engaged when a public authority seeks, collects, stores, processes, compares or disseminates personal information or opinions about an individual, even if this information is in the public domain, though safeguards had to exist against unlawful release of the information.[78] The intended use of the information was considered relevant in *Friedl* v. *Austria*,[79] while the necessity of protection of personal information

---

72 Application No. 1306/61. para. 21.
73 *McVeigh, O'Neill and Evans* v. *UK* (1981) 5 EHRR 71; (1981) 25 DR 15
74 As above at para. 227.
75 *Kinnunen* v. *Finland* (Application No. 24950/94) (unreported), 15 May 1996.
76 The EComHR did not consider the case further as his details had been taken in 1985, before the convention came into force in Finland, and he had failed to exhaust domestic remedies to attempt to have his records expunged.
77 (1987) 9 EHRR 433, para. 48.
78 (Application No. 28341/95) 5 May 2000, para. 59.
79 (1995) 21 EHRR 85, paras 49–50.

was reiterated in *Peck* v. *UK*,[80] and in *Z* v. *Finland*,[81] it was stated that the more intimate the information, the greater the obligation on the state to protect confidentiality.

The retention of fingerprint and DNA samples under the *Criminal Justice and Police Act* 2001, was considered on appeal to the House of Lords in *Marper*.[82] The law was challenged, invoking Article 8 privacy rights and Article 14, the right against discrimination. The Court of Appeal had ruled that the retention of fingerprints did interfere with Article 8 rights, but that adverse consequences to the individual were not out of proportion to the benefits to the public and that whilst all citizens were entitled to be regarded as innocent, the different treatment of those who had previously been the subject of a criminal investigation could be justified. The question of discrimination was the source of some dissension, with Lords Woolf and Waller holding that there was a 'perfectly clear, objective distinction' between those from whom prints and samples had and had not been taken, and they could legitimately be treated differently. Lord Sedley on the other hand, felt that 'to have been charged or investigated but not convicted is both as involuntary and as stigmatic a condition as the majority of those listed [under Article 14]' and that it should therefore be considered under the list as 'other status', so that discrimination against this group would require justification.[83] Of concern however, was the solution posited to such discrimination: that if there were a comprehensive DNA register then no such discrimination would exist. Sedley LJ did not consider that, lawfully compiled, such a database would be an unacceptable invasion of privacy, in fact, such a resource available to the police and courts would be 'a real and worthwhile gain in the endeavour to ensure that the guilty, and only the guilty, are convicted of crimes'.[84]

At the House of Lords, after extolling the virtues of DNA and the benefits (in terms of crimes solved) reaped by the retention of samples from those whose records would have been expunged under s. 64 of *PACE*, Lord Steyn concluded that: 'in respect of retained

---

80 (2003) 36 EHRR 41.

81 (1998) 25 EHRR 371.

82 *R* v. *Chief Constable of South Yorkshire Police (Interviewee) ex parte LS (by his mother and litigation friend JB) (FC) (Appellant) R* v. *Chief Constable of South Yorkshire Police (Interviewee) ex parte Marper (FC) (Appellant)* (2004) UKHL 39.

83 *Ibid.*

84 *Ibid.*

fingerprints and samples article 8(1) is not engaged. If I am wrong in this view, I would say any interference is very modest indeed'.[85] This interference was then justified under 8(2), including agreement with Lord Waller in his prior judgement, that it 'is in the public interest in its fight against crime for the police to have as large a database as possible',[86] with no adverse impacts upon those whose samples were retained: 'The retention … does not affect the appellants unless they are implicated in a future crime'.[87] Lord Brown concluded with a justification for the House of Lord's decision to reject the appeal, stating that:

> … it seems to me that the benefits of the larger database brought about by the now impugned amendment to *PACE* are so manifest and the objections to it so threadbare that the cause of human rights generally (including the better protection of society against the scourge of crime which dreadfully afflicts the lives of so many of its victims) would inevitably be better served by the database's expansion than by its proposed contraction. The more complete the database, the better the chance of detecting criminals, both those guilty of crimes past and those whose crimes are yet to be committed. The better chance too of deterring from future crime those whose profiles are already on the database. And these, of course, are not the only benefits. The larger the database, the less call there will be to round up the usual suspects. Instead, those amongst the usual suspects who are innocent will at once be exonerated. Were these appellants to succeed in their challenge, the cause of justice would be seriously impeded.[88]

The issue may not have been concluded by this resounding dismissal of the appeal and support for the NDNAD (indeed the only note of dissension came from Baroness Hale, who did find an interference with Article 8(1), though she found the interference justified under 8(2)), with an appeal to Europe possible as well as challenge to the

---

85 *R* v. *Chief Constable of South Yorkshire Police (Respondent) ex parte Marper (FC) (Appellant)* [2002] EWCA Civ 1275: Waller LJ, at para. 31.
86 As above at para. 66.
87 As above at para. 37.
88 As above at para. 88.

latest legislative changes in the *Criminal Justice Act* 2003. For, it was stated at the Court of Appeal that:

> The line between those unconvicted people who have faced charges and those who have not, while not a bright line, is not arbitrarily drawn. It does not tarnish the innocence of the unconvicted in the eye of the law. But it recognises that among them is an indeterminate number who are likelier than the rest of the unconvicted population to offend in the future or to be found to have offended in the past.[89]

Yet the *Criminal Justice Act* 2003 now extends sampling to arrestees, not just those charged, a move that some interviewees viewed as excessive:

> Taking DNA from arrestees and retaining it is wholly disproportionate, especially given the dangers of unauthorised access or the ways in which the DNA samples could be used in the future. The idea of the police having such important information of so many people is worrying. People could obtain the information, and then they could sell it. Of course the police say they would never do that, but that is not that point. Rules and regulations are needed, not good intentions.[90]

It is open to question whether Lord Sedleys' assertion holds for arrestees as well as those charged, if not, the latest enlargement of police powers and the NDNAD needs further justification. As one interviewee pointed out, while taking samples from convicted persons may fit within Article 8(2), they had no hesitation in finding the powers to retain DNA samples from arrestees as unjustified, and discriminatory:

> Legal powers to take DNA are excessive ... There is no doubt that the retention of DNA samples for those who have been convicted of serious offences can be justified. What we have seen though is a pushing back of the boundaries so that it is now disproportionate. Certain groups in society come into contact with the police more often, so they will be disproportionately

---

89   *Op.cit.* n. 82. Sedley LJ, para. 86.
90   Interviewee 2/P/C.

affected by the police powers to take DNA samples. The suburban housewife might be more concerned about the NDNAD if she thought there was a chance of her being on it.[91]

Indeed, in their briefing for the second reading of the *Criminal Justice Bill* 2003, JUSTICE identified concerns arising from the 'further expansion of the category of persons from whom such information may be obtained and retained'.[92] They stressed that the issue of necessity, and appropriateness of retaining information on innocent persons was of great importance and required 'general and open public debate', arguing that:

> If such a [universal] database is considered appropriate then all persons, arguably, should be compelled to provide samples. If the database is not considered appropriate, it is difficult to see the logic in allowing the police to retain information from those charged but not convicted, as under current law, or to extend the compulsory powers to obtain samples to those who are merely arrested and not even charged. To amend *PACE* to create laws which fundamentally affect the civil liberties of the citizen by adding to the categories of people who are liable to have their samples obtained and retained does not promote this debate. Indeed, it may be perceived to be 'legislation by stealth' in relation to an important issue of privacy and civil liberties.[93]

The permitting of non-consensual sample taking in a wide range of situations, and samples which may later be retained and stored indefinitely, raises many issues including the status of the privilege against self-discrimination and the presumption of innocence. This privilege and the consequences of non-compliance with a sampling request must then be considered in light of the current position with regard to police powers to take and retain samples, and their use during police investigations, in particular since the DNA Expansion Programme.

---

91   Interviewee 1/P/C.
92   JUSTICE Briefing for the second reading and committee stages in the House of Lords, *Criminal Justice Bill* 2003, June 2003.
93   *Ibid.*

Chapter 2

Forensic identification: the criminal investigation

DNA and police investigations

Police investigations have been characterised as 'case constructions': 'a process ... in which, once a clear suspect has been identified, the objective of the inquiry becomes the one-sided collection (and sometimes 'manufacture') of evidence to support the police version of what happened' (Field and Thomas 1994: 74). While Walker (1999) theorises as to the constructed nature of 'truth' during investigations, as well as 'guilt', the case construction literature emphasises the critical importance of police goals 'which lead the police to interpret events in particular ways, to neglect certain lines of enquiry, and to suppress specific items of information' (Redmayne 2001: 13). The 'objectivity' and 'neutrality' of forensic science could eradicate such practices, but even the selection of items for forensic analysis during an investigation is usually a part of building a case against a suspect(s); i.e. not trying to find a suspect but getting proof against the suspect they already have (Roberts 1994a). Walker and Stockdale (1999: 148) suggest that 'the hope that science may provide an antidote to the police construction of criminality, especially through interrogation, seems forlorn' not least because of the fact that the great majority of criminal investigations involve little or no physical trace evidence (Steer 1980: 71).

Forensic scientists' abilities to assist in criminal investigations are also clearly circumscribed by the skills used in the collection of evidence from the crime scene:

> Forensic scientists do not make physical evidence 'objective' simply by subjecting it to analysis in the laboratory. If bias has been employed in selecting evidence in the field or in deciding which evidence should be examined or reported, or both, no amount of scientific testing can correct for this prejudice. (Lucas 1989: 721)

The situation may have changed since the Philips Royal Commission in 1981 reported that the utilisation of forensic science was rare, with limited value and there was widespread police ignorance of application; although Home Office research in 1996 still reported that 'little pro-active use is made of forensic science', with widespread ignorance of forensic science within the police (Tilley and Ford 1996: vi). Whilst forensic science is clearly now utilised to a much greater degree, such ignorance has still been attested to more recently, and recent training initiatives on 'DNA awareness' have only been delivered to 11,000 police officers (less than 10 per cent of the total number of serving officers).

The DNA Expansion Programme, and the Forensic Integration Strategy more generally, both seek to alter investigative practices to utilise new technologies and give the police new methods for detecting crime, although new technologies have long been harnessed to investigate crime. However, there may now be a powerful motivation in that the closing down of other avenues of investigation necessitates resort to science and technology:

> through a range of changes in the criminal justice system; disclosure; the way that suspects are dealt with; even the way that policing has developed, some of the more traditional ways of investigating crime and identifying suspects have fallen away ... Therefore there is a greater reliance on this technology to identify the offenders. You are not going to get admissions these days, the use of informants is not as effective as it was, even societal factors such as the public not relating to the police as they once did ... as other things have fallen away, forensic evidence is what is left.[1]

Forensic science is then perhaps utilised as a means to circumvent public cooperation: 'there are huge pockets of the community where

---

1 Interviewee 1/P/C.

there is a huge distrust of the police and they won't help, so DNA can overcome that'.[2] However, DNA cannot overcome a lack of public cooperation fully, as DNA cannot substantiate a charge alone and further evidence is still required for a successful prosecution.

The training of constables as well as senior officers has been highlighted as an essential requirement of developing the effectiveness of forensic science in investigations. Problems were referred to by analogy by one senior scientific manager:

> Over the last few years, if an identification had been made using either fingerprints or DNA, it tended to be allocated to just whichever bobby went to the original crime. So, in effect, you've got this Rolls Royce piece of evidence and you're giving it to the junior mechanic.[3]

There may also be difficulties arising where police have a poor understanding of what DNA can prove: 'The police can be blinded by their own science and believe it will save them from investigating a case properly. Even some senior police don't understand what DNA can actually prove, that just having a DNA match won't prove a case.'[4] Such problems belie a lack of understanding about the interpretation of DNA results; that a DNA match in itself is meaningless without proper interpretation and contextualisation:

> The interpretation of the DNA is more important than the result itself. There can be all sorts of reasons for a DNA profile appearing somewhere – we have to look at all the possibilities ... Because it is so powerful, it can't discriminate between minor contact and major contact. You have to be able to interpret the DNA result.[5]

Coleman (2004: 9) observes that it has been stated that it is 'quite natural' for a senior police officer to have limited or little knowledge of forensics, as many senior officers are rarely involved in serious criminal investigations, or may not have engaged in front-line duties for some years. He points out that the impact of such ignorance is significant however, with appreciation of the effectiveness of spending

---

2 Interviewee 6/L/C.
3 Interviewee 9/P/C.
4 Interviewee 2/L/C.
5 Interviewee 6/L/C.

on forensics not properly understood or communicated to less senior officers. Potential problems encountered when insufficiently trained officers attempt to rely upon forensic evidence include the continuation of a thorough investigation after a 'hit':

> There tends to be a reliance on forensic evidence in terms of once you have it, other avenues aren't followed up. You need to guard against a 'silver bullet' mentality: we have a DNA match, case closed. DNA is sometimes conceptually difficult for police to grasp ... Rather than look for the cigarette end, for which someone may come up with a plausible explanation, you need to look for the DNA associated with the commissioning of the offence, so you need to get the forensic knowledge right ... forensic knowledge levels in the police service are fairly low – you need to have safety nets, to make sure that people act properly on the information they've got. Police officers can rest on their laurels if they get a forensic hit and they need to not be complacent. Anecdotally, they will put it to the offender and hope to get an admission out of it.[6]

Abbreviated or skewed investigations are then a potential risk, with the temptation for police to use DNA to prove a case, or supplement a lack of evidence:

> The police can be over-reliant on the DNA, if they find a match, they think, right let's investigate this, rather than investigating all the evidence. It can skew the investigation ... There is a temptation probably to just run to court with a DNA match and save time and bother carrying on an investigation, they could just rely on their DNA match because that will carry a lot of weight with the jury. There is a danger then that DNA could be used to supplement weak cases, because juries are convinced by it, so DNA could be used as a crutch to hold up weak cases. Investigations can be distorted, it shouldn't be a case of who was there, but what happened when they were there.[7]

Police officers themselves admit that there can be dangers:

---

6 Interviewee 1/P/C.
7 Interviewee 2/L/C.

You can slip into this lazy approach that 'we've got DNA we needn't bother doing the rest of the work'. What it does though is give you a concrete line of inquiry, which still needs corroborating with other evidence. There's a lot of good old-fashioned detective work also needed.[8]

Erroneous police conclusions at early stages of an investigation can lead to unwarranted prosecutions and convictions, which can result in demands that police investigations be subject to scrutiny for this is where 'the roots of miscarriages of justice are to be found', due in part to a lack of 'advanced verification procedures' (Zuckerman 1992: 324). Increasingly faith is placed in forensic science to fulfil a supporting or 'verification' role in investigations, however, forensic science may serve to hide from critical gaze detection practices where forensic evidence has been afforded 'apparent credibility, leaving the process of detection, evidence gathering and investigation hidden. The canopy of science obscures the primitive analytic tools that persist. These technological advances, even those enhancing information processing, have little altered police effectiveness' (Manning 2001: 84).

There are problems then with the training of police officers in forensic awareness and the dangers of the 'silver bullet' mentality. Misunderstanding the strength of the evidence and what can be actually be determined by a DNA match may lead to missed opportunities to detect offenders effectively and swiftly, and possibly to the collapse of cases from poor preparation:

> Will the police remember that good detective work, the kind that cannot be accomplished by a telephone call to the … DNA databank, is still a requirement for a successful identification? Will they remember that no forensic evidence is any good unless it is recovered from the crime scene, sometimes by sifting for hours through apparently meaningless debris? (Baird 1992: 75)

A 'lazy approach' is of particular concern; the initial statement from the FSS regarding potential DNA evidence is a one-page report with only initial results and basic information, stating that there has been a preliminary match, produced quickly so as to be used at interview. Only if a suspect does not indicate a wish to plead guilty will the

---

8 Interviewee 2/P/C.

FSS go on to do full testing procedures and produce a full statement for trial.[9]

In addition, there are also important considerations when accepting DNA 'matches', for match statistics are, according to Saul (2001: 93), 'misleading in some crucial respects'. Simple matches denote the presence of someone at a crime scene at some point in time. In effect, particularly at scenes that may be public areas, Saul argues, 'a match may not mean very much' (2001: 93). The Home Office itself states that 'in many cases of minor interpersonal violence, DNA is relatively easily recovered but makes no material impact on the subsequent investigation as the identities of those involved are frequently not in question' (Forensic Science and Pathology Unit 2005: 16). Leary and Pease (2002: 8) also stress: 'a match is not a conviction', using an analogy presented to them by an expert, who described DNA as:

> 'a fresh filling placed between two slices of stale bread'. By this was meant that while the science may be good, police operations and training (the first stale slice) and the vicissitudes of prosecution and conviction (the second stale slice) limit the quality of the whole sandwich experience.

However, Home Office Circular 58/2004, which amends section 23 of HOC 16/95, states that suspects can be charged upon the basis of DNA matches as a result of speculative searches of the NDNAD, only 'so long as there is further supporting evidence'. In addition, such dangers should be protected against by s. 23 of the *Criminal Procedure and Investigations Act* 1996, which states that: 'where a criminal investigation is conducted all reasonable steps are taken for the purposes of the investigation and, in particular, all reasonable lines of inquiry are pursued'. As the ACPO (2003: 36) DNA guidelines state, it is crucial to obtain additional evidence.

In addition to the sampling of arrestees for matching with crime scene samples, or a speculative search against the NDNAD for the prosecution of relevant offences, forensic DNA has also leant itself to further applications in criminal investigations such as intelligence screens, is also being used as an 'intelligence' tool, and is undergoing research for potential future uses such as producing offender 'identikits' or familial searching (see Chapter 6). In addition

---

9 See Bramley (2004: 20). Recently, more developed testing kits may preclude this two-stage process, providing a full result upon first testing.

to changes to investigatory practices in light of new technologies of identification, and presenting new challenges and problems in crime detection, forensic identity databases have also been used to assist in 'mass screens' of volunteers.

Targeted intelligence screenings

Although now associated with DNA screening, and apparently meeting with public approval, the police use of 'mass screening' techniques has a long and controversial history. In May 1948, in the 'Blackburn baby' case, fingerprints were taken from the entire male population of Blackburn where a three-year-old girl had been sexually assaulted and murdered, the perpetrator having left fingerprints next to the cot in the hospital from where the child was abducted. The fingerprints of the suspect eventually came from set of prints number 46,253, whereupon a local man was convicted and executed for the murder (Eddy 1955). In 1954, the Metropolitan Police undertook a mass screen after the murder of a woman on a golf course, with the palm prints of 10,000 local male residents taken. Identification of the suspect, later convicted, was made on physical examination of set of palm prints number 4,604, demonstrating the timely processes used at that time.[10] These investigations did much to bolster support for fingerprints and the mass screening process, though controversy over such tactics did surface in allegations in the House of Commons that in 1957 the Metropolitan Police had been ordered to fingerprint all Irishmen.[11]

In the UK controversy ensued however when in January 1976 police planned to take fingerprints from 15,000 people, including all residents over the age of 12 in the Blakelaw district of Newcastle-Upon-Tyne, following the murder of an old lady. This was the first time that such young volunteers had been sought, raising a storm of protest (Levenson 1980: 707). The Home Secretary assured the public that no pressure would be brought to bear on citizens, that the consent of parents would be sought, and all fingerprints would be subsequently destroyed.[12] By May 1976 the fingerprints of several hundred schoolchildren had been taken and the National Council for Civil Liberties, in a prescient response, voiced concerns that the use

---

10 See the Metropolitan Police Service Centenary Fingerprint Bureau Pack, available at http://www.metpolice.gov.uk.

11 Hansard, HC (series 5) vol. 580, cols. 1391–92 (23 May 1957).

12 Hansard HC (series 5) vol. 922, cols. 591–92 (23 January 1976).

of techniques such as mass fingerprinting would: 'bring nearer the day when the public would be asked to accept such blanket police techniques as unavoidable, and was a very serious step on the path to a system of universal databank holding information on individuals which was in the hands of the police or government' (Levenson 1980: 707).

In the first case to utilise a mass DNA screen, indeed the first use of DNA in a criminal investigation in the UK, a sample from a man confessing to the second of two rapes occurring in rural Leicestershire proved him not to be the rapist. It also proved that the two rapes had been perpetrated by the same offender. Police then proceeded in January 1987 to take DNA samples from all the males of three local villages aged between 16 and 34. The 5,500 samples taken failed to match the crime stains. However, months later, it was brought to the attention of the police that one man had given a sample on behalf of a work colleague, Colin Pitchfork. Both men were arrested and Pitchfork's sample matched the crime scene samples. Pitchfork confessed and was convicted in January 1988.[13]

Since this first use of a mass DNA screen, the police have increasingly resorted to screens to solve serious crimes. By the end of 1999, 120 mass screens had taken place with an average of 4,000 samples collected,[14] leading some to conclude that: 'mass screenings demonstrate that policing by consent is still a viable option' (Walker and Cram 1990: 488). The use of mass screens in the UK now appears less controversial, while in some international cases much larger screens have taken place, with a screening of 16,400 men in western Germany in the hunt for the killer of an 11-year-old girl (Imwinkelreid and Kaye 2001). The Australian police have also utilised the mass screening technique with success in several high-profile cases although this proved controversial with the issue of consent in such screens being demonstrated as being illusory, and rights then to refuse compliance negated:

> This erosion of rights is perhaps most clearly evidenced in the recent cases of mass testing in Wee Waa and Norfolk Island, where non-compliance became not so much an exercise of choice but rather an act equated with an inference of guilt ... Arguably,

---

13 See Walker and Cram 1990: 480; Hibbs 1989: 619; Wambaugh 1989.
14 'Rights fears over DNA plan', BBC news, 30 July 1999 (http://news.bbc.co.uk/1/hi/uk/408097.stm).

this is best characterised by the familiar question heralded in media reports of the time: 'Why wouldn't he give a sample if he has nothing to hide?' There has been enough challenge to the reality of informed consent within forensic procedures without the added strain concerned with the actuality of volition in mass-testing situations. (Findlay and Grix 2003: 281)

The use of mass screens has also been used to contrast the police use of DNA in the USA and the UK. In 1966, the Supreme Court in the USA stated in *Schmerber* v. *California*,[15] that: '[t]he interests in human dignity and privacy which the Fourth Amendment protects, forbids any such intrusions on the mere chance that desired evidence might be obtained' (Peterson 2000: 1232). Again in 1969, in *Davis* v. *Mississippi*[16] the Supreme Court ruled that 'dragnet' fingerprint screens violated the Fourth Amendment, as there are no warrants, probable cause, or individualised suspicion. The US National Institute of Justice characterises the UK use of mass screens or 'intelligence-led screens', as a 'primary investigative tool' where it has been used with success since 1995 in at least 17 high-profile cases. The US National Institute of Justice (1998: 6) states that UK officials believe that the DNA testing program 'has actually reduced overall law enforcement costs by eliminating extensive traditional police investigations in some cases'. This is in contrast to the use of DNA sampling procedures in the USA where the 'databanking' (retention and use of DNA samples in a large database) of voluntary samples has been characterised as being 'deeply flawed' by civil liberties experts (Peterson 2000: 1232).

Police intimidation, public reluctance to cooperate, and repeated approaches for samples have been cited as consequences of a penchant for mass screens, castigated as a 'waste of money'.[17] Pressures to submit to such screenings in high-profile cases are huge, with sanctions for non-compliance and immediate suspicion cast upon those who refuse to cooperate. The use of mass screens is a case of requiring the local population to prove their innocence via a blood sample, rather than the police using conventional investigative techniques to raise suspicions against particular individuals that then require rebuttal. Indeed, in examining the use of very public mass screens in New South Wales, Saul (2001: 78) argues:

15 *Schmerber* v. *California* (1966) 384 US at 769–770.
16 *Davis* v. *Mississippi* 394 US 721 (1969) at 727.
17 'Rights fears over DNA plan', BBC news, 30 July 1999 (http://news.bbc. co.uk/1/hi/uk/408097.stm).

There is a tendency for DNA testing to replace trial, since a charge becomes determined by the apparently definitive and publicly conclusive DNA test. The presumption of innocence is reversed, undermining a key element of the right to a fair trial, even though a myriad of scientific, statistical, and procedural issues may affect the accuracy of a particular DNA test.

During 'Operation Minstead', 1,000 black men in South London were 'profiled' in the hunt for a serial rapist, and those men were then requested to volunteer for DNA tests. Of those, 125 initially refused, leading to 'intimidatory' letters from the police urging reconsideration, and five were arrested with their DNA taken post-arrest and added to the NDNAD. Such actions have raised questions of legality, with arrests only lawful with 'reasonable suspicion' of an individual having committed a criminal act. If the police are to arrest on non-compliance with a DNA request, then that casts non-compliance as a crime, a step that worries civil libertarians and may lose the spirit of cooperation essential in these circumstances.[18] Despite such concerns, the use of mass screenings and the retention of the samples voluntarily submitted are just the latest development in the expansion of forensic identification databases. Such databases are also being put to other uses and are forging an institutional role in the 'risk society' as a risk-aversion technology tasked with bringing certainty to the criminal process, saving police resources and securing community safety; a mighty weapon in the 'war on crime'.

Ethical disclosure of DNA evidence

Pre-interview disclosure of scientific evidence has been singled out as raising problems for investigators, as a scientist explained: 'A suspect will either tell lies and try and explain the scientific evidence, if they are told too much, or will admit it. So, the biggest improvement that could be made with scientific evidence is actually nothing to do with science – it's to do with pre-interview disclosure'.[19] The police need to ensure that scientific evidence is not unnecessarily disclosed to suspects, thereby permitting suspects the opportunity to provide an innocent explanation for the evidence:

---

18 Ford, R. and Tendler, S. 'Innocent men forced to give DNA samples', *The Times*, 9 July 2004.
19 Interviewee 3/L/P.

[There are] lots of issues around pre-interview disclosure ... So you can have this marvellous piece of evidence, i.e. a fingerprint, and before they get interviewed, the suspect knows what it is and where it is, and so they can arrive at an 'explanation' for the interview, and so losing the use of the evidence ... You don't have strictly in legal terms to disclose that amount of detail. It's the trick of the thing – they need sufficient information to know what they are answering to, but not enough to concoct a story to explain away the scientific evidence. Bobbies have been telling legal advisors everything so your work is wasted. About 30 per cent of scientific evidence can be wasted in this way as they [suspects] can claim legitimate access. The very high burden of proof means that if you can come up with a reasonable story of how your fingerprints were found where they were, then you won't get a conviction – it probably won't even get to court. But if you simply tell the legal advisor that you have scientific evidence, but don't tell them what it is or where it is, then they have to think. This is a key aspect that still hasn't been well gripped nationally.[20]

More worryingly perhaps, some police had seemed to positively advocate keeping forensic evidence details from the suspect, at least until forced to disclose it pre-trial:

There's a risk of giving too much away during the interview stage. Tactically what you want is the suspect to give you an account of their involvement without the issue of DNA coming into it. The skill in the interview is to get the suspect to give an account without giving anything away. We have had problems with police being harried by solicitors and giving away the DNA evidence and then them advising their clients to explain it away. At some stage during the interview you would probably disclose it, although not always. It will always be disclosed before trial but if you don't need to disclose it at interview then you don't.[21]

ACPO have published guidelines for police officers on how to handle DNA evidence during interviews with suspects. This states

---

20 Interviewee 9/L/P
21 Interviewee 2/L/P.

that interviewers will 'prefer' to hear a suspect's account before they disclose details of evidence, although the guidance states that it is 'in the interests of all parties concerned for some information to be disclosed to the suspect and their solicitor before or at the beginning of the interview' (ACPO 2003: 40). However, ACPO warn against 'premature disclosure', which may 'provide the suspect with an opportunity to fabricate an explanation to support a claim of lawful access or to give a false account to explain the reasons why the evidence exists' (ACPO 2003: 41). They advise that the suspect should establish their position without the disclosure of DNA evidence (though a suspect must know why they are being interviewed), as innocent suspects have no reason to fear non-disclosure, and indeed may benefit from providing a full account 'uncontaminated' by knowledge of the evidence. Guilty suspects meanwhile 'should not be given the opportunity to fabricate a defence or an alibi around the police evidence' (ACPO 2003: 42).

Officers are reminded that there is no legal obligation to disclose information pre-interview and they are to decide how much information to disclose at interview stage, the Crown Prosecution Service (CPS) then deciding what documents to disclose to the defence. However, if a legal representative asks if there is DNA evidence, the interviewer is not permitted to lie or deliberately mislead. ACPO concludes the guidance by reminding officers:

> Police must use the introduction of DNA evidence in an ethical manner. Officers should not attempt to mislead legal advisers or suspects by implying that the suspect has left DNA at a scene or on recovered items when they have not. This would be unfair to the suspect and highly likely to be deemed unlawful. The court would rule evidence gained by such deception inadmissible. (ACPO 2003: 42)

Previous reports have indicated that 'the availability of forensic evidence appears to result in a high proportion of guilty pleas' (HMIC 2002: 5), implying that DNA matches can be used tactically by police investigators, not just to evidence a case at court, but to prevent a case going to trial. Guilty pleas coerced in light of DNA or fingerprint evidence are then considered 'good' outcomes in a system striving to minimise trials and secure more convictions. The use of DNA evidence as a 'lever' in the police station also requires research, particularly when s. 62 (10) of *PACE* enables the drawing of adverse inferences at trial from a refusal to consent to sampling (although the use of this may now be limited by the expansion of police powers meaning that consent is rarely required). Such research should include further consideration of issues concerning: the ethical use of DNA evidence; the protections afforded suspects; the rights of suspects not to assist the police in their investigations; and the role of legal advice when facing DNA evidence. Indeed, lawyers attested to the impact that forensic evidence would have on their advice to clients: 'If you're representing a defendant, and you're in a position where the prosecution are saying that they have DNA then that would have a huge impact on your advice'.[22] Further anecdotal evidence suggests that most lawyers will advise clients to plead guilty when informed that there is a DNA match, without further investigation into the actual strength or reliability of that evidence.

Consequences of non-compliance with requests for samples

An order authorised under the *Magistrates' Courts Act* to take fingerprints from those refusing to consent did not provide for a sanction for non-compliance, but there was also no legal right to resist and the police had the authority to use 'reasonable force'. In *R v. Jones*,[23] Jones's resistance (biting officers, leading to assault charges), was only lawful because the police were not properly complying with the order obtained under s. 40, by taking her fingerprints at the police station and not the courthouse. The defendant was then entitled to resist and the police were guilty of an assault against her:

> It must be remembered that many people find it humiliating to be fingerprinted and regard such a requirement as an infringement of the liberty of the subject. The provisions of s. 40 of the Magistrates' Courts Act 1952 were the result of considerable public debate and the safeguards in the section are to be strictly regarded. It is an important protection for the subject who is at liberty that his fingerprints may be taken against his will only in the court building where the order was made. The subject who insists on this is acting within his rights.[24]

In contrast, Parliament included in s. 8 of the *Road Traffic Act* 1967 penalties for non-compliance with a lawful request for a breath

---

22 Interviewee 1/P/C
23 *R v. Jones* [1978] 3 All ER 1098; see also *The Times* 6 February 1978; [1978] Crim LR 684; [1978]; Telling (1978).
24 *R v. Jones* [1978] 3 All ER 1098, 1101.

sample from a police officer (or later, a blood or urine sample). Under the statute, refusal – without reasonable excuse – to provide a sample is to commit a crime, with the penalty to match that imposed if a sample had proved the driver to be over the alcohol limit. The intention being to avoid drivers evading prosecution and possible conviction by refusing a sample (they would also not receive lesser punishment for not providing a sample, so there is incentive for a driver to provide a sample and hope). Obtaining samples was vital to prove the commission of an offence, but additionally, must be taken without delay as the metabolism of alcohol could result in a guilty driver evading conviction if police had to seek recourse to the courts to order a sample.

The *Criminal Justice and Court Services Act* 2000 gave the police powers to test detainees for the presence of class A drugs by way of a urine or non-intimate sample. If failing to comply with the request without good cause, he is liable to prosecution, punishable with up to three months in prison. The reasoning for permitting penalties for non-compliance is common to that used in arguments for compulsory sampling in road traffic offences; it circumvents the problem of avoidance of conviction of the correct offence by the defendant's refusal (as the timeliness of the sample is of importance, making it vital that the police can obtain the sample in time to prove the offence).

More controversially, *PACE* s. 62(10) provides for the drawing of adverse inferences at trial for refusal to consent to bodily samples; if a person refuses to provide an intimate sample they may be warned that this refusal may harm their defence at trial. If a suspect continues to refuse to consent to a request in the correct form without good cause, the court can draw such inferences as it saw proper, meaning that 'refusal to supply a sample was capable of amounting to evidence of guilt and failure to supply a sample could be used to corroborate other evidence' (Alldridge *et al.* 1995: 277). Section 62(10) was strongly criticised for dismantling the burden of proof: 'If the accused does refuse to supply a sample, it means that the attention of the jury is focused on the defence rather than on the nature and strength of the prosecution's case' (Easton 1991: 28).

Perhaps of greater concern is the potential use by the police of s. 62(10) as a 'lever' to obtain a sample by using the threat of adverse inferences to persuade reluctant suspects to provide a sample. This invokes debate over protections afforded suspects and the rights of suspects not to assist the police in their investigations. The argument most often relied upon is that there are no valid reasons for an innocent suspect not to provide fingerprints or DNA samples, whereas there are a variety of reasons why a suspect may wish to remain silent under questioning, so differentiating the two situations. However, this has been contested; there may indeed be several reasons for innocent non-compliance (as is accepted when serving police officers refuse to submit a sample to the Police Elimination DNA Database):

> First, many individuals will not accept that existing laws or practices will guarantee that the privacy of their non-criminal activities will be observed ... Second, some individuals may object to the procedure for obtaining samples ... Third, some people will object to participating in a criminal investigation without the backing of statutory compulsion or prior evidence of suspicion. Indeed, some will simply object to aiding the police at all. (Gans 2001: 173)

There is also potential for the police to use sample requests as an investigatory or surveillance tool, with the strength of such, as Gans (2001: 174) observes, 'obvious to suspects, as well as investigators, perhaps to the point of generating additional evidence of consciousness of guilt ... DNA request surveillance is potentially more powerful than traditional methods of interrogation.' Prison authorities in New South Wales, Australia, have been reported as changing the security classifications of those prisoners refusing to provide samples to police upon request (Gans 2001: 173). When faced with a sample request, there must be a choice made between two adverse consequences: giving the sample or revealing a fear of giving the sample, forcing the individual into a coerced position which in itself can generate self-incrimination in the absence of pre-existing suspicion (2001: 178). Indeed, Gans (2001) asserts that 'so called' volunteers in mass screens are under considerable pressure to comply, making the sampling compelled self-incrimination, and risking losing traditional limits of investigative compulsion.

There remains contention also over the evidential weight of inferences from refusal to consent at trial. Whilst no one can be convicted by the drawing of adverse inferences alone (*CJPOA* 1994 s. 38), there are questions where a defendant may have refused a sample and remained silent – do two adverse inferences add up to guilt? In *R* v. *Smith*[25] it was held that refusal to provide a sample could

---

25 *R* v. *Smith* (1985) 81 Cr.App.R. 286.

corroborate other evidence, but could not lead to a conviction alone. Clarification of the weight of DNA 'matches' and adverse inferences is vital if we are to increasingly rely upon database 'mining' techniques. In such a situation, evidence of the 'match' generated by the database and adverse inferences from a refusal to consent to a sample could be combined to form the basis of a prosecution. This raises the likelihood of defendants convicted exclusively on the basis of a DNA 'match': 'the DNA database makes it likely that an increasing number of cases will come to court where the prosecution presents only DNA evidence. Such cases pose difficult evidential problems for fact finders, especially if the defence adduces exculpatory evidence' (Redmayne 1998: 453). In a case mentioned in debate in the House of Lords in 1998 a Mr Easton, an elderly gentleman suffering from Parkinson's disease and largely housebound, was charged with burglary after a DNA match on the national database.[26] In this instance, the CPS halted the prosecution when it became clear that Mr Easton had not partaken in any housebreaking and that the match was a false positive: an example however, of the dangers of basing convictions upon DNA matches generated by the database, possibly supported by 'adverse inferences'.

As discussed the European Court of Human Rights has held that the non-consensual taking of an intimate sample could contravene Article 8, with even minimal physical interference with a person against their will requiring justification (*X* v. *Netherlands*).[27] However, the Council of Europe Recommendation does not forbid the use of coercion in forensic sampling, but states that:

> use of these techniques should take full account of and not contravene such fundamental principles as the inherent dignity of the individual and respect for the human body, the rights of the defence and the principle of proportionality in the carrying out of criminal justice.[28]

The recommendation goes on: 'where the domestic law admits that samples may be taken without the consent of the suspect, such sampling should only be carried out if the circumstances of the

---

26 Lord Phillips of Sudbury, HL Debs, vol. 625 col. 961 (8 May 2001).
27 Commission Decision of 4 December 1978, App.8239/78.
28 Recommendation No.R (92) 1 (10 February 1992) at p. 6.

case warrants such action,'[29] The ECtHR held in *Kruslin* v. *France*,[30] that for state powers to be 'in accordance with law', they must be clearly set out in legislation, compatible with the rule of law, and its consequences accessible to the person. In this case, as in *Malone* v. *UK*,[31] it is the requirement that the power be compatible with the rule of law that offers the greatest protection against over-zealous police and legislature, as 'there must be some practical and meaningful control incorporated into the domestic law which will protect against arbitrary interferences or misuse of discretionary powers' (Alldridge *et al.* 1995: 276).

Whilst there may be alternatives to coercion, i.e. creating a separate offence of refusing a sample and allowing adverse inferences to be drawn, neither achieve the aim of actually getting the sample, prosecuting the crime successfully, and adding the sample to the database. It is no surprise therefore that they are being ultimately rejected in favour of powers to forcefully coerce individuals. While such tactics have been characterised as 'affording brutality the cloak of law' in the USA,[32] and the UK government have previously rejected methods of 'deep interrogation' in Northern Ireland in the 1970s, the forcible taking of samples now appears to be not only legal but publicly touted as 'necessary' for the prevention of crime. However, critics such as Walker and Cram (1990: 493) assert that such methods are 'unconscionable ... no matter what their results'.

The reality however, is that the powers available to the police to forcibly take a sample are rarely required, most detainees and suspects choosing to consent, or consent not being required by law. Additionally, in light of the increased encouragement to take samples to expand the DNA database in particular, the position of the sampling laws in light of the legal privilege against self-incrimination must be considered. In the instance of bodily samples, the privilege against self-incrimination is particularly pertinent, considering the incriminatory nature of the samples that are requested during the criminal process, their use at trial and the weight accorded them by judges and juries alike.

---

29   Recommendation No.R (92) 1 (10 February 1992) at p. 7.
30   App. 11801/85, (1990) 12, EHRR 547.
31   *Malone* v. *UK* (1984) 7 EHRR 14.
32   Frankfurter J in *Rochin* v. *California* 342 US 165 (1952) at p. 173.

The privilege against self-incrimination and bodily samples

In considering the extension of police powers to obtain DNA samples from citizens, Corns suggests that the 'ratchet effect' witnessed – where police powers are continually extended – may lead to the loss of important civil rights, including the right to silence and the privilege against self-incrimination:

> Herein lies one of the fundamental contradictions which is generated by the incorporation of DNA technology into criminal justice practices. On one hand, DNA technology becomes useless unless the suspect is either persuaded or physically forced to provide a bodily sample, yet on the other hand, the very legitimacy of the Anglo criminal procedure and practice is premised upon the general assumption of innocence and the right to silence. It is conceptually difficult to reconcile the forceful taking of a suspect's blood with the rhetoric of the presumption of innocence, the right to silence and the privilege against self-incrimination. (Corns 1992: 18)

As Scutt (1990:10) warns, 'the allegation that the accused's DNA pattern is reproduced in body fluids at the crime scene immediately conjures up a highly suspicious prejudicial atmosphere in which the presumption of innocence tends to be replaced with a presumption of guilt'. The presumption of innocence gives rise to a disparate group of rights, such as the right against self-incrimination: 'a general immunity, possessed by all persons and bodies from being compelled on pain of punishment to answer questions which may later be used to incriminate them'.[33] Such rights are explicitly expressed in international documents such as Article 14(3)(g) of the International Covenant on Civil and Political Rights, which asserts that citizens have the right 'not to be compelled to testify against himself or confess his guilt'. Article 6 of the ECHR does not expressly mention either the privilege against self-incrimination or the right to silence, however, the ECtHR has consistently declared that Article 6 states only minimum rights and that it should receive an expansive application,[34] describing the rights as 'lying at the heart of the notion

---

33 Lord Mustill in *R* v. *Director of the Serious Fraud Office, ex parte Smith* [1993] AC 1, 3.

34 See *Delcourt* v. *Belgium* (1979–80) 1 EHRR 355 at para. 25; *Moreiva de Azvedo* v. *Portugal* (1992) 13 EHRR 731, para. 66.

of a fair procedure'.[35] The rationale for such rights was summed up in *Murray* v. *UK*:

> There can be no doubt that the right to remain silent under police questioning and the privilege against self-incrimination are generally recognised international standards which lie at the heart of the notion of a fair procedure under Art 6. By providing the accused with protection against improper compulsion by the authorities these immunities contribute to avoiding miscarriages of justice and to securing the aim of Article 6.[36]

While under common law the citizen is under no duty to provide evidence against himself, the right against self-incrimination was first restricted by road traffic legislation and there are provisions in company law and customs laws that restrict the general right.[37] Indeed: 'Parliament has made many inroads into the privilege against self-incrimination. Many statutes require individuals to answer questions, provide information, and produce documents in a variety of contexts, with threat of criminal sanctions for non-compliance' (Dennis 2002: 132). The right to silence was significantly diminished by the *Criminal Justice and Public Order Act* 1994, ss. 34 and 35, which provided for the drawing of 'proper' adverse inferences at trial, should a jury believe there to be no real explanation for the defendant's silence when facing a case to answer.[38] In the *Attorney General's Reference No.7 of 2000*, there was no doubt that the privilege against self-incrimination was not absolute and that many inroads had been made on that privilege by Parliament in a range of statutory contexts.[39] The status of, and rationale for, the right against self-incrimination was subsequently reiterated by the Privy Council: 'The right not to incriminate oneself is an important right, but not an absolute right, and it is directed to improper compulsion, coercion and oppression likely to result in forced confessions and miscarriages of justice.'[40]

---

35 *Murray* v. *UK* (1996) 22 EHRR 29, para. 45; *Saunders* v. *UK* (1997) 23 EHRR 313, para 68; *Heaney and McGuinness* v. *Ireland* [2001] *Criminal Law Review* 481.
36 (1996) 22 EHRR 29 at 60–61; see also *Funke* v. *France* (1993) 16 EHRR 297, para. 44.
37 For example, *The Road Traffic Act* 1988, s. 172.
38 See *R* v. *Cowan and other appeals* [1995] 4 All ER 984.
39 *Attorney General's Reference No.7 of 2000* [2001] Crim LR 736.
40 *Brown* v. *Stott* [2001] 2 All ER 97, 113.

The distinction between being forced to answer incriminating questions and the provision of a bodily sample has led to debate over whether the right against self-incrimination is even relevant in consideration of the legality of coerced sampling (Ashworth 2002: 18–22). The possible argument that the compulsory taking of bodily samples, including fingerprints, may constitute self-incrimination, was raised in Scotland, in *Adair* v. *McGarry*:

> If a man's fingerprints could not be obtained without some involuntary action on his part, and were to be obtained only by tormenting him until he agreed to give them, I could understand the argument. But if, as I am led to believe, fingerprints can be obtained with very moderate force *nolens volens* of the patient, and if this is done when he refuses to give them, then there is no question of the man being compelled to give evidence against himself … He is entirely passive, and he is not compelled to do anything requiring any exercise of his own will or control of his body.[41]

The argument that the ordering of the taking of fingerprints may contravene the right against self-incrimination was heard in *George* v. *Coombe*[42] where the defendant objected to the taking of fingerprints (under a s. 40 order from the Magistrate's Court), arguing that:

> as fingerprint evidence was the most convincing evidence of identity, such evidence was equivalent to an oral or written confession and that as a defendant could not be compelled by the law to make a confession, it was not a proper exercise of the justice's discretion to order that his fingerprints be taken.

It was held however, that this was a 'misconceived argument', on the basis that confessions are excluded where they are involuntary because an involuntary confession is unlikely to be reliable. The judges ruled that fingerprints were still reliable evidence whether compelled or not, and that reliability was not affected by the circumstances of their taking. The Court relied upon *Nowell*,[43] where evidence of a medical examination had been admitted, although the defendant argued that he had submitted to the examination, after repeated refusals, only

---

41   *Adair* v. *McGarry* (1933) SLT 482, 493.
42   *George* v. *Coombe* [1978] Crim LR 47.
43   *Nowell* [1948] 1 All ER 794.

when a police surgeon told him it might be to his advantage. Such a comment was not construed as inducement, and did not render the evidence unreliable.

Similarly, in *R v. Apicella*,[44] a sample taken from the defendant by prison authorities whilst undergoing treatment for a sexually transmitted disease, was equated with an oral confession by his defence. They argued that the sample, used by the prosecution to prove that the defendant suffered from the same disease contracted by victims of the sexual assault in question, should not have been taken without consent. The appeal was dismissed on the grounds that a basic principle of the law is that evidence which is relevant should be admitted unless there is a rule of law which says that it should not be: as the appellant had not been tricked into medical treatment, the use of the evidence was fair. This case was heard before the introduction of s. 78 of *PACE* and was decided using the common-law discretion exercised to exclude evidence in *R v. Sang*. It seems likely however, that even post-*PACE*, such an argument – that a fingerprint or bodily sample equated with a confession, and when taken using compulsion would render it inadmissible – would still fail.

The Privy Council affirmed in *Brown v. Stott*,[45] that compulsion to answer a question put by police under s. 172 of the *Road Traffic Act* 1988 did not infringe human rights, classifying the right against self-incrimination as a 'testimonial immunity' which protected people against being forced to speak. This meant that the obligation to answer a question was distinguishable from the taking of samples and the obtaining of documents, 'since neither of these require the person to speak and the evidence obtained is already in existence'.[46] In addition, the crucial question was whether s. 172 was a disproportionate response or one that undermined the suspect's right to a fair trial. Lord Bingham agreed that the High Court may be entitled to distinguish between the giving of answers and the provision of physical samples, but that this distinction should not be 'pushed too far' (Starmer *et al.* 2001: 212–13).

In the USA, the case of *Schmerber v. State of California*,[47] considered the legality of compulsory blood tests. The defendant, taken to hospital after a car crash, had a blood sample taken by a doctor

44   *R v. Apicella* [1986] Crim LR 238.
45   *Brown v. Stott* [2001] 2 All ER 97.
46   *Brown v. Stott* [2001] 2 All ER 97, 102.
47   *Schmerber v. State of California* (1966) 16 L.ed. 2d 908.

without his consent, fulfilling a police request. Upon conviction of drink-driving, the defendant appealed claiming that the compulsory blood test violated the Fourteenth Amendment (which insists upon 'due process of law'), the Fifth Amendment (which protects persons against being compelled to be a witness against themselves) and finally, the Ninth Amendment (which protects against 'unreasonable searches and seizures'). The appeal failed despite the dissenting opinion of Black J who stated that:

> to reach the conclusion that compelling a person to give his blood to help the state convict him is not equivalent to compelling him to be a witness against himself strikes me as quite an extraordinary feat ... It is a strange hierarchy of values that allows the state to extract a human being's blood to convict him of a crime because of the blood's contents but proscribes compelled production of his lifeless papers.[48]

This echoes the opinion in a Canadian case, where the right against self-incrimination was described as fundamental to the system of justice: 'so that it spans both statements and bodily substances obtained from the accused at the behest of the state'.[49] The Canadian court held that: 'while the evidence obtained from the seized bodily substances may be highly probative of whether an accused committed an offence, it is nevertheless subject to a general rule of exclusion in order to preserve the innate dignity of the individual from being interfered with, absent lawful authority' (Peck 2001: 465).

The argument then that requiring answers to questions may infringe the right not to incriminate oneself and yet the requirement to supply a bodily sample that will prove incriminating is not considered an infringement seems to require greater exposition by the English courts. As commented in *Brown v. Stott*: 'It is not easy to see why a requirement to answer a question is objectionable and a requirement to undergo a breath test is not.'[50] In the USA, the courts have drawn a distinction between a test where a suspect is not required to do anything (such as a blood test), and the case of compelling the production of papers where he would have to produce

---

48 Quoted at Brennan, J. [1967] *Law Quarterly Review* (83) 18.
49 *R v. Stillman* [1997] 1 SCR 607.
50 *Brown v. Stott* [2001] 97, 116.

them himself.[51] In the majority opinion of the Supreme Court in *Schmerber*, it was held that the privilege against self-incrimination:

> protects an accused only from being compelled to testify against himself, or otherwise provide the state with evidence of a testimonial or communicative nature, and that the withdrawal of blood, and use of the analysis in question, in this case did not involve compulsion to these ends.[52]

The ECtHR has sought to draw a distinction between physical evidence and evidence independent of the suspect. In *Saunders* v. *UK*,[53] it was held that the protection of Article 6 did not extend to material obtained 'through the use of compulsory powers but which has an existence independent of the will of the suspect, i.e. documents, and bodily samples'.[54] This appeared to contradict the decision in *Funke* v. *France*,[55] where it was held that the privilege against self-incrimination did extend to the handing over of potentially incriminatory documents. Dissenting opinion in *Saunders* v. *UK* pointed out that the overruling of *Funke* was done without cogent reasons, and that it was open to 'grave doubt' whether the distinction between oral and physical self-incrimination was sound:

> Why should a suspect be free from coercion to make incriminating statements but not from coercion to co-operate to furnish incriminating data? ... the will of the accused is not respected [in either case] in that he is forced to bring about his own conviction ... can it really be said that the results of a breath test to which a person suspected of driving under the influence has been compelled to have an existence independent of the will of the suspect?[56]

The case of *JB* v. *Switzerland*,[57] again held that the privilege against self-incrimination did not attach to documentary evidence as such evidence has an existence independent of the will of the accused.

51 Brennan, J. [1967] *Law Quarterly Review* (83) 18.
52 Brennan, J. [1967] *Law Quarterly Review* (83) 16.
53 *Saunders* v. *UK* (1996) 23 EHRR 313.
54 *Saunders* v. *UK* (1996) 23 EHRR 313 at para. 69.
55 *Funke* v. *France* (1993) 16 EHRR 297.
56 *Saunders* v. *UK* (1996) 23 EHRR 313, 355.
57 *JB* v. *Switzerland* [2001] *Criminal Law Review* 748.

Relying upon this tenuous distinction between evidence independent of the will of the accused (i.e. documents) and 'speech', the decision in *Heaney and McGuinness* v. *Ireland*,[58] dismissed the Irish government's argument that the 'fight against terrorism' constituted a significant public interest in compelling a person to speak, 'destroying the very essence' of the privilege against self-incrimination and the right to silence (Ashworth 2001: 867).

A rationale for distinguishing between testimony, documents, and bodily samples is that bodily samples cannot be subject to a lie; the evidence exists prior to the investigation, so cannot be fraudulently tampered with in light of possible criminal charges.[59] Another distinction has been posited as being that between indirect and direct compulsion. Direct compulsion destroys the 'very essence' of the right (as in *Heaney*) whereas indirect compulsion, where the right is preserved but adverse inferences may flow from its exercise, do not automatically entail a penalty and so do not involve direct compulsion (Starmer *et al.* 2001: 214). It would not appear that the domestic or Strasbourg courts would consider the use of fingerprints and bodily samples as an infringement of the privilege against self-incrimination (Starmer and Woolf 1999: 113), although why this is so has not been convincingly argued to date in domestic courts, with the argument that taking samples without 'defying the will' of the suspect does not lead to a contravention of the right against self-incrimination appearing particularly weak. It cannot be easily argued that breathalyser tests, urine or blood samples and fingerprints, taken without consent, do not require the will of the suspect. Such reasoning requires 'full and careful discussion',[60] with much more work required by the European and English courts.[61] As Ashworth (2001: 859) concludes, 'the first year of the [*Human Rights*] Act has brought stark conflicts of authority as to the reach of the privilege against self-incrimination'.

There are clearly then great difficulties in arguing that the privilege against self-incrimination is violated by enforced sampling, as well as a failure to successfully argue that other rights, such as Articles 8 and 14, are contravened by police powers to take non-consensual bodily samples. Indeed, even if a breach of human rights were found, the admissibility of such evidence has been acknowledged as, in general,

---

58   *Heaney and McGuinness* v. *Ireland* [2001] *Criminal Law Review* 481.
59   *JB* v. *Switzerland* [2001] *Criminal Law Review* 748, p. 21.
60   Commentary to *JB* v. *Switzerland* [2001] *Criminal Law Review* 748, 750.
61   Case comment, Ormerod, D. [2001] *Criminal Law Review* 739.

a matter for nation states to regulate.[62] *Khan* v. *UK*,[63] confirmed that evidence obtained in contravention of convention rights will still be admissible at trial, and that its exclusion is a matter for the judge in his consideration of the fairness of the trial. There is nothing to suggest therefore, that samples obtained in breach of Article rights may not still be admitted in evidence, particularly as the powers of the state to demand samples are increasing, with the justification of the 'prevention of crime' appearing to trump individual human rights.

The DNA Expansion Programme

Portrayals of the infallibility of DNA and its unrivalled ability to 'solve' crime have led to determined effort and financial investment in significantly increasing its use. Indeed, one of the NDNAD 'strategic objectives' is stated as being to demonstrate value for money from the database, especially in crime detection and through this, crime reduction.[64] The 'Forensic Integration Strategy' from the Home Office also aims to 'achieve a step change in the impact of forensic science on police performance in order to make major contributions to crime reduction and closing the justice gap' (Home Office Science Policy Unit 2004: 18). This was reinforced in the *Home Office Strategic Plan 2004–08* which stated that the police detection rate will be raised in order to bring more offenders to justice 'by improving police effectiveness and deploying new technology, including enhanced DNA testing … across the country to target criminals more effectively' (Home Office: 2004c: 10).

The DNA Expansion Programme was announced by the Prime Minister in September 1999, committing the government to an expenditure of £182.6 million to increase the collection of DNA samples and to build the NDNAD. This money was in addition to £19 million per annum from individual police forces, taking the total value of investment in the programme to March 2005 to over is £300 million (Home Office Forensic Science and Pathology Unit 2005). In 2004–05, the NDNAD has been provided £61 million (with NAFIS and IDENT1 taking a further £13 million) (Home Office

---

62 *Schenk* v. *Switzerland* (1988) 13 EHRR 242.

63 *Khan* v. *UK* (App.no. 35394/97, 12 May 2000), see also [2000] Criminal Law Review 684.

64 *NDNAD Annual Report* 2003/4 available at www.forensic.gov.uk. 3.

Science Policy Unit 2004: 14). The primary 'aim' of the programme was to input 3 million samples onto the NDNAD by April 2004, or 'a DNA profile for all known active suspect offenders'.[65] Before the Expansion Programme, an average of just over 200,000 offenders were being sampled per year. Since the programme, between April 2000 and March 2005, 2,250,000 persons have had their DNA loaded onto the NDNAD (Home Office Forensic Science and Pathology Unit 2005). The government provided extra funding for: police forces to increase the sampling of suspects; the recruitment of 650 additional Crime Scene Examiners and other staff; equipment purchases; and the collection and analysis of more DNA material at crime scenes (Home Office Science Policy Unit 2004: 12). The DNA Expansion Programme also provided funding during 2003/04 for an upgrade of 22,000 subject samples, taken since 2001 and reported as matching crime scene samples. Of these, 6,000 have been upgraded from SGM (Second Generation Multiplex) to SGM Plus profiles and have been compared again with the crime scene samples, with 52 per cent confirming the original match.[66]

It is claimed that science and technology 'play a vital role in modern policing', with the NDNAD 'revolutionising' crime detection (Home Office Science Policy Unit 2004: 1), with reports that DNA 'has not merely enhanced existing police capacity, but has even begun to replace 'the slow, tedious and expensive traditional investigative methods of police interviews' (Watson in White 1999: 325). The government 'targets' for the NDNAD, and police targets to take samples from suspects in particular offence types (i.e. the recent focus on DNA in volume crimes) mean that sample taking is now a routine element of police detention procedures. By 2001–02, DNA was used in approximately half of all cases received by the Forensic Science Service from the police, a significant growth from a quarter of cases in 1997–8 (Comptroller and Auditor General 2003). The increase is a result not only of greater understanding of forensic DNA potential and decreasing costs, but the speeding up of the process; the 'turnaround' time for DNA analysis being five days, down from almost a year in 1997 (Comptroller and Auditor General 2003: 6). The *NDNAD Annual Report* 2002–03, reported that on average just over 97 per cent of matches are declared within one working day, with

65 Caroline Flint, Ministerial Written Answers – Hansard, HC (series 5) vol. 426, col. 298W (3 November 2004).

66 *National DNA Database Annual Report* 2003–04: p. 16. available at www. fss.gov.uk.

100 per cent of violent crimes being reported within one working day. Special initiatives have seen even this reporting time shortened in pilot projects.[67] (The discrepancy between these statistics may be due to a lack of common criteria and the confusing vocabulary employed.)

DNA and criminal detection rates

Criminal detection rates have become the bane of the police, with the Audit Commission in 1993 strongly criticising poorly organised and 'reactive' investigative work and the lack of evaluation of the effectiveness of investigations. The Labour government have made much of 'closing the justice gap' – the difference between the amount of offences committed, and the number of people convicted for committing those offences. Detection rates have been steadily declining, dropping from 41 per cent in 1979 to 27 per cent in 1992 (Audit Commission 1993). Recent criminal statistics report a further drop, with detections for sexual offences down 4 percentage points on the previous year, while the overall crime detection rate in 2003/04 was 23.5 per cent (47 per cent for violent crimes) (Home Office 2004d: 103–4). However, there are indications that resort to DNA in criminal investigations can significantly improve detection rates, although it remains marginal when looking at the broad picture of criminal detection.

From the establishment of the NDNAD in April 1995, to March 2004, there were 584,539 suspect-to-scene matches and 38,417 scene-to-scene matches reported.[68] The DNA Expansion Programme evaluation now declares that the NDNAD provides the police with approximately 3,000 'matches' per month (with over 40,000 matches being declared in 2004/05). The clear-up rates for crimes where DNA evidence is available is significantly higher than for those crime scenes with no DNA evidence recovered, with the overall detection rate of 26 per cent rising to 40 per cent, (although the government have claimed a rise to 43 per cent),[69] where DNA is successfully recovered. Different

---

67 *National DNA Database Annual Report* 2002–3: p. 24. available at www. fss.gov.uk.

68 Forensic Science Service, Press Release, 2004, available at www.forensic. gov.uk.

69 Caroline Flint, ministerial written answers – Hansard, HC (series 5) vol. 426, col. 289W (3rd November 2004).

crime types can improve further; in domestic burglary the detection rate rises from 16 per cent to 41 per cent (see Home Office Forensic Science and Pathology Unit 2005: 16).

Of course, not all 'matches' result in a conviction, or even an arrest. Indeed, in 2004–05, the Home Office reported 19,873 'DNA detections' (detected crimes in which a DNA match was available) from 40,169 'offender-to-scene' matches reported by the FSS, a match-to-detection rate of 49 per cent (Home Office Forensic Science and Anthology Unit 2005: 12). However, on average each crime detected with DNA results in a further 0.8 crimes being detected, so there were a further 15,732 detections associated with those directly detected from the initial investigation, giving a total of 35,605 detections for the year (Home Office Forensic Science and Pathology Unit 2005: 15). The Home Office estimates that 20 per cent of the DNA detections result in a custodial sentence, preventing a further 7.8 crimes being committed (though it is not clear how these rates are calculated) (ACPO 2003: 9). The limitations of such statistics are exacerbated by: poor uniformity of data; highly variable return rates between different forces; poor recording of the use of DNA in detections; and 'the variable role played by DNA matches in the detection process' (Williams *et al.* 2004: 60).

The improvements in detection rates when DNA evidence is available may also require caution: 'These stark improvements, however, are balanced by the fact that we still load DNA from relatively few crime scenes' (Smith 2004: 14). There has been a 10 per cent increase in crime scene visits since 1999, with 913,717 visited in 2004/05. With a priority placed on using DNA to clear up more 'volume' crime however, in 2004/05 there were 1.5 million volume crimes, of which 45 per cent had a crime scene examination (Home Office Forensic Science and Pathology Unit 2005: 4). In the UK in 2004/05, just 12 per cent of these examined crime scenes resulted in DNA material being located, with a successful DNA sample being loaded onto the NDNAD for 45 per cent of these crime scenes. With 16.2 per cent of all crime scenes examined, this means that just 0.87 per cent of recorded crime produced a DNA sample that was loaded onto the NDNAD during 2004/05.[70]

Further, not all samples loaded onto the database result in a 'match' and if they do, only 49 per cent of matches result in a detection. This means that in 2004/05, a total of just under 0.35 per cent of recorded

---

70 *National DNA Database Annual Report* 2003–04. Available at www.fss.gov. uk, see p. 23.

crime could be claimed to have been 'detected' via DNA. Even adding into the equation the additional 'detections' from initial matches, the relevance of the NDNAD in crime investigation as a whole remains distinctly marginal and of course, in many of these cases there may have been a detection even without the DNA match (the DNA match was the first link to the suspect named in just 58 per cent of cases, meaning that in nearly half of these detections the police already had the name of the suspect provided by the NDNAD) (Home Office Forensic Science and Pathology Unit 2005: 15). There is also a wide variation between police forces in how many samples are sent for analysis, and how many crime scenes result in successful DNA samples. Of course, the Home Office itself admits that: 'in many cases of minor interpersonal violence, DNA is relatively easily recovered but makes no material impact on the subsequent investigation as the identities of those involved are frequently not in question' (Forensic Science and Pathology Unit 2005: 16).

Yet such statistics are meant to 'clearly' demonstrate, 'the value of the police continuing to take samples from the widest possible range of suspects'.[71] Objective assessment of the 'success' or otherwise of the DNA Expansion Programme on the basis of crime detection rates is therefore near impossible. Some commentators are now admitting: 'it is now generally acknowledged that the projected outputs for the DNA Expansion Programme were overly ambitious' (Coleman 2004: 9). Even some police officers concede that perhaps the ability of DNA to solve the crime problem has been overstated:

> DNA and fingerprints gives us the ability to shortcut the investigation, particularly a DNA match on the database ... It's impacted upon the public's thinking though, they expect too much from it. DNA isn't always helpful – a lot of the time it doesn't take us anywhere. People tend to think that DNA is the solution to everything and it isn't. And there are a lot of crime scenes where you will never find DNA. It's only useful then if you can get DNA and it actually means something.[72]

In addition, at the end of March 2005 there were 240,301 unsolved crime scene profile records on the NDNAD: a significant number of

---

71 *National DNA Database Annual Report* 2002–3. Available at www.fss.org. uk, p. 24–5.
72 Interviewee 9/L/P.

crimes where DNA is present, but a suspect sample has yet to match (Home Office Forensic Science and Pathology Unit 2005: 10).

Further, the Home Office (2004d: 104) continues to report that forensic sample 'matches' are not being followed up by investigators, or are not pursued for further crimes and are simply dealt with for the crime for which they were arrested and not all crimes which they may have committed, lowering potential detection rates. With the HMIC warning of the 'black hole' whereby potential detections are not efficiently turned into arrests, it could be assumed that the actual total number of people imprisoned as a result of the NDNAD is smaller than even these rudimentary calculations suggest. The Police Standards Unit is addressing the ongoing significant number of 'load failures' (samples taken from arrestees not making it onto the NDNAD). Such variation, and the huge financial commitment to the DNA Expansion Programme, demands that critical attention is paid not only to ensuring that public financial investment is reaping significant rewards, but also that potential encroachments upon civil liberties (in retaining DNA indefinitely) are justified by the resulting improvements in crime detection, and whether the 'tremendous opportunities for use and abuse' are being sufficiently utilised, and protected against (Townsley and Laycock 2004: 3).

DNA evidence and deterrence

The creation of a DNA database of all the active criminals of the nation, it is held, could lead to a drop in crime when offenders realise that they can no longer evade arrest and conviction. This argument is often invoked when supporting a compulsory national database: 'they may be deterred from offending upon release, or failing that, lay themselves open to the increased prospect of early arrest' (Hudson 1997: 127). Within a generation, crime will be reduced by creating a population aware that they will not evade detection, and also by the swift punishment and further deterrence of those who still transgress. As the President of the Police Superintendent Association has commented, a national database would enable criminals to be identified before they became serial offenders.[73] Indeed, the reasoning behind the decision to take samples from those suspected of committing a recordable offence (which can include minor property offences), rather than simply those suspected

---

73 'News in Brief', (1998) *Nature*, 393: 106.

of serious or violent crimes (as in most other countries), came from statistics demonstrating that the majority of men found guilty of sexual assaults had previous convictions for minor crimes. Offenders would be caught early in their 'career': 'a person who sets out to be a serial rapist could be denied his ambition because he would be identified from the database after the first assault' (and placed then on VISOR) (Martin *et al.* 2001: 229).

As seen, the DNA Expansion Programme is part of the government's bid to 'close the justice gap' in ensuring more offenders are prosecuted. Supporters of the programme also suggest however, that criminals 'may be deterred from offending upon release' (Hudson 1997: 127), while Lord Brown supports the enlargement of the NDNAD to deter 'from future crime those whose profiles are already on the database'. The Human Genetics Commission has stated that while aware of a potential deterrent effect, there was also evidence of changes in criminal behaviour – 'countermeasures' – to avoid leaving DNA evidence: 'We are slightly concerned about the potential for escalation in the seriousness of crimes in an attempt to destroy DNA evidence' (Human Genetics Commission 2002: 149). When offenders are 'forensically aware', this may influence criminal behaviour:

> when the suspect is arrested they will probably know that they have been arrested on the basis of a [forensic] 'hit'. There are high levels of forensic awareness, the offenders clearly know the power of this technology. They change their MO to avoid leaving DNA or fingerprints ... Stolen cars are now more often burnt out to try and make sure they don't leave any clues.[74]

Research into criminal careers highlights a potential flaw in the belief that the larger the NDNAD, the more 'useful' a deterrent or an investigative tool it will become. In reality, because of the 'churn' of the offending population (whereby many offenders on the NDNAD will already have ceased offending while many who have just commenced their 'criminal career' will not appear on the NDNAD for some time), the 'useful life' of a profile on the NDNAD is only as long as the offenders' criminal careers, which are typically short, thus: 'the need to remain realistic over the shortness of time for which most of those contributing criminal justice samples will remain relevant for crime detection purposes' (Leary and Pease 2002:

---

74 Interviewee 1/P/C.

3). Such research directly contradicts Lord Brown, who claimed that the benefits of enlarging the database are 'manifest'. Rather, to reap the greatest benefit from the huge sums expended on the NDNAD and the DNA Expansion Programme there needs to be proper focus upon maximising its effectiveness, whilst at the same time protecting against possible undesirable consequences and making sure that the incursions into individuals civil liberties are justified by the results.

Forensic science and criminal investigation: a case for caution?

In 1996, Tilley and Ford wrote that the future of forensic science was not clear, pointing at the potential of the NDNAD to strongly influence patterns of usage as well as impact upon more traditional forms of forensic analysis (Leary and Pease 2002: 8). In the intervening years the use of forensic science has become more widespread, often to great effect, in police investigations and it is increasingly understood that forensic science is available in broad range of cases although the efficient use of forensic science remains of concern (Walker and Starmer 1999). What has become clear is that the government will legislate to empower the police to utilise technology, with public interest in the fight against crime and the dependence upon information in the risk society outweighing public interest in privacy or consensual policing.

The non-consensual taking of bodily samples has been tested for compliance with human rights and passed, as has the retention of the information derived from such samples. Penalties for refusal to supply a sample in road traffic offences are universally accepted, with adverse inferences presently able to be drawn from refusal to supply bodily samples in other cases. The potential remains for future legislation to bring *PACE* into line with road safety laws, and allow for penal sanctions for refusal to consent to bodily samples being obtained. Additionally, there have been serious implications flowing from the provision of 'special' powers during times of perceived emergency or heightened threat. An example being legislation enacted to provide police with extra powers in the light of 'terrorist' threats (such as the IRA in England and Al Qaeda internationally). These have then been 'normalised': legislation enacted in light of particularised threats in response to a particular need then become 'acceptable' and so these provisions find their way into the more general criminal law, to be used on 'ordinary' criminals. So from 'cold hits'; confirming identities;

directing investigations; circumventing public non-cooperation; supporting a criminal charge; use as evidence at trial; use as data in academic research; and exonerating the wrongly convicted, forensic identity databases would appear to have multiple uses in the fight against crime. Yet not all investigations result in a conviction or other substantive outcome (in fact only the smallest minority of crimes are successfully 'cleared up'), and some result in miscarriages of justice (either innocent suspects being convicted, or guilty offenders escaping conviction).

It is now recognised that, 'the seeds of almost all miscarriages of justice are sown within a few days, sometimes hours of the suspect's arrest'.[75] For, despite the huge variation in circumstances in criminal investigations, 'what remains fairly constant ... is the high significance of judgements made at this early stage. As the case against a particular person begins to take shape, so (in most cases) does the investigator's belief that the person is guilty' (Ashworth 1998: 93). This is not to deny the power of forensic identification technologies to preclude the investigation of innocent suspects; indeed, DNA testing in particular can be very effective in eliminating innocent suspects swiftly. However, there is a case to be made that faith in forensic science has been too easily used to shore up falling confidence in police investigative competence without questioning the fallibility of forensic science itself. (Further, the expansion of DNA testing has in many respects had a very marginal impact upon criminal detection 'success' rates, with less than a half of a per cent of crimes 'solved' using DNA in 2004/05.)

There are a number of reasons for scepticism about the power of forensic science to eliminate miscarriages of justice however, with a critical one focusing on quality. The training and use of SOCOs (Scenes of Crime Officers) or SCEs (Scenes of Crimes Examiners) as part of an investigating team is essential, and scrimping on exhibit collection and analysis negatively affects the quality of forensic evidence.[76] Home Office research has concluded that much forensic

75 Mullin, C. in testimony to Royal Commission on Criminal Justice (Runciman Commission) (1991) Report (CM 2263) London: HMSO, para. 13. Quoted in Belloni and Hodgson (2000: 22).

76 These officers are vital as the initial collection of evidence is a key link in the chain of events leading to successful (forensic) testing, but it is also a vulnerable link (NIJ 1998: 7). The Audit Commission (1993) noted that between 1987 and 1991 numbers of SOCOs went up by 16 per cent whilst recorded crime went up by 40 per cent. It estimated that about one in three relevant cases was being attended.

analysis done in-house or by external suppliers (as opposed to the FSS which carries out the majority of forensic science analysis required by police) was not quality controlled or quality assured, with the risks of such to justice and to credibility 'obvious' (Tilley and Ford 1996). Additionally, economic considerations impact upon when, and why scientific expertise is utilised with pragmatism playing a role, and fiscal priorities being formed within the 'institutional norms and pressures of the criminal process' (Roberts 1994a: 782). Indeed, 'unless the forensic science budget is treated for practical purposes as unlimited, there is a clear potential for periodic budgetary crises with knock-on effects on patterns of forensic science usage' (Tilley and Ford 1996: 20). Such fiscal and budgetary concerns are heightened by the planned privatisation of the FSS.

There can also be found a close association between certain offence types and investigative strategies, in addition to institutional and organisational arrangements, which are 'more significant than either scientific principles or criminal justice policy in determining the role of scientific evidence in any given case' (Roberts 1994a: 789). Perhaps more important than efficiency and effectiveness concerns, convictions of innocent men and women which continue to be overturned by the appeal courts demonstrate that forensic evidence must be handled and utilised with great assiduity and integrity. The management and organisation of forensic science by the police needs astute supervision and constant regulation to prevent abuse and mistake. Further, the use of forensic identity technology to support legal reforms which threaten traditional criminal procedural protections for suspects (such as the right to silence and the privilege against self-incrimination) necessitate public, as well as legal, attention with the construction of large forensic identification databases undermining traditional legal protections.

Examination of the legal developments that have led to the retention of fingerprints and bodily samples goes some way to an understanding of the driving forces behind the growth of identity databases. Police powers have been extended to keep up with science and technology, raising the question of whether the technology itself is dictating the development of the law and police powers. It appears that once there is a technical capability to determine identity 'scientifically', which requires legal powers to empower the police to utilise the capability, the government obliges. As the technology also becomes more innocuous (e.g. breathalysers to take breath samples, fingerprints being taken by holding the hand on a screen and 'buccal' mouth swabs – a simple cotton bud in the cheek), obvious objections to interfering with people's bodily integrity have disappeared, and principled objection to the procedures have failed to prevent the extension of police powers. Indeed 'it could be argued that the criminal justice system as we know it is being appropriated by the very technologies designed to assist its pursuit' (Kellie 2001: 174). In the risk society technologies to minimise risk are being incorporated into criminal processes regardless of their 'fit' with traditional practices and their ethical underpinnings.

It is for the courts to now clarify the laws regarding sampling in response to the rapid legal changes taking place in the wake of government and police enthusiasm for their increased use. The courts have found the retention of bodily samples of those charged with criminal offences to be compliant with human rights in the interests of crime prevention, in spite of the possible arousal of 'strong feelings' around such a policy.[77] It must now be determined if justification for the retention of samples stretches to arrestees also, however, challenges to police powers and practices are notoriously difficult, particularly with respect to consensual interactions between police and citizens, such as in the case of mass screens of volunteers in response to a serious crime. It may be necessary to require the courts to regulate police practices through the exclusion of evidence (Gans 2001: 178).

One of the dominant characteristics of the modernisation agenda is the demand for justice to be 'speeded up' with the government accusing defence lawyers of 'stringing-out' trials, indeed almost all government statements now emphasise the need to bring more defendants to trial, and quicker. Constraining principles, in particular human rights demands, have themselves been marked 'more by concerns about the potential effects on case throughput rates and of defence challenges on human rights grounds than by enthusiasm to embrace a stronger human rights culture ... concern with delay reduction, [is] driven by the adage *"justice delayed is justice denied"* (Raine 2001: 119). Laws concerning investigation, pre-trial and trial processes have been modified in attempts to improve upon the perceived poor record of the consistent conviction of guilty defendants. The adversarial system is increasingly adopting 'the *instruments* of inquisitorial investigation' (Jorg *et al.* 1995: 48). However, it can be cogently argued that protecting and respecting the rights of suspects

---

77 Morris, S. (2002) 'Police allowed to retain DNA of ex-suspects', *The Guardian*, 23 March: 7.

is not an impediment to evidence gathering, and serves the public interest. Indeed, invoking the amorphous 'public interest' serves to nullify rather than support the argument for greater police powers:

> We must refuse to accept references to the 'interests of justice', 'the public interest', and even (more emotively) 'the interests of victims' – unless it is carefully spelt out how exactly these rather sweeping claims have been arrived at. We need to identify the values that underlie such statements, and then consider what values should be recognised in criminal justice. (Ashworth 1998: 87)

It is clear that there are values other than truth-seeking, even during criminal investigations, that must be pursued and protected (Ashworth 1996: 227). As Choo asserts: 'what the public interest demands is that offenders are brought to conviction in a civilised and publicly acceptable manner' (Choo 1993: 13). The problems of supervising low-visibility activities such as criminal investigations (which must necessarily sometimes be secretive) and finding a balance between unfettered discretion and giving police sufficient powers, are yet to be overcome.

Conclusion: forensic identification and the criminal process

There is broad agreement that there should be constraining principles and higher goals, restraining pure crime-control aims. As Zander stated in the Runciman Report: 'the integrity of the criminal justice system is a higher objective than the conviction of any individual'.[78] Similarly, others highlight the 'moral integrity of the system' (Choo 1993). Cases such as *R v. Mullen* reassert this concept of 'moral integrity', highlighting the inherent tensions between allowing the appeals of the palpably guilty where their conviction was not secured 'fairly' or within the boundaries of proper police or prosecutorial behaviour, and retaining the confidence of the public that the guilty are consistently convicted. The Court of Appeal still places considerable importance on integrity of process and the *Criminal Appeal Act* 1995 specifically allows for the overturning of 'unsafe' convictions, however 'safety' may have been impacted upon. Similarly, the *Human Rights Act* places emphasis on 'fairness', with Article 6 articulating a series

---

78 Royal Commission on Criminal Justice, 1993: 235.

of minimum rights pertaining to the 'fairness' of the criminal justice system and processes.

Forensic identification evidence is then invaluable in assisting with this priority of rectitude, and efficiency: forensic science able to 'shortcut' investigations, and the 'accuracy' and 'objectivity' of science able to circumvent rules concerned with fairness. Forensic identification evidence is then used successfully to support the dismantling of long-standing legal safeguards and suspect protections, for science will protect the innocent. Police powers can concurrently be 'safely' expanded to enable the obtaining of sufficient information to successfully prosecute the guilty. However, whilst forensic science may aid in exculpating innocent suspects, it can also convict the innocent. Forensic science may yet come to usurp 'fairness' and render obsolete the presumption of innocence. The impact of such change can be evidenced further in examination of the criminal trial, including considerations of fairness, and the impact of forensic identification evidence at trial. There is then a critical consideration of the role of the criminal trial in this new criminal process and the part played by forensic identification technologies. The contribution of forensic science to 'rectitude' must then be considered, with the rules and practices regarding the presentation of fingerprint and DNA evidence in court scrutinised. The criminal trial, whilst becoming a rarer event, can be seen to be moving further from a process concerned with fairness and procedural justice, to one with accuracy of outcome as its primary goal, a goal which it is believed can be achieved by utilising forensic expertise.

Chapter 3

Forensic identification: the criminal trial

The criminal trial: fairness or truth?

It is asserted that forensic science is aimed at assisting courts to arrive at accurate verdicts. While verdict accuracy is clearly vital, there are other issues to be considered within the context of the criminal trial. Indeed, debate remains on the appropriate confines of a definition of the purpose of the criminal trial. If it is assumed that forensic science is introduced into trials to assist with truth-finding (and does not impact upon procedural fairness or integrity for instance), then consideration of debate over the true purpose of trials is essential before the value of forensic identification within trials can be properly assessed.

Galligan writes that the criminal trial is 'an inquiry into whether legal standards have been breached in a manner for which the accused can be held sufficiently responsibly for the imposition of punishment' (Galligan 1996: 139). However, Galligan also alludes to a wider social and moral dimension, such as that indicated by Bradley and Hoffman (1996: 1272): 'Criminal trials are a form of civic theatre that allows us to define who we are as people, helps to educate all of us about that definition and provides us with an opportunity to foster our self-confidence in the fundamental morality of our society'. Criminal trials may not simply involve then, the consideration of the specific facts of the case, but may invoke debate over the appropriateness of the law, penal policy, the legitimacy of policing and so on: 'the true purpose of a fair hearing ... is not merely to ensure the accurate *application* of authoritative standards, but may extend, in appropriate cases, to contesting their legitimacy' (Allan 1998: 501).

It is asserted that because the criminal trial is the 'central locus' where individuals encounter the state: 'commitments to truth and to those values that should coexist with truth are, therefore, deeply embedded in the institutions and procedures of criminal adjudication' (Maguire-Shultz 1992: 21). This 'embedding' of the truth perhaps stems from historical demands for adjudication to establish 'truth' (such as the drowning of alleged witches or trial by ordeal, which are examples of extreme attempts to arrive at accurate verdicts). Accounts of the purpose of the rules of criminal procedure then tend to focus upon the technical or succinct exposition that trials are held for the determination of guilt in regard to criminal charges. As Rawls (1973) states: 'The desired outcome is that defendant should be declared guilty if, and only if, he has committed the offence with which he is charged. The trial procedure is framed to search for and establish the truth in this regard'. Indeed, Ashworth (1998: 50) asserts that the 'fundamental purpose' of the criminal process is to ensure the accuracy of outcomes, requiring 'the taking of steps to avoid or minimise the risks of mistaken assessments of evidence leading to wrongful acquittals or convictions'.

Twining (1990: 77) asserts that the aim of adjudication is rectitude of decision-making, to be achieved 'by the correct application of substantive law to the true facts of the dispute', and that such facts are determined 'through the accurate evaluation of relevant and reliable evidence by a competent and impartial adjudicator applying the specified burden and standard of proof'. This rationalist model of adjudication thus adopts a 'correspondence' theory of truth, where 'facts' have an objective existence in the world that can be communicated to a court, through reconstruction from inferences (Dennis 2002: 98). There has however, according to Dennis (2002: 99), long been scepticism about how far legal processes 'are suited to serving the epistemological aspirations of the rationalist model'. He states (2002: 100) that facts do not have 'an independent, static quality which can be discovered by an impartial inquirer. Rather, they are, or may be, socially contingent, a product of the social process used to determine them and hence possessing a dynamic and dependent quality'. Indeed, 'at each point of the criminal justice process "what happened" is the subject of interpretation, addition, subtraction, selection and reformulation. This is a continuing process … involving not simply the selection and interpretation of evidence, but its creation' (McConville *et al.* 1991: 12).

This means that, as Carson (2003: 127) succinctly argues: 'The trial is not a scientific procedure. We cannot, correctly, make inferences about the quality of the process (the trial) from its product (the verdict) when we cannot know the accuracy of that product'. The trial then should be viewed more accurately as a passive review of the finished product of a criminal investigation in that: 'it can probe it but it cannot reconstruct it and it cannot present an alternative to a defective police case' (Zuckerman 1992: 337–8) making it 'entirely inappropriate to regard a criminal trial as being concerned solely with the determination of the truth' (Choo 1993: 91). Summers (1999: 500) concludes: 'it is simply not so that the exclusive business of a trial court in all disputed cases is to find the actual truth'. The adversarial model in particular represents a 'contest' where the factfinder is persuaded of the merits of competing versions of the 'truth', with the accepted version forming the official account. An alternative view then is to conceive of rectitude as closely related to, and assisting with, the *legitimacy* of decisions. Legitimacy incorporates notions of integrity and acceptability:

> In essence, the idea of integrity signifies an aspiration that an adjudicative decision should as far as possible be factually accurate and also consistent with other fundamental moral and political values embedded in the legal system. In this way a decision may claim both factual accuracy and moral authority. The acceptability of a decision is then very largely a function of its accuracy and integrity. (Dennis 2002: 41)

This means accepting that in certain circumstances criminal process outcomes may account for community sentiments 'about the justice of the application of the substantive law to the facts of the dispute' (Dennis 2002: 41). Thus, a verdict may serve alternative public functions, with rectitude not always the pre-eminent goal of the trial process (Dennis 2002: 44). Indeed, a minimum notion of fairness and the protection of human rights indicates higher values than truth (Ashworth 1979: 421). Thus:

> trials, particularly criminal trials, seek truth, but they also express norms about the value of individuals, the role of government, the appropriate methods of truth-seeking, and the preferability of some risks over others. These value preferences are encoded in concrete legal institutions and procedures. (Maguire-Schultz 1992: 20)

There are substantive values,[1] reflected in procedural values,[2] upon which verdicts must be based, because as Dennis (2002: 45) asserts, 'it is not in the public interest that verdicts should be returned which lack moral and expressive authority'. Truth-finding then is the primary means of securing a legitimate verdict, but it is legitimacy that is the ultimate aim. This means that a factually inaccurate or doubtful conviction can never be legitimate, but a decision may be factually correct and yet still lack legitimacy (2002: 46). Thus the notion of rectitude being the overriding aim of the criminal trial must be questioned, with other ends sought over and above outcome accuracy. The potential for divergence between substantive truth and formal legal truth being: 'the price we pay for having a complex multi-purpose system in which actual truth, and what legally follows from it, comprise but one value among a variety of important values competing for legal realisation' (Summers 1999: 511).

Despite this, in his review of the criminal courts, Auld LJ concluded that: 'A criminal trial is not a game under which a guilty defendant should be provided with a sporting chance. It is a search for truth …' (2001: 459). This 'justice as truth' standpoint is not novel, with Bentham (1827: 743) arguing strongly in favour of 'free proof', which, he claimed, was the best method for arriving at the truth. If there are values considered during the criminal process, then the 'truth' must clearly be one of them:

> those who advocate rights and fairness must also accept the value of truth, in the sense of a need both for convictions of those who are factually guilty, and for the acquittal of those who are factually innocent. In a similar way those who advocate truth must adopt a limited commitment to both rights and fairness. (Nobles and Schiff 2000: 33)

Verdicts which correlate with the substantive truth are: 'essential to the credibility and integrity of law' (Paciocco 2001: 440), for; 'without judicial findings of fact that generally accord with truth, citizens would, over time, lose confidence in adjudicative processes as fair

---

1 Such as respect for human autonomy and dignity, security of person and property from unjustified interference, privacy, and freedom from discrimination.
2 Such as the presumption of innocence, fair trials according to principles of natural justice, and probity on the part of state agencies entrusted with coercive powers.

and reliable tribunals of justice and as effective means of dispute resolution' (Summers 1999: 498). The ineffectiveness of trials at reaching the truth however, means that the acquittal of the innocent is then the more vital outcome:

> the searing injustice and consequential social injury which is involved when the law turns upon itself and convicts an innocent person far outweigh the failure of the justice and consequential social injury involved when the processes of law proclaim the innocence of a guilty man.[3]

In contrast, Lord Devlin noted (1960: 113) that, 'when a criminal goes free, it is as much a failure of abstract justice as when an innocent man is convicted,' while a Law Commission report of 1972 stated that 'it is as much in the public interest that a guilty person should be convicted as it is that an innocent person should be acquitted'.[4]

Increasingly, due process protections are portrayed as inhibiting the search for the truth, casting the adversary process as ineffective, and the rules of evidence obstacles to justice:

> In the interests of finding the truth, the exclusion of relevant information must justify itself. Admission need not … the relationship between truth and justice is a nuanced one … society should choose to sacrifice the truth by excluding information relevant to guilt only reluctantly, and even then, to no greater degree than is absolutely necessary. (Paciocco 2002: 435)

Although, it must be remembered that it is 'the role of the trial courts to determine whether the defendant is "legally guilty" not whether he is "factually innocent"' (Roberts 2003: 445). As alluded to in broader conceptions of the trial, they do not test 'facts' alone, but 'hinge upon matters of interpretation and judgement rather than upon questions of factual accuracy … the criminal trial therefore, is as much about the construction of "the truth" as it is about its discovery' (Greer 1994: 61). This is particularly so because the criminal justice system relies upon concepts which have particular constructions within the

---

3 Deane J of the High Court of Australia in *Van de Meer* v. *R* (1988) 82 ALR 10 (H.C.) quoted in Plaxton (2002): 408.
4 Criminal Law Revision Committee (1972) 11th Report: Evidence (General), (CM 4991) para. 27.

system which may have no direct comparison outside of the criminal justice context (Nobles and Schiff 1996: 319). Meaning that:

> For a non-scientific system like the law, the problems of attempting to present its findings of fact as the truth are almost overwhelming ... Indeed, attempts at understanding the criminal trial as a scientific process that operates to seek out the truth are clearly flawed theoretically, epistemologically, and practically. (Nobles and Schiff 2000: 19)

Justice then, cannot be easily translated as the reaching of an accurate verdict and other important considerations must remain, as the Court of Appeal has indicated: 'the integrity of criminal process is the most important consideration ... Both the innocent and the guilty are entitled to fair trials'.[5] Similarly, the ECtHR has held that the question of whether the accused had been secured his Article 6 rights cannot be assimilated to a finding that his conviction was safe in the absence of any inquiry into fairness (Roberts 2003: 448). Whilst periodically cases such as that of Tony Martin[6] highlight continued public support for 'fairness' to override substantive truth in certain scenarios, indications are that 'justice as truth' is gaining pre-eminence over procedural justice, and most often directs the criminal process and ultimately, the criminal trial.

Society may be committed in principle to the acquittal of the innocent and the conferment of substantive rights, but limited resources and competing demands, as well as the improbability of designing and implementing perfect procedures, means that 'it invariably fails in practice to provide the necessary resources for procedures adequate to prevent mistakes in their identification or application in particular cases'.[7] Others argue that this concern with rules, process, and procedure should not be permitted to supersede concern for accuracy, in spite of the often subjective evaluations of accuracy. It is claimed that 'dignitarian' theorists fail to understand that while treatment in accordance with legal standards is an essential element of according respect, accurate outcomes cannot be undervalued: 'accurate decisions themselves constitute an important

---

5   Roch LJ in R v. *Hickey and others* [1997] CA unreported, transcript 30 July 1997.
6   *R v. Martin (Anthony)* [2001] EWCA Crim 2245.
7   As above at p. 512.

element of fair treatment, which in turn constitutes an important element of respect for persons' (Galligan 1996: 78).

Of course, defendants are not the only participants in the criminal process and as such, are not the sole consideration or beneficiary of the protection of rights. There are strong arguments that accurate verdicts benefit others, even the public as a whole. Considerations of fairness should also not be limited to the defendant and may also have widespread benefactors: 'Fairness of the proceedings involves a consideration not only of fairness to the accused but also ... of fairness to the public'.[8] The 'public interest' was invoked by Kennedy LJ in the case of *R* v. *Kelt*,[9] where a sample of blood taken from a robbery scene while Kelt was being held under suspicion for murder was admitted at his trial for the robbery, despite the law stating that samples taken by the police must not be used in subsequent, or unconnected investigations (*PACE* ss. 62 and 64). Kennedy LJ gave ss. 62 and 64 an expansive interpretation:

> The police must act in good faith, but the public interest would not be served if a sample lawfully obtained in connection with an investigation could not be compared with blood left at the scene of another serious crime. If a serial rapist were to be arrested and were to give a sample in the course of the inquiry into an offence which he did not commit, it can hardly have been the intention of Parliament that the sample which he gave could not then be compared with a whole series of specimens obtained from rapes which he had committed.[10]

In subsequent cases where DNA evidence was relied upon by the prosecution despite being illegally held by the police, 'reliability' of the evidence was used as a rationale for its admissibility. In *R* v.*Cooke*,[11] DNA evidence was distinguished from other evidence such as confessions, asserting that where the truth of coerced confessions may be at issue, the veracity of DNA evidence is unquestionable in that the manner in which the evidence was obtained does not effect its safety or reliability. The intrinsic reliability of the evidence permitted the Court of Appeal to overlook any irregularities in its acquisition, demonstrating a reluctance to exclude highly probative

---

8   Lord Taylor in *Smurthwaite* [1994] 1 All ER 898 at 902–3.

9   *R* v. *Kelt* [1994] 2 All ER 780.

10   As above at 768.

11   *R* v. *Cooke* (1995) 1 Cr App R 318.

scientific evidence: the end justifying the means.

The case of *Cooke* contrasted, however, with that of *Nathaniel* of the same year.[12] Nathaniel was arrested and charged with the rapes of two Danish students in September 1991, had a blood sample taken, but was acquitted. Under s. 64, these samples should have been destroyed but in January 1993 they were matched to a rape from 1989. Upon arrest a further sample was taken and used as evidence in the subsequent prosecution. His appeal was successful because Nathaniel was promised that the original blood sample was only for the trial of the two Danish students and would be destroyed upon acquittal. To allow the evidence to be used four years later in a totally unrelated trial was deemed to have had an adverse effect on the fairness of the trial. Lord Taylor CJ suggested that four separate considerations persuaded the court: there had been a clear breach of s. 64; the appellant had been misled by promises not honoured; the appellant was told the sample would be destroyed and he was informed that if he refused to provide a sample, the jury could draw inferences from his refusal.

The ruling in *Nathaniel* seemed to directly contradict the decision in *Cooke*. This confusion was considered by the House of Lords in *Attorney General's Reference (No 3 of 1999)*,[13] where it was held that DNA evidence held in breach of s. 64 was not automatically excluded but that the trial judge had a discretionary power to admit such evidence. Lord Steyn relied upon a concept of 'fairness' as including, but not exclusively, the public interest. The House of Lords contended that the defendant still had the ability to challenge the DNA evidence. This undermined the protection that Parliament had attempted to provide suspects in enacting s. 64, with little disincentive for police *not* to use DNA profiles unlawfully held. The ruling, whilst significant as an interpretation of s. 78, was made immaterial by the enactment of the *Criminal Justice and Public Order Act* 2001 which removed the obligation to destroy samples.

In light of recent prioritising of 'truth' as the basis of legitimacy within the criminal justice system, the law is increasingly turning to science to furnish courts with methods for establishing the 'truth': 'The increasing dominance of ideas associated with truth, as the basis for justifying practices within the legal system, creates pressures on that system, for what can objectively count as truth lies not in

---

12   *R v. Nathaniel* [1995] 2 Cr App R 565.

13   *Attorney General's Reference (No 3 of 1999)* [2001] 2 WLR 56.

law, but in science'.[14] Forensic science then is stepping into the breach, to lend legal decisions and outcomes legitimacy through (supposedly) infallible, non-partisan methods of fact determination: 'Jurisprudence based on natural law and positivism has a tendency to look for and locate an "absolute" ground or foundation. In the criminal trial, that expert support comes from forensic science and the presumed certainty of the scientific method' (Kellie 2001: 173). This then requires critical examination of the ability of forensic science to facilitate rectitude, and the use of forensic identification evidence by the courts.

Forensic science and rectitude

Scientific evidence is intended to assist in decision-making and lend certainty to verdicts, in which context DNA has been called: 'the single greatest advance in the "search for truth" … since the advent of cross-examination'.[15] Forensic science is thus hailed as a guarantor against miscarriages of justice and indeed, most often admirably fulfils this remit. However, experience should warn against unquestioning acceptance of forensic science, having caused, or at least contributed, to several high-profile miscarriages of justice, demonstrating that where forensic science is relied upon 'it is one thing for the science to speak, quite another for the courts to achieve the necessary comprehension of what is being said' (Kingston 2000: 708).

The benefits of forensic technologies have been questioned in the context of the practical realities of court practices and procedures, as discussed by Freckleton (1992b). He suggests that forensic science and law are 'mismatched', with the legal system unable to act as a quality regulator of forensic science, ensuring neither reliability or accountability:

> the legal system has not functioned in such a way as to facilitate accountability of forensic science as a reliable discipline … recent high profile miscarriages of justice cannot be explained away as simply 'extraordinary phenomenon'. Furthermore, the system is not structured in such a way that expert witnesses, particularly in the criminal field, will regularly be subjected to rigorous and well informed cross examination and expose deficiencies in the quality of scientific work. (Freckleton 1992b: 10)

---

14   *Ibid.*
15   *People* v. *Wesley*, 533 N.Y.S. 2d 643, 644. (N.Y.Co.Ct 1988).

No scientific test is infallible and each must have construct validity (where the adequacy of scientific knowledge must be sensitive to the purpose for which it is required). Problems encountered by forensic scientists include the fact that they have no or little control over materials, while there may be divergent opinions over what is required, in addition: 'each scientist may find different things from the same raw material and reach differing opinions/conclusions. Science is a "dynamic social institution"' (Walker and Stockdale 1999: 121). There are further difficulties with individual techniques or disciplines, in particular those which rely upon statistics, for while statistics permit predictions about uncertainties, 'they do not establish facts' (Maguire-Schultz 1992: 28).

The leap from laboratory to courtroom often takes place without proper critical assessment however, and there exist important contextual differences that often make the two incompatible:

> First, science generally perceives itself as being predominantly about truth. In contrast, legal adjudication has truth as one goal, but sees other goals as equally or more important ... Second, even to the degree that the law, like science, does seek truth, there are significant differences in the two field's assumptions about the character and sources of truth. Whereas science envisions truth as a substantive quest, law tends towards procedural and functional definitions. (Maguire-Schultz 1992: 20)

Despite reservations concerning the desirability of forensic evidence in court, its acceptance is widespread, and largely uncontroversial. It is most often the uncritical acceptance of scientific evidence that proves problematic, with 'scientism' encouraging the erroneous perception of science as able to determine 'truth', with legal outcomes then reflecting such truths, even within a system not working with equivalent standards:

> The media systematically misreads law's claim to determine the 'truth' of a person's guilt, as if the legal system had a scientific commitment to that truth as fact. But, while one of the central features of scientific truth is the replicability of results ... the legal system cannot hope to live up to this standard. Whereas its rhetoric of 'beyond reasonable doubt' points to a scientific standard of truth, the reality (at best) is that a particular jury, after a particular trial, was extremely certain that the defendant had committed the offence. (Nobles and Schiff 2001b: 297)

The emphasis placed upon scientific reports despite their often problematic presentation in court leads to uncertainty, dispute, and even error, demanding greater scrutiny of the role of forensic identification expertise in the courtroom.

The basis of admission of scientific evidence remains expressed in *Folkes v. Chadd* of 1782, where Lord Mansfield stated that, 'the opinion of scientific men upon proven facts may be given by men of science in their own science. When such a person is called as a witness, his opinion is admissible on any relevant matter'.[16] Forensic scientists are then afforded special privilege by being able to give evidence of opinions as well as fact (one of the difficulties which then arises is in distinguishing which is which). The primary task for defence experts includes verifying prosecution forensic evidence and undertaking further tests if necessary (although there are often obstacles to re-testing).[17]

Defence experts may also be required to clarify findings and interpretations of prosecution evidence, often to overcome the scientific illiteracy of lawyers. Experts can then be instrumental in advising on strategy and how to challenge the prosecution case. Finally, the defence may call upon their expert to give oral testimony on an alternative finding or interpretation of evidence (Roberts 1994b). Despite an apparently essential role, a study in 1993 estimated that whilst 30–40 per cent of contested Crown Court trials involve scientific evidence, there is a defence expert in only 3 per cent of these (although they only counted when the prosecution evidence was challenged and defence experts can help in more ways than this obvious one, Zander and Henderson 1993). It may be fairly safely presumed that the proportion of cases involving scientific evidence and experts over a decade later may have increased.

Experts must be not only expert in their field, but must also be expert in presenting evidence.[18] Often however, scientific evidence has been problematic, with jurors reporting difficulty in following

---

16   *Folkes v. Chadd* (1782) 3 Doug K B 157.
17   To begin with, it is rare for disputes between scientists to occur and the necessity of retesting must often be evidenced. There may be resistance to the borrowing of notes or facilities and samples, with priority given to prosecution. Finally, costs of testing for the defence may be prohibitive.
18   JUSTICE (1986) 'Witnesses in the Court', London pp. 8–10. Although experts present oral evidence in very few cases, with their court appearances then receiving disproportionate attention.

reports presented orally, while commentators note the possible undue influence of experts or the partisan presentation of scientific evidence.[19] Experts need to be wary of straying from evidence that falls within their expertise, while there is a temptation:

> to dwell on the analytical tests employed and the manner in which these were carried out, matters which are often unimpeachable, without giving sufficient weight to the provenance of the material under test, how this was collected and presented and what inferences may safely be drawn from the results obtained. (Walker and Stockdale 1999: 120)

Forensic scientists begin their work far earlier in the criminal process and other people and protocols will have been involved. However, it is most often only the presentation of their conclusions at the very end of their work, and the manner in which those conclusions are presented, that are afforded any critical attention.

Informed cross-examination of expert testimony is vital as if the wrong questions are asked then evidence may be lost, although it may also be easy for counsel to obfuscate non-controversial findings; most scientists will concede some room for error but debate between scientists as to how certain their findings are can lead to an impression that findings are contested, when it may simply be a difference in verbal communication techniques.[20] This raises the perennial problem of jury persuasion by extraneous factors:

> the court's impression of the strength of scientific evidence can be influenced by such wholly unscientific factors as to the extent to which an expert is experienced in court-craft, has learned a few 'tricks of the trade' and is sufficiently self-possessed to take the initiative. (Roberts 1994b: 504)

Other difficulties with experts have been summarised as involving 'charlatans, incompetence and partisanship'.[21] While steps have been taken to address two of these problems with the establishment of the Council for the Registration of Forensic Practitioners (CRFP), whilst calls continue for court-appointed expert witnesses to circumvent the problems of partisanship. The success of such measures and

---

19   *Ibid.*
20   For more details on expert evidence at trial see Roberts (1994b).
21   Prof. Badenoch, CRFP and EWI Conference, London, 8 April 2002.

the potential for neutral experts remains unclear although it has been stated that in future, acceptance of evidence from non-CRFP accredited witnesses will become the exception. However, qualifications in themselves do not provide a guarantee of quality, and appreciation of accreditation must not come at the expense of thorough and informed cross-examination. Such cross-examination may be scarce however: 'the check and balance upon which both the adversarial and the inquisitorial systems depend, the informed and effective cross-examiner making forensic scientists accountable for their views, is often more rhetoric than reality' (Freckleton 1996: 4). There is demand then for both effective peer review (though this system is now in question as a guarantor of veracity in light of recent scandals with falsified scientific papers on stem cell research being published in esteemed peer-reviewed journals), and scrutiny of the technology and scientific techniques, as well as competent cross-examination:

> what is very important is that there are robust review procedures in order to ensure that we are not deceived by apparently excellent technology that later proves to be less than excellent. There is a history of mistakes by forensic scientists ... The technology is to be encouraged but the peer review and testing must be of the most robust kind.[22]

In addition, many miscarriages of justice highlight the perennial problem of disclosure, adequate and timely disclosure being essential for prosecutions involving forensic evidence.

Disclosure of forensic evidence

Disclosure of evidence prior to trial is an essential element of securing the 'equality of arms' vital to fairness. Miscarriages of justice have demonstrated that non-disclosure can have disastrous consequences, although in line with the recent onus on prosecutorial powers, amendments to disclosure rules have attempted to equalise the disclosure burden. Moves to ensure equality of discovery have as their basis a negative view of the stricter rules of disclosure placed on the prosecution. Such moves have been rationalised in terms of securing convictions, with defendants unable to run 'ambush' defences. The accuracy of verdicts has also been implicated, with

---

22   Interviewee 3/L/P

equal discovery requirements called a 'quality control issue' (Gianelli 1998: 414). However, equal discovery rules may erode the privilege not to have to assist the prosecution.

With reference to forensic evidence, it has been stated that 'convenient and comprehensive disclosure', is of the utmost importance: 'in order to provide the defence with every opportunity to prepare and develop a case using what is still relatively novel, potentially prejudicial and often extremely complex scientific evidence' (Findlay and Grix 2003: 276). In *Maguire and Others*,[23] it was ruled that forensic scientists advising the prosecution are under a duty to disclose material of which they know, which may have 'some bearing on the offence charged and the surrounding circumstances of the case'. The disclosure is to be to the retaining authority, who must then disclose it to the defence, there being a duty because 'we can see no cause to distinguish between members of the prosecuting authority and those advising it in the capacity of a forensic scientist'.[24]

However, what is to be disclosed can still be a matter of contention. In *R* v. *R*,[25] a blood sample provided to the defence was given in confidence and privileged material under s. 10(1)(c) of *PACE*, and therefore need not be disclosed to the prosecution, unless the appellant consented. In *R (on application of DPP)* v. *Croydon Magistrates Court*,[26] the prosecution provided a case summary which prompted the defence to request an adjournment to obtain further information on DNA profiles mentioned, which was granted. The Director of Public Prosecutions (DPP) challenged the decision, submitting that the obligation to supply advance information had been complied with. The judicial review held that 'DNA profiling' did not constitute a 'document', and that while there exists an obligation to provide an accurate and fair case summary, there was no obligation to submit a detailed report on the DNA profiles for advance disclosure. This ruling was constructed upon a restrictive definition of 'document', contrary to that relied upon in other cases where a broad definition has been applied to numerous modern evidential contexts.

A case summary must be sufficient for an accused to decide upon a plea, the mere mention of DNA profiles cannot be sufficient as this precludes critical assessment of the DNA evidence. DNA evidence

---

23   *R* v. *Maguire and Others* [1992] 2 All ER 433, 447.
24   *Ibid*.
25   *R* v. *R* (1994) 1 WLR 758.
26   *R (on application of DPP)* v. *Croydon Magistrates Court* [2001] EWHC Admin 552.

may be flawed, prove worthless, be open to interpretation or may even support a defence. To base a plea upon the mention of DNA evidence would seem highly presumptive. The scope then of the obligation of advance information is in need of clarification. The *Criminal Justice Act* 2003 s. 35(1) demands that the details of all expert witnesses instructed by the defence are disclosed, with sanctions against the defendant for defence non-disclosure (Wilcock and Bennathan 2004). Whilst desirable that there be a balance between the cost and length of pre-trial processes, there is a risk of: 'guilty pleas based upon scant information in order to take advantage of maximum sentence discount'.[27] The mention of fingerprint or DNA 'matches' should not lead to assumptions about the quality or significance of the evidence, an issue which has demanded attention in reaching common acceptable standards for both fingerprint and DNA evidence.

Identity 'matches': acceptance of fingerprint and DNA evidence

The Court of Criminal Appeal was not much troubled by fingerprint evidence, when it suggested in 1955 that the only answer to fingerprint evidence in court was to claim that its presence was legitimate (Eddy: 1955). The history of fingerprint evidence then largely concerns the context and manner of taking fingerprints, and the standards applied for declaring 'matches'. While the standard for fingerprint 'matches' has recently changed, and the 'science' of fingerprinting has of late been questioned (particularly in the US since the *Daubert* ruling), the introduction of fingerprint evidence still rarely raises issues. This common view of reliability led pioneers of DNA profiling to call it 'DNA fingerprinting': 'purposefully attempting to "piggyback" on the tremendous power that fingerprinting was known to have' (Mnookin 2001: 40). DNA evidence has had a more chequered history in the courts, with early cases questioning its reliability and validity, though these early challenges appear to now have been resolved in favour of general admissibility. The weight of such identification evidence, and its almost unquestioned admissibility, may be traced to 'cultural' perceptions of the infallibility of science, and the authority accorded experts in society. Such cultural beliefs are then influencing the reception of such evidence at trial, as well as having a wider impact of the nature of trials and the criminal process.

---

27   *R (on application of DPP)* v. *Croydon Mag's Court* [2001] Crim LR 980.

Fingerprint evidence on trial

From its introduction into courts, fingerprint evidence was presented using the language of certainty, contrary to the norm of expert witnesses presenting 'opinion':

> According to the norms of the professional community, identifications must be certain and absolute, or they must not be made at all. In fact, the primary professional organisation for fingerprint examiners passed a resolution in 1979 making it professional misconduct for any fingerprint examiner to provide courtroom testimony that labelled a match 'possible, probable or likely' rather than 'certain'. (Mnookin 2001: 28–9)

Such testimony had an important impact upon the reception of fingerprinting, coming to have a 'cultural authority':

> It came to be seen as especially powerful, especially compelling form of evidence, one that simply could not be challenged as erroneous. Because the reliability of fingerprinting was not challenged in court, it came to have a great deal of epistemological authority – both within the courtroom and outside of it. That fingerprinting is generally viewed as a tremendously reliable technique hardly needs to be established – it is common knowledge – almost without dispute. (Mnookin 2001: 39)

Early fingerprint cases dealt with the identification of convicted offenders in order to establish their antecedents for the purposes of sentencing. In 1915 in *R v. Bacon*,[28] the appellant claimed that previous convictions were not his and some were his brother's. The Court examined fingerprint records with an expert from Scotland Yard, and claimed to have: 'no doubt that they are all the same, and that they tally with the fingerprints of the accused'.[29] The first case before the appeal courts to rely solely upon fingerprint evidence was that of *R v. Castleton*,[30] in 1910. Castleton's conviction, based upon fingerprints left on a candle at a crime scene, was upheld, the fingerprint evidence taken to be conclusive. Such opinion of fingerprint evidence was not unanimous however, with Madden CJ in Victoria, Australia, stating in

---

28   *R v. Bacon* [1915] 11 Cr.App.R. 90.
29   As above at 91.
30   *R v. Castleton* (1910) 3 Cr.App.R. 74.

1912 in *Rex* v. *Parker*,[31] that whilst fingerprint evidence was relevant and admissible, it was far from being conclusive. This opinion was highly criticised however, on appeal to the High Court of Australia, where it was held that fingerprint individuality was now; 'so generally recognised as to require very little, if any, evidence of it'.[32] In the USA, the first court of last resort to consider the admissibility of fingerprint evidence was the Illinois Supreme Court in *People* v. *Jennings* in 1911.[33]

In 1934, the defence in the Scottish case of *Hamilton* v. *HM Advocate*,[34] submitted that it would be unsafe to convict on fingerprint evidence alone as, like all expert evidence, it was liable to error. In response, the appeal court held that 'the experience of the method of identification by fingerprints, in different countries and over a long period, has established its reliability'.[35] The experts in the case had claimed fingerprint evidence to be 'infallible', a claim that the appeal court considered at some length:

> This may well be thought (in words at least) to put the case too high, but the substance of their evidence was that, over an area of experience of great extent, and over a tract of time of highly significant duration, the fingerprint method of identification had never once proved to be unreliable. There was no counter-evidence ... The value of fingerprint evidence depends on the reliance that can be placed on the result of expert investigation and experience – in an immense number of cases, examined over a very extended period of years – to the effect that identity is never found to exist between the skin ridges on two different person's fingers. This is what leads the experts to claim infallibility for the fingerprint method. I deprecate the use of the word 'infallibility' in this connexion at all. What the experts obviously mean is, not absolute, but practical infallibility – that is to say, a presumption of truth, the reliability of which may be accepted, not because it is irrebuttable in its own nature – but because long and extensive experience is shown to provide no instance in which it has even been successfully rebutted.[36]

---

31 *Rex* v. *Parker* (1912) VLR 152.
32 Quoted in *The Law Times*, 14 October 1933: 288.
33 *People* v. *Jennings*, 96 NE 1077 (1911).
34 *Hamilton* v. *HM Advocate* [1934] S.C. (J) 1.
35 As above at 3.
36 As above at 3–4.

It was held that the fingerprint evidence was competent, whether it was sufficient for a conviction on its own was a question for the jury. In an apparently dissenting note, one judge argued that while two expert witnesses had testified that the accused's fingerprint matched the print on the bottle:

> the day may come when that will be enough, but that day has not yet quite come. This is a somewhat novel mode of criminal investigation. It will not do for the Crown simply to lead evidence of two experts who say they were the man's fingerprints. As I say, that day may come when that may be enough, and then it will be for the accused to endeavour to challenge or shake that evidence.[37]

The court ruled that the fingerprint evidence had been correctly put to the jury, a view endorsed by *H.M. Advocate* v. *Rolley*,[38] where the sole evidence of a palm print found on a sideboard was presented, the jury directed that the palm print evidence was: 'competent, admissible and sufficient evidence of identification provided you accept it. The value of the evidence is a matter for you'.[39] In England, evidence of fingerprints found in a stolen car was held in *R* v. *Court*,[40] to be insufficient to prove a charge of possession, the admission of the fingerprints was not challenged, just their probative value. It was held that although the defendant failed to explain his fingerprints, this only gave rise to suspicion which was not enough to plug a gap in the evidence: the gap being evidence of possession.

The admission of unlawfully obtained fingerprints was considered in *Dumbell* v. *Roberts*,[41] where the court ruled that there was 'an overriding discretion to exclude such evidence ... if such evidence had been obtained oppressively, e.g. by false representations, trick, threat or bribes'.[42] In *Callis* v. *Gunn*,[43] reliance was placed on the law as stated in *Kuruma*,[44] where Goddard LJ stated that the test to be applied in considering whether evidence was admissible is whether

---

37 As above at 5.
38 *H.M. Advocate* v. *Rolley* (1944) S.C. (J) 154.
39 As above at 156.
40 *R* v. *Court* [1960] *Criminal Law Review* 631.
41 *Dumbell* v. *Roberts* [1944] 1 All ER 326.
42 As above, Scott LJ at p. 330.
43 *Callis* v. *Gunn* [1963] *Criminal Law Review* 846.
44 *Kuruma* [1955] AC 197.

it is relevant to the matters in issue. In *Callis*, the failure to admit fingerprint evidence was appealed by the prosecution, having been excluded on the grounds that the defendant had submitted his fingerprints despite there being no court order (under the *Magistrates' Courts Act*), and no caution that he could refuse consent. The appeal was allowed, ruling that fingerprint evidence was admissible subject to the overriding discretion of the court, excluding evidence only if it had been obtained by trick, false representation, threats, bribes, or the like. In *Callis* there had been none of the aforementioned so the evidence should have been admitted.[45] The House of Lords appeared to end the problem of whether unlawfully obtained fingerprints were admissible in *R* v. *Sang*,[46] ruling that a trial judge had no discretion to exclude relevant evidence merely because it had been obtained by improper or unfair means (with the exception of confessions).

In the USA there have been according to Lee and Tirnady (2003: ix), 'cracks in the fingerprint edifice'. In 1995, a proficiency test that found 20 per cent of fingerprint examiners tested made at least one false match – a false positive being the most serious of errors (2003: ix). In 1998, after serving two years of a life sentence, Richard Jackson was released after prosecutors conceded that the three fingerprint experts had been wrong in linking Jackson to the murder. There have since been a spate of challenges to fingerprints since the introduction of the *Daubert* test,[47] for the admission of scientific or expert evidence. In the first of a series of cases, the status of fingerprint evidence as 'scientific' was challenged in the 1999 case *US* v. *Byron Mitchell*,[48] where the judge held that fingerprint evidence did satisfy the *Daubert* criteria of reliability. In *US* v. *Cline*[49] however, it was held that fingerprint expertise was in need of 'traditional' scientific testing; lacked an adequate body of peer-reviewed literature; and lacked uniform standards (Saks 2003: 1185). Despite such deficiencies, fingerprint evidence still passed the *Daubert* test, the court concluding that the shortcomings; 'meant that alternative, less rigorous criteria

---

45 The Irish High Court had considered the admission of unlawfully obtained fingerprints in People (*Attorney General) and O'Brien* v. *McGrath* (1960) 98 ILTR 59, ruling that the fingerprints, taken improperly, were relevant and should not be excluded simply because they were obtained illegally.

46 *R* v. *Sang* [1979] 2 All ER 1222.

47 *Daubert* v. *Merrell Dow Pharmaceuticals*, 509 U.S. 579 (1993).

48 *US* v. *Byron Mitchell*, (1999) Cr.No. 96-407–1.

49 *US* v. *Cline*, 188 F. Supp. 2d 1287 (D.Kan. Feb. 21, 2002).

needed to be employed in order to facilitate admission' (Saks 2003: 1185).

In a more controversial case, *USA* v. *Llera-Plaza, Acosta and Rodriguez*,[50] fingerprint evidence was initially excluded, the judge later reversing his decision. In early hearings, witnesses for the defence had stated that the fingerprint expert: 'is operating within a vocational framework that may have numerous objective components, but the expert's ultimate opining is likely to depend in some measure on experiential factors that transcend precise measurement and quantification'.[51] However, since Judge Pollak had initially held that fingerprinting was not a science, the court, as in *Cline*, found that less needed be asked of fingerprinting by way of verification. In order to facilitate admission, fingerprint examiners were classed as 'specialists' as opposed to 'scientists', a 'back door' to admission that *Kumho Tire* at the Supreme Court had attempted to lock (Saks 2003). Judge Pollak, after further presentations of evidence from the government, reversed himself, stating that he now believed in the reliability of fingerprinting 'without reservation'. Thus, as Saks (2003: 1185 n. 76) points out, 'both *Daubert* and fingerprint expert testimony emerged from the collision intact'.

Critics claimed that *Daubert* was ignored, suggesting that 'fingerprint expert evidence actually does not meet the requirements of *Daubert*' (Saks 2003: 1186–7). The opinion in *Llera-Plaza* was considered in *US* v. *Havvard*,[52] in which it was stated that 'latent print identification is the very archetype of reliable expert testimony', satisfying all of the *Daubert* criteria. Critics however, maintain that the recent challenges are united: 'by their failure to conduct any thoughtful analysis under *Daubert* and *Kumho Tire*' (Saks 2003: 1171). Judicial confidence in fingerprinting is not always shared, with the infallibility of fingerprints still questioned in scientific, as well as legal circles: 'The idea that there is something about fingerprints that is fundamentally different from any other area of human knowledge concerns me. There have to be errors. It is a human process'.[53] Indeed, there is still no international or universal standard for what constitutes a fingerprint 'match', a problem that has led to considerable scrutiny and recent reform.

---

50 *USA* v. *Llera-Plaza, Acosta and Rodriguez* (2002) Cr.No. 98-362-10,11,12.
51 As above at p. 46.
52 *U.S.* v. *Havvard*, 117 F.Supp. 2d 848 (S.D.Ind.2000).
53 Jim Fraser, President of the UK Forensic Science Society, in Randerson and Coghlan (2003: 6).

Fingerprint 'matching': the fingerprint standard

When fingerprints were first utilised in criminal investigations, there were no set criteria to determine a 'match', although a numerical standard was evolving. Whilst there is consensus that fingerprints are unique and that finding a number of similarities will prove identity beyond doubt, there are no statistics on which to base such beliefs and 'no way of quantifying the cut-off point at which sufficient similarity proves identity' (Redmayne 2002a: 25). Stoney (1991: 197) suggests that 'on perceiving enough points of identity, the expert makes a "leap of faith" and becomes "subjectively certain" of identity'. Practitioners came to believe that finding 12 similar ridge characteristics was the point at which to make such a leap and declare a match. However, in 1924, New Scotland Yard adopted a 16-point standard, though not all police forces upgraded to this standard until 1953, when a common approach was agreed, resulting in the National Fingerprint Standard requiring 16 similar ridge characteristics.

Such a high threshold was sought in order that fingerprint matches would be beyond legal challenge. This standard was monitored by the National Conference of Fingerprint Experts, resulting in a slight amendment whereby a match could be declared with 10 points of similarity if any other mark at the same scene could be matched with 16 points of similarity, a system that operated for many years. As the science of fingerprint analysis developed there became a consensus that considerably less than 16 points could establish a match with some experts suggesting 8 points would still ensure a safeguard against false matches, whilst others suggested the abandonment of a numerical standard altogether. Other countries at that time operated with 8, 10, or 12 points or had no numerical standard.

In 1988, the Home Office and ACPO commissioned research that concluded that there was no scientific basis for the retention of the numerical standard, particularly one as high as 16 points. Additionally, the Audit Commission published a paper calling for the greater utilisation of fingerprint analysis and changes to rules.[54] Such sentiments began to be noted by the courts, with Otton LJ in *R v. Giles*,[55] refusing leave to appeal where a trial judge had admitted evidence of a fingerprint match with 14 points of similarity and

---

54 Audit Commission (1988) *Improving the Performance of the Fingerprint Service*, Police Papers No.2 London, paras 16,20.

55 *R v. Giles* (unreported, Court of Appeal (Criminal Division) 13 February 1988).

one of 8 points. An ACPO report in 1994 recommended changing to a non-numerical system while the publication in 1995 of *A Review of the Sixteen Point Fingerprint Standard In England and Wales* stated that fingerprinting: 'was not an exact science' but involved judgement (Evett and Williams 1995: 11). Change to a non-numerical system was endorsed by the Chief Constable's Council in 1996.[56] Meanwhile, a judge admitted evidence of a match based upon 12 points of similarity,[57] although a year later evidence of ten similar ridge characteristics was not admitted in *R* v. *Holt*.[58] In *Reid* v. *DPP*,[59] Leggatt LJ held evidence of a 12-point match that had been properly admitted. Likewise, in *R* v. *Charles*, an appeal on admission of a fingerprint with 12 points of similarity, Lord Bingham stated that the fingerprint expert had:

> relied on the comparison between them, on the similarities and absence of dissimilarities, on his professional experience during a long career, and on his expert knowledge of the experience of other experts as reported in the literature. He concluded that the possibility of the disputed print and the control prints being made by different people could in his judgement be effectively ruled out. In cross-examination ... he agreed he was expressing a professional opinion and not a scientific conclusion.[60]

The Fingerprint Evidence Project Board hoped that by April 2000 there would be the necessary protocols and procedures to enable experts to give their opinions without arbitrary numerical thresholds, courts being then able to draw conclusions as they saw fit. This target was endorsed by *R* v. *Buckley*,[61] where the courts set down new guidance on the admission of fingerprint evidence:

> fingerprint evidence like any other evidence, is admissible as a matter of law if it tends to prove the guilt of the accused. It may so tend, even if there are only a few similar ridge characteristics

56 Thames Valley Police 1996 Report of the Quality of Fingerprint Evidence Review.
57 Judge Gordon in *Allen* (unreported) 30 June 1995.
58 *R* v. *Holt* 5 November 1996 (unreported).
59 *Reid* v. *DPP* (unreported, 2 March 1996, Divisional Court).
60 *R* v. *Charles* (unreported) CA (Crim) 17 December 1998: Lord Bingham of Cornhill (p. 9e).
61 *R* v. *Buckley* (1999) 143 SJ LB 159.

but it may, in such a case, have little weight. It may be excluded in the exercise of judicial discretion, if its prejudicial effect outweighs the probative value. When the prosecution seek to rely on fingerprint evidence, it will usually be necessary to consider two questions: the first, a question of fact, is whether the control print from the accused has ridge characteristics, and if so how many, similar to those of the print on the item relied upon. The second, a question of expert opinion, is whether the print on the item relied upon was made by the accused. This opinion will usually be based on the number of similar ridge characteristics in the context of other findings made on the comparison of the two prints.

It was ruled that where there were fewer than eight similar ridge characteristics, it would be unlikely that a judge would admit evidence of a match, and nor should the prosecution seek to adduce such evidence. However, if there are more than eight points, the judge may exercise his discretion in favour of admitting the evidence, depending upon other circumstances of the case, considering in particular; the experience and expertise of the witness; the number of ridge characteristics; and whether there are dissimilar characteristics; the size, quality, and clarity of the print relied upon. It was also asserted that in cases where fingerprint evidence was admitted, it would generally be necessary for the judge to warn the jury, as with all expert evidence, that it is evidence of opinion only and that it is not conclusive, but rather it is up to the jury to determine guilt in light of all the evidence.[62]

On 11 June 2001 the 16-point standard was officially replaced by non-numerical standard 'after extensive consultation with the Lord Chancellor, the Attorney General and other criminal justice system stakeholders'.[63] Instead, there are:

> objective criteria which must be satisfied and must be capable of demonstration, e.g. in a court, before any decision is made. There are also prescribed verification procedures which must be adhered to at all times before that decision is

---

62   *Ibid.*
63   Lord Rooker Hansard, HL (series 5) vol. 625, col. 2699 (25 February 2002).

communicated to an investigating officer and eventually to the courts.[64]

The change to a non-numerical standard reflected the desire of police to bring more fingerprint identifications to court. It was also suggested that the abandonment of a national standard would lead to more vigorous cross-examination of experts and fingerprints being challenged more often. Experts will be required by courts to prove their experience,[65] and that verification procedures had been adhered to.[66] Despite safeguards and checks, mistakes have been, and will continue to be made: 'certainly if mistakes can occur under the old system where 16 points of similarity were required it would be foolhardy to expect that mistakes will not be made when fewer points of agreement are required' (Armer 2001: 1660). In 1998, Scottish Police Officer Shirley McKie was tried for perjury for testifying that a fingerprint on a doorframe at a murder scene was not hers. Four fingerprint experts testified to a match with McKie, whilst two American experts gave contrary testimony, seeing McKie finally acquitted. Controversy continues over how the erroneous 'match' got through the Scottish Criminal Records Office procedures and why the experts still refuse to admit their error.[67]

The case of *Chiori* v. *UK*[68] was taken to the European Court of Human Rights, claiming unlawful imprisonment. Chiori was charged with burglary following the matching of his fingerprints with those at the scene. The fingerprint officer claimed 'no doubt' about the identification, this the only evidence against Chiori. Two independent experts later found the match erroneous. The prosecution offered no evidence, explaining that their fingerprint examiner had made an error of judgement. The defence expert claimed that there had been a serious flaw in the checking procedures which, had they been performed correctly, would have identified the false positive, concluding that there was compelling evidence of gross negligence and incompetence on the

---

64   As above at col. 2701.
65   They should have passed the Advanced Fingerprint Course, have years of experience, and be included on the National Register of Fingerprint Experts.
66   In a Fingerprint Bureau each identification is checked by three different experts – each decides independently on identification and then the Head of Bureau or designated deputy makes final verification.
67   See www.shirleymckie.com and www.onin.com for details.
68   *Chiori* v. *UK* (1999) ECHR App. No. 44926/98.

part of the Metropolitan Police Fingerprint Department (although this was without malicious intent). Chiori sought compensation for time spent in custody and claimed that there was no redress as police and fingerprint officers were immune from prosecution. Chiori's case was dismissed due to the fact that the case had not been pursued through the domestic courts and the time limit had been exceeded.

The difficulties with attaining a consensual standard for fingerprint 'matches' mirror some of the problems that have beset DNA evidence. Lack of scientific consensus exacerbates difficulties at trial, with continued debate on the presentation of 'match' statistics curtailed by judicial attempts to set guidelines for the reception and presentation of DNA evidence.

DNA on trial

While the legislature in the 1990s was extending the circumstances in which DNA samples could be taken and widening the powers of the police to search databases speculatively, the first reported case of a DNA-based conviction was in 1987 in R v. Melias,[69] where a match with a semen crime stain induced a guilty plea. Soon, cases relying upon DNA profiles began to reach the appeal courts (such as the case of R v. Kelt,[70] concerning the admissibility of a DNA sample). In R v. Deen,[71] a retrial was ordered for a case originally tried in 1990, when forensic application of DNA profiling was still in its infancy. The appeal had raised a number of criticisms of the statistical formulae used and the summing up. The Lord Chief Justice, calling the case 'an early exercise in a new field', heard evidence that the prosecution had fallen foul of the 'prosecutor's fallacy' (mistaking the likelihood ratio for the match probability).[72]

Again in R v. Gordon,[73] the prosecution relied upon a DNA match to identify the accused as a double rapist. Of the five scientists giving evidence, one testified as to being unsure as to a complete DNA match. The accused appealed submitting that there was insufficient exclusion of the possibility of a mismatch, meaning that the prosecution had failed to prove guilt beyond a reasonable doubt. A retrial was ordered because of uncertainty over the quality of the DNA evidence, although not its validity. This case demonstrated that

---

69   R v. Melias (1987) The Times, 14 November.
70   R v. Kelt [1994] 2 All ER 780.
71   R v. Deen (1994) The Times, 10 January.
72   Ibid.
73   R v. Gordon (1995) 1 Cr.App.R. 290.

while DNA technology and techniques were accepted, the statistical evaluations could yield misleading evidence. Gross exaggerations of the significance and value of the evidence cast doubt on the evaluative stage of the process, with the risk that juries may accept 'matches' as conclusive where they are not, as Redmayne (2002: 19) explains: 'when DNA evidence began to be used in court, a problem quickly emerged. The problem was how to present DNA statistics – 'match probabilities' – to juries'. Indeed, in one case, the judge permitted the jury to alter the match probability figure presented if they accepted that the figure may have been different had a Sierra-Leonian database been used.[74]

The issue of DNA evidence and *PACE* s. 78 was considered in *R v. Denis Adams*,[75] one of the first cases reliant upon a DNA match. The Court of Appeal rejected the reasoning that complexity of evidence was a ground upon which it could be excluded for reasons of fairness. However, the court ordered a retrial because the use by the defence of Bayes theorem had 'plunged the jury into inappropriate and unnecessary realms of theory and complexity deflecting them from their proper tasks'.[76] The Court rejected the proposition that DNA could only be used to support other evidence: 'There is no principle of law that DNA evidence is in itself incapable of establishing guilt'.[77] This was reaffirmed on appeal after the subsequent retrial (*R v. Adams (No.2)*).[78] Again during his trial for rape, the DNA evidence was challenged, and rebutted with an alibi, and again, Bayes theorem was put to the jury. The appellant claimed that if the prosecution are allowed to present statistical evidence based on a DNA profile, then the defence should be able to adduce statistical evidence, arguing that Bayes theorem is logical and that the judge should encourage the jury to use the theorem instead of relying on their common sense. The judge had told the jury that they could decide themselves whether to use Bayes, the court agreeing that the defence were allowed to reply to the prosecution case by way of statistics. The Court of Appeal ruling again stated that there was no objection in

74   *R v. Musa-Gbengba* (1998) Crim LR 478, Judge Gordon gave a novel direction on the statistical significance of DNA evidence, allowing the jury to alter the match probability figure of 1 in 14,000.

75   *R v. Denis Adams* [1996] 2 Cr.App.R. 467; see also J of CL (1997) 61(2) 170 and Crim LR [1996] 898.

76   *Ibid.*

77   *R v. Denis Adams* [1996] 2 Cr. App. R 467, 469.

78   *R v. Adams (No.2)* [1998] 1 Cr.App.R. 377.

principle to relying on DNA evidence alone but soundly rejected the use of Bayes theorem in jury trials.[79]

The weight to be given DNA evidence, its presentation and ability to prove guilt were considered in R v. *Doheny and Adams*.[80] An expert in *Doheny* testified that it was his opinion that the offender was the defendant. The trial judge directed the jury that if this evidence was to be believed, guilt had been conclusively proved. This was contrary to the real meaning of the DNA evidence, that whilst there were a very small number of others that could match the DNA profile, the defendant was only one of this small group (appeal for *Doheny* allowed). In R v. *Adams* (Gary), both the expert and prosecutor had fallen foul of the prosecutor's fallacy, though this did not invalidate the verdict as the defendant had been identified by the victim. However, it was vital in light of the increasing use of DNA evidence that the profiling process be understood and that the manner in which the evidence is presented be made as clear as possible, thus R v. *Doheny and Adams* attempted to set out guidelines to minimise the risk of the misuse of DNA evidence, including:

1 Any issue should be identified and resolved before trial in pretrial review

2 The expert witness should not be asked his opinion on the likelihood that it was the defendant who left the crime stain, nor when giving evidence should he use terminology which may lead the jury to believe that he is expressing such an opinion.

3 It is inappropriate for an expert witness to expound a statistical approach to evaluating the likelihood that the defendant left the crime stain, since unnecessary theory and complexity divert the jury from their proper task. [81]

DNA evidence now rarely raises admissibility issues, having made the transition 'from a novel set of methods for identification to a relatively mature and well studied forensic technology' (Imwinkelreid and Kaye 2001: 458). Indeed, defendants have continued to be convicted

---

79 *Journal of Criminal Law* (1998) 62(5) 444.

80 R v. *Doheny and Adams* [1997] 1 Cr.App.R. 369; see also J of CL (1998) 62(1) 33 Crim LR [1997] 669.

81 R v. *Doheny and Adams* [1997] 33 Crim LR [1997] 669 at 672.

on DNA evidence such as in *R v. Lashley*,[82] and *R v. Smith*.[83] However, the DNA 'match' in *Lashley* left him as a suspect along with seven to ten other men in the UK, with no other evidence linking Lashley to the crime or even the area. The only evidence Lashley could then proffer was an outright denial and a claim of mistaken identification. As such, his refusal to testify could not be held against him and used to supplement the DNA evidence to reach a conclusion of guilt, and his conviction was overturned. In *Smith* however, the appeal was rejected where the DNA match left Smith a suspect along with 43 other men in the UK, because 'there was also quite clearly evidence of this man having been arrested some shortish distance away'.[84] This ruling raised the possibility that should your DNA be found at a crime scene of which you have been in the vicinity, or even live nearby, this could be sufficient to lead to a conclusion of guilt, surely as unacceptable a state of affairs as being convicted on a DNA match plus inferences drawn from silence.

The courts have since considered the weight of DNA evidence in the cases of *R v. Watters*[85] and *R v. Mitchell*.[86] Watters was convicted of four burglaries based on a DNA match from cigarette butts found at the scenes of burglaries, the prosecution relying upon the similarity of the burglaries to claim the same people had been responsible for each. The prosecution also relied on facts that the defendant was a smoker, lived locally, and was male. The appellant argued that the DNA evidence was weak (the match probability was 1 in 79,000), and additionally, if the defendant had a brother – which he does, this was reduced to 1 in 267. The expert testifying claimed that the DNA evidence should not have been used in isolation as this in itself did not constitute proof, as Kay LJ confirmed: 'in every case one has to put the DNA evidence in the context of the rest of the evidence and decide whether taken as a whole it does amount to a *prima facie* case'.[87] The Court of Appeal concluded that the case should not have been put before jury because of the confusion over the brothers (the other brother was also suspected of being in the burglary team), and

---

82   *R v. Lashley* CA 9903890 Y3 (8 February 2000).

83   *R v. Smith* CA 9904098 W3 (8 February 2000).

84   As above at para. 10.

85   *R v. Watters* CA (Criminal Division) unreported, 19 October 2000.

86   *R v. Mitchell The Times*, 8 July 2004.

87   Kay LJ *in R v. Watters* CA (Criminal Division) unreported, 19 October 2000.

the matters relied on were at best weak – if they couldn't exclude the brother then all the jury should do was acquit.

In *R v. Mitchell*,[88] the appellant successfully argued that the fact that DNA swabs taken from the victim were not his strongly supported his defence of mistaken identity. The trial judge had summarised that the DNA evidence was entirely neutral and could not assist the jury, the Court of Appeal disagreeing, finding that a 'non-match' was powerful evidence in favour of the accused, which the jury should consider. The court concluded that when considering DNA evidence, judges should take great care not to raise scientific speculative possibilities and so detract from evidence that the defence could rely upon.[89]

The move towards convictions based largely or solely on DNA evidence was not met with universal approval by interviewees. Some commented that with the passing of the *Criminal Justice Act 2003*, permitting the admission of previous convictions in certain circumstances, DNA evidence would be easily supplemented and would almost always prove sufficient to convict:

> As soon as there is a suspicion against you and your DNA matches, then that is going to convict if you put that before a court. Now, when people have DNA matches, and their previous convictions are revealed ..., then you could be convicted just on that, which is clearly wrong considering the potential problems with DNA, so you essentially get convicted for having a previous conviction.[90]

An over-reliance on DNA was of concern to several interviewees, one commenting that it was an attitudinal problem: 'People have a blinkered attitude to DNA and fingerprints, that it is conclusive evidence and then don't look for any other explanations or other alternatives and not looking at other issues raised. With forensic evidence, people can sometimes be conned into missing the obvious'.[91] This was then compounded by poor handling of DNA evidence, and the nature of experts:

> Most lawyers don't understand such evidence and a lot of judges don't. Even now, we find a lot of judges have summed up DNA evidence incorrectly, particular before *Doheny and Adams* ... We

---

88   As above.
89   *Ibid.*
90   Interviewee 1/P/C
91   Interviewee 6/P/C

can't scour all the judgements to see how many judges are still getting it wrong ... The vast majority of people in the legal arena have no mathematical or scientific background ... Lawyers are very bad at understanding science so it means they have no ability to challenge experts, they just rely on their own experts and because experts tend to see things the same way, it isn't a real challenge.[92]

Most problematic was the use of statistics to represent matches to juries, one interviewee expressing the view that complex statistics should not have a place in a courtroom, demanding too much of the participants:

You've got this bizarre situation where, with DNA, forensic scientists can't give definitive opinions, where they can with other types of evidence, such as ballistics and fingerprints. So you fall into the trap of dealing with statistics and you have to try to turn the jury into statisticians. There need to be some safeguards. It's almost drawn too much of the science into the courtroom – that needs to be dealt with by the people who understand it. It can unravel otherwise. You can get prosecution and defence using the same statistic in very different ways. How do you get people to understand that?[93]

The dangers, and persuasiveness, of statistics, was also highlighted by another interviewee:

I have some reservations about the way statistics are presented in court, particularly to juries. Presenting a statistic such as 1 in 5 million doesn't mean a lot to a jury though it looks hugely convincing. It is difficult to explain exactly what that statistic really means.[94]

Such sentiments echo conclusions from studies undertaken in the USA and Australia, finding that acceptance of DNA evidence belies problems with its use in court. Findlay and Grix set out a series of problems, including 'white coat syndrome': where evidence can only be understood and 'disentangled' by experts, and becomes a contest

---

92 Interviewee 6/P/C
93 Interviewee 1/L/P
94 Interviewee 3/L/P

between these experts. Further, the authority of opinions presented at trial can be established or challenged in a number of ways, holding potential for further juror confusion when required to 'arbiter what is fact from opinion' (Findlay and Grix 2003: 274) with the existence of professional alliances between experts and lawyers often alienating jurors further (2003: 174). There are also language difficulties, DNA often requiring 'demystification'. Jurors are required to enter the realms of genetics and statistics, with some likely to be 'unduly influenced by overtly probabilistic evidence because it exudes an "aura of precision"' (Schklar and Diamond 1999: 160). Findlay and Grix (2003: 274) also found jurors had:

> high expectations for the significance of DNA evidence. This may be based more on popular culture rather than scientific understanding. Such disproportionate expectations can produce frustration ... but overall did not significantly diminish the jurors belief in the probative importance of DNA.

This problem was identified a decade earlier when it was stated that the subjectivity in testing and reporting DNA profiling surprised many jurors: 'one of the many problems surrounding DNA evidence is the vocabulary used to describe it. This in itself tends to mislead as to the accuracy of DNA test results' (Farrington 1993: 806). This problem is exaggerated by the trend to incorporate DNA as an essential feature of prosecutions, the DNA evidence represented as 'compelling', with jurors expectations of DNA 'compounded through media representations of DNA as conclusive proof of a person's guilt' (Findlay and Grix 2003: 274). In contrast to such media representations, Findlay and Grix conclude that DNA evidence remains relatively new with a lack of established authorities or conventions on the presentation and challenging of such evidence, a view supported by the observation by Gans and Ubas (2002: 4) who note:

> the interpretation of DNA evidence requires expertise from several fields, notably genetics, statistics, laboratory technique, and crime-scene analysis. On a number of occasions, Australian courts have permitted a person qualified in a single field to present an opinion based on several fields.

Jury interpretation and confusion are not the only problems which beset DNA evidence, with many problems occurring before trial, at the collection and analysis stage. The infamous USA case of *People*

v. *Castro*,[95] was the first occasion in which DNA evidence was successfully challenged, on the basis of the unreliability of the testing procedures and protocols, the laboratory failing 'in its responsibility to perform the accepted scientific techniques and experiments'.[96] Such failings at early stages of the DNA process negate the validity of any 'match' data at trial: 'statistics as to probability assume that the biological tests have been carried out and interpreted according to acceptable scientific standards. However, some recent cases in the US suggest that such an assumption may be far from safe' (Walker and Cram 1990: 489). The US National Institute of Justice (2000: 7) has conceded that while the science behind DNA is solid, weaknesses are possible in 'human errors, breaks in the chain of evidence, and laboratory failures'. What can then be safely assumed is that:

> the effects of the trial process are to expose the messy complexity that lies behind such sanguine assertions of truth. Opposing teams of lawyers hire biological experts to attack each other's truth claims, with consequences that would delight contemporary sociologists of scientific knowledge: the most robust scientific claims are shown to be contestable products of dubious technical procedures, questionable leaps of causality and loosely controlled discretionary judgement. (Rose 2000b: 13)

In research studying the impact of DNA evidence on trials in Australia, it was found that DNA cases were more likely to reach court, but DNA evidence (and also incriminating fingerprints) assumed its greatest strength in influencing jury decisions, with juries 33 times more likely to convict where prosecutors produced DNA evidence (Briody 2002: 170).[97] However, the presence of scientific evidence does not relieve a jury of their primary task, which must be based upon matters of judgement, however impressive the science: 'no matter how sophisticated forensic science may become, there are no "techno-fixes" when it comes to matters of judgement'.[98] This is particularly so in rape trials where the presence of DNA increases the chances that the defendant, unable to argue mistaken identity

---

95   *People v. Castro*, 545 N.Y.S.2d (N.Y.Sup.Ct. 1989).
96   As above at 996.
97   See also Briody 2004: 231–52.
98   Marx, G. (1998) 'DNA "Fingerprints" may one day be our national ID card', *Wall Street Journal*, 20 April.

in defence, will contest consent instead. Further research from Australia suggests that as a result of DNA evidence, defendants are deterred from submitting early guilty pleas by long sentences and the difficulty in victims successfully convincing juries in matters of consent. Thus, the reporting of sexual offences is being discouraged, an unintentional and undesirable consequence of the burgeoning use of DNA evidence in rape cases (Findlay and Grix 2003: 281).

In a study in the USA, the presence of DNA evidence resulted in a variance in sentencing severity (DNA convictions leading to harsher sentences), the researchers concluding that the finding may have been: 'an example of the old adage: you take up some of my time and I'll take up some of yours. After all, the DNA evidence ... clearly demonstrated the guilt of the defendant, yet he still refused to plead guilty' (Purcell *et al.* 1994: 153). Whilst other variants in verdict and sentence could be explained primarily by other correlates such as age, race, and offence seriousness, the authors (Purcell *et al.* 1994: 156) conclude that 'one inescapable fact remains: DNA testimony is already having a significant, if little understood, impact on rendering justice in serious felony cases'. With defendants convicted on the basis of DNA 'matches' alone, such 'matches' postulated as lending certainty to a conviction, the trial ignores the reality that:

> findings may be tainted by the manner in which the sample was collected or the manner in which it was stored. It depends on the ability or the integrity of the scientist who carries out the tests – we all know of cases in the past where the integrity of scientists has been questioned ... at the end of the day there cannot be certainty.[99]

The criminal trial: certainty and rectitude

Identification technologies currently available do not permit the examination of every single difference between individuals, and, particularly in the case of fingerprinting but also in DNA analysis, relies upon human interpretation. Scientists are then unable to say with complete certainty, that there is a 'match'. Instead, they can say is that there is (usually) a very high probability that the fingerprint or DNA evidence originated from the individual rather than an

---

99 Lord Thomas of Gresford, Hansard, HL (series 5) vol. 625, col. 969 (8 May 2001).

unrelated person (assuming that all the stages of the process have been executed faultlessly). The use of probabilities brings with it the problems of complex statistics, with experts themselves highlighting the potential for 'misinterpretation of the value of statistical evidence' (Bar 2003: 1). It may not be the case that identification evidence is erroneous, but attention must be paid to the possibility that 'DNA results can be, and sometime are, manipulated, misapplied, or misunderstood by the courts' (Urs 1999: 317). This is particularly so, when during the criminal process 'DNA evidence has become the scientific litmus test of culpability, based on statistical probabilities that are perceived, and often presented as scientific certainties' (Kellie 2001: 175).

Forensic identification evidence on its own is thus compelling, but not conclusive, and the courts need to demand independent corroborative evidence to prove involvement of the suspect in the crime.[100] However, in a society which increasingly views the 'risk' of the guilty escaping conviction as more serious or injurious (to the community of potential victims, and public confidence in the criminal justice system) than the conviction of the innocent, forensic identification evidence (as 'neutral' and 'objective') gains special status. The risk of injustice has been balanced with the risk to public safety, with addressing insecurity prioritised above the risk of injustice. The danger then, is that the faith in forensic science to facilitate convictions, and bring certainty to the criminal process will lead to such evidence going unchallenged, risking:

> the notion that the forensic evidence is somehow beyond the structuring operations of mediation and potential error: to a degree, unless the evidence is contested by other scientists, the forensic evidence may risk appearing tautologically scientific, that is, self-evidently factual and thereby incontrovertible ... A silent witness that is immune from challenge would produce a technological tyranny that would undermine the adversary process. (Blake 1989: 110–11)

On an individual basis (micro-level), forensic identification technology can ensure the innocent are exculpated, while helping secure the detection, and conviction of the guilty. At the macro-level there are perhaps greater concerns, with the reform of the criminal process

---

100   See FSS, *National DNA Database Annual Report 2002–03*, p. 17.

in the risk society eroding the presumption of innocence, negating protections against wrongful conviction, and downgrading the status afforded 'fairness'. The adversarial process may then risk being undermined by forensic identification evidence, with a perceptible shift towards inquisitorialism and legal processes founded upon justice as 'truth'. The 'risk' of failing to convict offenders is shaping reform agendas, with the removal or diminishment of suspect and defendant protections justified by reference to the 'certainty' achievable through utilisation of scientific techniques and technologies. If trials can achieve rectitude and certainty through science, then fairness can become a subsidiary concern. On a micro-level analysis this may be an improvement, the system notorious for consistently achieving neither rectitude or certainty, but denigration of the concept of fairness and the shift to a concept of justice as 'truth' will have negative impacts itself on both rectitude and certainty as long-standing protections against miscarriages of justice are removed or downgraded. Indeed, an 'unfair' system itself can be characterised as a miscarriage of justice, where State powers are used oppressively, or without due cause.

However, consideration of the rules of evidence in terms of their aiding or hampering accurate verdicts is simplistic. There is no real consensus upon the true purpose of the criminal trial and trials cannot easily be cast simply in terms of convicting those guilty of criminal offences. Instead, there must also be: 'a consideration which has force independently of considerations pertaining to guilt and innocence. This is the consideration of the public interest in the moral integrity of the criminal justice system' (Choo 1993: 10). This 'moral integrity' has also been called the principle of 'judicial legitimacy', a principle premised upon:

the idea that a court does not behave legitimately unless it fulfils its public duty of protecting the innocent from wrongful conviction and protecting the moral integrity of the criminal process, while at the same time keeping in mind the public interest in bringing offenders to conviction. (Choo 1993: 13–14)

The use of such techniques is demonstrated by the establishment of a 'cold case review' between the police and FSS with unsolved murders, and rapes being reinvestigated.[101] With increased utilisation

---

101   See James *et al.* (2000) for examples of cases.

of forensic science techniques, criminal investigations can be opened and re-opened time and again with each new identification method appearing to pinpoint the identity of the perpetrator; developments in forensic science could then lead to ridiculous scenarios: 'scientific progress never ends. What happens when new science supersedes the old – new science previously thought to support a now, manifestly flawed conviction secured in a retrial after the original acquittal has been quashed?' (Roberts 2002: 422). With the double jeopardy rule diminished, and Strasbourg jurisprudence forcing a re-evaluation of the rights of victims, it may be envisaged that following a failed prosecution, a victim may press the police and prosecution for a reinvestigation and retrial rather than bringing legal action against the police for their failure to secure a conviction. In *Aydin* v. *Turkey* it was held that when a serious crime is committed there must be 'a thorough and effective investigation capable of leading to the identification and punishment of those responsible',[102] while in *Stubbings* v. *UK*,[103] this included an effective prosecution.

Conclusion: forensic identification and the criminal trial

In sweeping aside traditional tenets of justice under the banners of 'modernisation', 'rebalancing', 'narrowing the justice gap', or 'security for all', the government has attempted to align criminal justice priorities with those prominent in the risk society; taking greater account of the 'risk' of not convicting guilty offenders, while downgrading the importance of avoiding miscarriages of justice. Managerialism and efficiency concerns focus solely upon the risk of resource depletion, or increasing costs beyond public acceptability, at the cost of concern with system moral integrity or process legitimacy. The promise held out by forensic science for the successful discovery and appraisal of the substantive truth during the criminal process has promoted the pursuit of substantive justice above procedural justice. This is not to propose that process values are *always* ignored, indeed s. 78 of *PACE* is an explicit attempt to uphold 'process values' and the *Human Rights Act* brought into sharp focus procedural integrity and fairness. However, protections designed to uphold the 'moral

---

102   *Aydin* v. *Turkey* (1997) 25 EHRR 251, para. 103.
103   *Stubbings* v. *UK* (1996) 23 EHRR 213.

integrity of the system', and the regard paid to this integrity as worthy of respect over and above the consistent conviction of the guilty, are being unofficially ignored (for example, via unchecked police misconduct), and officially eroded (for example, via law and procedural reform).

As demonstrated in the previous chapter, police powers have been extended to facilitate the use of forensic identity technologies as they have developed. Such developments become successively less controversial, with extensive powers to take bodily samples attracting little in the way of public or political resistance. This expansion of police powers has not been coupled with greater protections for suspects, with many historical safeguards bring downgraded or restricted. Reforms of evidential law are now primarily focused upon assisting the arrival at a verdict in line with the 'truth', rather than being concerned primarily with fairness to the accused. This 'truth' is increasingly revealed utilising forensic techniques, rendering obsolete traditional protections against unreliable or partial evidence.

Despite imperfection, attempts to adopt principles such as human rights as the basis for criminal justice decision-making and organisation may mark the best hope for constraining the trajectory, speed and extent of reform being witnessed and proposed. However, risk aversion may now be so dominant that normative constraints appear weak. Rights are easily derogated from using justifications predicated upon 'security' and 'public safety', and so on. Fiscal constraints also appear powerless, as witnessed in the US where there appears to be unlimited spending limits on 'homeland security'. Fiscal concerns have also not impacted upon decision-making in the UK in crises such as the BSE scandal, the solution chosen by the government costing millions of pounds. The trajectory then towards a quasi-scientific criminal process designed to search for 'the truth' is evidenced by the propagation of inquisitorial procedures and legal reforms that introduce greater defence burdens while easing prosecution burdens and increasing prosecutorial (including police) rights. Forensic science is playing a crucial role in these developments, which demands analysis of the development of forensic identity databases.

Chapter 4

The development of forensic identity databases

The development of forensic identity databases

The influence of ideology underlying the criminal justice system may not be limited to its own operation and outcomes, but has wider implications and consequences; a difficulty in pinning down the purpose of the criminal justice system is that not only is the system impacted upon by social values, but the system itself impacts on the society in which it operates (Rutherford 1993: 1). Late modern society has been characterised as fragmented, fearful, mistrustful, and insecure, symptoms manifest by ubiquitous fear of crime and victimisation. In tandem with this is a 'general disillusionment' with policing and in particular, traditional criminal investigation (Maguire 2000: 317). Reforms instigated in light of such 'disillusionment' and altered priorities of the criminal process are then impacting upon other social policy goals and concerns, which are in turn supporting and fuelling the shifting aims of the criminal justice system.

A common understanding of 'justice' as an outcome of the criminal process is changing in line with these altered priorities, both in society and within the criminal justice system. Additionally, the status of science as pivotal to the successful achievement of criminal justice and social policy aims has seen the role of technology not simply assisting in policy implementation, but policy formulation. Science and technology capabilities drive as well as support policy, making understanding their development essential to analysis of current trends, and the future potential of forensic identification technologies. As detailed, the law has extended the situations in which bodily samples can be taken, what can be taken, and restricted when consent is necessary. The legislature has also extended police rights to retain the information derived from samples. While in the case of fingerprints a national database has been growing for years with little controversy, the establishment of the national DNA database has been the source of greater concern. Consideration then follows of how and why such databases have been created, before taking a 'healthy, sceptical' approach to their justification and claims made for them. As Stenning exhorts; 'we all need to be more sceptical about claims made in the criminal justice arena' (Stenning 2004); the operation and utility of forensic identification databases appearing an area where scepticism is lacking.

The 'information state' and criminal records

The nineteenth century saw a huge expansion in government information gathering with: the census; electoral rolls; registers of births, deaths, and marriages; and police reports all being established. Each brought greater bureaucracy, with data collection and storage of files forming the empirical foundation of the burgeoning social sciences. The system of national registration, in place during the World Wars, was dismantled in light of civil liberties concerns and perceived ineffectiveness, but personal data gathering again expanded with the advent of the welfare state. The period of expanding state surveillance during the twentieth century was then initially linked non-problematically to the provision of welfare and the taxation of citizens, its primary goal being the 'incorporation of the working classes into the political nation, if on limited terms, rather than direct domination' (Higgs 2001: 185). Bentham and Foucault understood however, that the accumulation of 'facts' meant power for the collecting authority (Lyon 1991: 606), power that the police became eager to harness.

In the earliest days of Scotland Yard, a formal Convict Supervision Office was established under the *Prevention of Crime Act* 1879, aiming to operate as a national surveillance body. This was the first systematic attempt to create a centralised source of police information for the purpose of suppressing deviancy (Higgs 2001: 187). At the same time as police professionalisation, expansion of detective branches, and the introduction of fingerprinting, the limitations of the Supervision Office became clear as it struggled to monitor thousands of criminals. Many attempts were made through the years to address police effectiveness, being boosted much later with the introduction of computers, primarily used to collate and store information. Computerisation went largely uncontested with approval for technological developments sealed with the creation of computerised criminal records. Computerised databases made the collation, integration, and accessing of data easier, and in 1969 the government funded the establishment of the Police National Computer (PNC). The computers purchased had capacity for a file on every adult in the country, but were soon upgraded. By 1973 each police force had at least one terminal with access to the centralised PNC, which held lists of all the cars, their owners, disqualified drivers, and stolen cars in the country, as well as an index to all the fingerprints held by the National Fingerprint Unit, an index to all criminal records held at the Central Criminal Records Office, a file on each person serving a suspended sentence, and all wanted and missing persons: 'The British Information State had come of age' (Higgs 2001: 191).

Information is now central to the operation of contemporary society, with personal information a vital strand in the constant expansion of knowledge witnessed in the last two centuries (Marx 1998: 1). Indeed, the central collection and analysis of information, especially that on individuals, is a feature of the modern western state which sets it apart from previous political formations (Higgs 2001: 175). Surveillance (as the continual garnering of personal data for detailed analysis) is occurring: 'routinely, locally and globally, as an unavoidable feature of everyday life in contemporary societies' (Lyon 2003a: 1). The police have access to numerous technological applications, including a digital national radio communication service (Airwave); Automated Number Plate Recognition (ANPR); Command and Control; and Holmes 2, while collating information for a number of databases, including VISOR, the violent and sex offenders 'register',[1] as well as police fingerprint (IDENT1), and DNA databases (NDNAD).

Fingerprint databasing

Following the Belper Committee recommendations,[2] Sir Edward Henry established a fingerprint bureau for the Metropolitan police

---

1 See the *Sex Offences Act* 2003, Part II: This requires police keep (up to date) an offenders date of birth; national insurance number; name and aliases; home address and any other addresses used, for a period specified for the monitoring of offenders in the community.

2 See Beavan 2003: 149–51.

on 1st July 1901.[3] The first conviction utilising fingerprint evidence was for burglary in 1902 with the first murder conviction resting upon fingerprint evidence in 1905.[4] Fingerprints quickly became instrumental in crime detection, with the fingerprint bureau responsible for identifying suspects in numerous high-profile cases, including many of the Great Train Robbery gang.[5] It was not until 1992 however, that technology existed to create an Automatic Fingerprint Retrieval system (AFR), linking fingerprint records around the country (previously carried out manually by the National Identification Service at New Scotland Yard). The National Automated Fingerprint Information System (NAFIS) was piloted in 1998, with rollout completed in March 2001.[6] In April 2004, IDENT1 went 'live', (after re-tendering at the cessation of the NAFIS contract), holding 6 million sets of fingerprints (12 per cent of the population), and over half a million crime scene marks, with capacity to hold 8.2 million sets and 1.2 million scene marks.[7]

IDENT1, as an 'identity platform' rather than a mere fingerprint database is, according to the Home Office (2001: 46–7), meant to 'enhance accuracy and efficiency and provide a platform for a wider range of identification services'. It will support LIVESCAN and also incorporate 'Palms', (funded by the Capital Modernisation Fund in April 2001 for £17 million),[8] a project to develop a national automated palm print identification system (Home Office 2001: 46–7). Palm prints can be recovered from around 20 per cent of crime scenes and, in about six per cent of cases, palm prints are the only marks recovered. Police record the palm prints of arrestees but currently have no effective method of searching these against other prints or marks from the scenes of unsolved crimes.[9] Further enhancements are under consideration, including the addition of shoeprints; the addition of facial images and video images; the creation of a Serious Crime Cache (SCC) of marks from serious crimes; an Operational Response

---

3   Metropolitan Police Service Centenary Fingerprint Bureau Pack, available at. www.metpolice.gov.uk.

4   *Ibid.*

5   *Ibid.*

6   See www.policereform.gov.uk/bureaucracy/change_proposal_reports/ Defendant_Management/Livescan_Implementation/page2.html   for details. (Accessed 2 June 2003.)

7   See http://www.pito.org.uk/what_we_do/identification/nafis.htm.

8   See http://www.pito.org.uk/what_we_do/identification/ident1.htm.

9   *Ibid.*

Database (ORD) to facilitate searching prints created for 'special events' such as a serious or serial crime; improved search algorithms to increase accuracy and confidence in responses not confirmed by a fingerprint officer (lessening the workload of fingerprint officers); and additional search capacity to cope with growing demand.[10] Project Lantern trialled mobile fingerprinting, with the police claiming that this will assist in the 60 per cent of cases where drivers stopped by ANPR Intercept Teams give false details.[11] Mobile fingerprinting, it is claimed, is required to free up time spent on establishing identity, and reduces the need for arrest powers, being a 'quick and direct route to establish identity', and an 'early warning access for police for suspected or wanted criminals'.[12]

Fingerprint comparison has been characterised as remaining 'a cornerstone of forensic crime scene investigation' (Home Office 2001: 46–7). Yet interest in other biometric identifiers, such as iris scans, has intensified with technological development, and many countries, including the UK, have plans to either introduce identity documents containing biometric information, or update existing documents to include fingerprints or iris scans. The UK government is intending to introduce identity cards with biometric details, and plans to include fingerprints in passports are well advanced, with fingerprint databases introduced for specific populations – in particular refugees, asylum seekers, and terrorist suspects.[13] Under European Council Regulation 2725/2000, the Eurodac fingerprint database was established, with the stated aim of permitting European immigration services to check the fingerprints of asylum seekers against those of other European countries (see Chapter 5).[14] With recent statistics putting the number of asylum seekers entering the UK alone in 2002 at 110,000 persons, the database has the potential to grow very large very quickly if the movement of people continues on this scale.[15]

---

10   See www.policereform.gov.uk/bureaucracy/change_proposal_reports/ Defendant_Management/Livescan_Implementation/page2.html   for details.

11   HC Home Affairs Committee (2004) *Identity Cards Fourth Report of Session 2003–04* Volume I HC 130-I London: HMSO, para. 6.4. p. 23.

12   *Ibid.*

13   See *Anti-Terrorism and Security Act* 2001 s. 36, amending s. 143 of the *Immigration and Asylum Act* 1999.

14   The Regulation came into force in 2002 although the database was not operational until early 2003.

15   Home Office (2002) 'Final agreement reached on EU fingerprint database for asylum seekers'. Press release: 28 February.

Such biometric information about non-criminal populations 'substantially expands the investigative capabilities of the police as technical standards for the use of the data are established and the technology advances' (Lingerfelt 1997: 11). The urge to create new – bigger and better – databases, with more information and biometric detail appears unstoppable, with the UK Passport Service agency and the Driver and Vehicle Licensing Agency establishing a working group in 2002 to extend and merge their records; a move to create a national database with details of citizen's fingerprints and iris scans included.[16] The National ID Card scheme will now most likely supersede such plans by including such information and biometric data. The 'success' of the national DNA database has paved the way for the ambitious plans for a national identity card.

In addition, across the country, and with very little public attention being paid, private companies have been 'selling' fingerprint database technologies to schools, to facilitate library lending schemes. Up to 2004 this had resulted in over 5,000 primary schools and 1,000 secondary schools having their own fingerprint databases of pupils. Limited comment on such developments to date have concluded that the children 'like' having their fingerprints taken, and that parents do not complain. However, it could be argued that schools have been seduced by technological 'gadgetry' (are forgotten library cards such a huge problem?), and that while there have been assurances given about the privacy of the data (which would be highly questionable faced with a police request for access after a serious incident in a school), there are potential objections simply on the grounds of 'acclimatising' children to surrendering their personal biometric information to authorities at such a young age (and for so paltry a reason). However, perhaps in the twenty-first century surrendering personal information will become an expected 'duty' of responsible citizens, and these children will have come to accept such obligations of 'freedom'.

The National DNA Database

The England and Wales National DNA Database commenced operation on 10 April 1995 governed by Home Office Circular 16/95, which stated that the database was for intelligence only, with matches found during speculative searches not to be used as the basis

---

16 See 'UK citizens' fingerprints and iris scans to go on database' at http://icwales.icnetwork.co.uk. Accessed 11 April 2002.

of prosecutions (Starmer *et al.* 2001: 85). However, legislation soon negated this circular, with prosecutions permitted upon matches from speculative searches. Until announcement of the DNA Expansion Programme, the £40 cost of taking and processing each sample had limited the number of tests submitted by police forces.[17] By February 2002, the database had reached its target halfway point with 1.5 million profiles stored.[18] The increased government investment funded a major expansion of the database to add samples at a faster rate. In 2003–04, 95 per cent of samples were loaded within 24 hours, the rest unable to be loaded because of police clerical errors, or results supplied by external suppliers not being in the required format.[19]

It is now claimed that the targets set for the expansion programme have been achieved, with the NDNAD holding 3,000,949 samples (from 2.71 million individuals – the discrepancy due to replication) as of March 2005, and 228,463 profiles from crime scenes (as at July 2004) (Home Office Forensic Science and Pathology Unit 2006). The UK now has the largest domestic forensic DNA database *per capita* in the world (Townsley and Laycock 2004: 3), with 5.24 per cent of the population on the database, compared with the closest European rate of 0.98 per cent in Austria, and 0.5 per cent in the USA. The database is projected to grow yet further with the new powers to sample arrestees yet to take full effect. It is predicted that the NDNAD will have reached almost 4.3 million samples by 2007–08, and it has been suggested that it will very soon encompass up to 10 per cent of the population (or at least 5 million individuals) (Jobling and Gill 2004: 739). Automation of DNA profiling processes has also meant a significant increase in the loading of samples, with the FSS more than doubling their load rate so that 40,000 samples can now be loaded each month.[20]

During 2001–02, the FSS received 395,050 criminal justice (suspect) samples from police forces. Since this peak, submissions have dropped annually to 350,962 in 2003–04.[21] Nationally, monthly submission rates average at 35,000 criminal justice samples, and 3,000 crime scene

---

17 'DNA database warning', available at www.bbc.co.uk/news, 1 September.
18 Home Office (2002) Press release: 21 February, available at www.home. gov.uk.
19 *NDNAD Annual Report 2003/4*, available at www.forensic.gov.uk p.10.
20 FSS (2004) Press release, available at www.forensic.gov.uk.
21 FSS (2004) *Annual Report 2003–4*, p. 19.

samples.[22] With arrest now sufficient for taking DNA samples since the enactment of the *Criminal Justice Act* 2003 (the provision coming into force on 5 April 2004), there may have subsequently been a steep increase in the number of samples taken from arrestees, with 170,000 profiles being taken in the first year alone.[23] During 2004–05, 521,117 new subject samples were added to the database, and 49,723 new scene-of-crime samples (Home Office Forensic Science and Pathology Unit 2006). The NDNAD includes samples from 139,463 individuals who have never been charged or cautioned with an offence (43 per cent of those arrested have no further action taken), as well as samples from more than 700,000 10–17 year olds.[24]

In addition to the database of criminal justice samples and crime scene samples, there are also now DNA databases for manufacturers of consumable goods used during the DNA testing procedures, the Manufacturers Elimination Database (the MED), to be used if any contamination is suspected. This database is in addition to the Police Elimination Database (the PED), which holds the DNA profiles of police personnel. The PED, established in 2000, had 92,127 samples as of March 2005 (80,574 of these are searchable records, with other records having been removed upon request and the rest remain awaiting analysis).[25] There have been, to date, 44 crime scenes where the testing has resulted in the DNA profile matching a profile of a member of a police service on the PED, resulting in the profile being eliminated from further inquiries.[26]

Many European countries have now also established DNA databases (though none as wide in scope as the England and Wales NDNAD (see Chapter 5)), often after undertaking public examination of issues surrounding DNA databases, with restrictions imposed upon the police use and retention of DNA samples.[27] In contrast, the inception of the NDNAD in England and Wales did not prompt significant

---

22 FSS (2004) Press release, available at www.bbc.co.uk/news.

23 *NDNAD Annual Report 2003–4*, available at www.forensic.gov.uk, p. 10.

24 BBC News, 'DNA Database continues to swell', 5 January 2006, available at www.newsvote.bbc.co.uk.

25 *NDNAD Annual Report 2003–4*, available at www.forensic.gov.uk, p. 13.

26 As above, at p. 24.

27 See for a recent example, The Irish Law Reform Commission, '*The Establishment of a DNA Database*' (LRC CP 29-2004) Consultation Paper, March 2004: 266.

protest or political opposition, with apparently few obstacles to general acceptance. Indeed, government investment in databases for policing is seen as beneficial:

> since its inception there appears to have been an acceptance that a well regulated index of offenders works for, rather than against the public interest. Even though it is a very costly venture it is expected that it will have considerable benefits in the future. (Schneider and Martin 2001: 232)

However, there may have been 'a rush to judgement that DNA databases are highly desirable, if not fundamentally necessary, in the fight against criminals' (Tracy and Morgan 2000: 667). Sometimes premature favourable judgements led Tracy and Morgan (2000: 682) to warn of 'expansionist tendencies', indicating that 'if society feels the need to expand its crime-solving abilities, these databases will be broadened accordingly' (2000: 670). They counsel adopting instead a 'healthy scepticism' about the capabilities of DNA databases to control crime (2000: 637). There follows then a consideration of the explicit justifications given for the expansion of forensic identification databases, incorporating potential rebuttals to positive arguments. As detailed, most of the controversy has centred upon DNA databases, with fingerprint databases ignored. Many issues are relevant to both, but the majority of critical points allude to DNA databases alone, accompanied as they are by particular concerns.

A sceptical approach to forensic identity databases

There have been a number of justifications for forensic identity databases expounded, with positive claims and statistics attesting to their 'success'. The money invested in forensic databases means it should not be surprising that they are portrayed in a positive light, while their success must be underlined to justify extensions to police powers to take samples from suspects (Redmayne 1998: 441). However, occasional media-friendly instances of dangerous criminals caught using such technology do not constitute sufficient evidence alone on which to base massive and expensive databases:

> isolated successes of DNA databases are interesting and laudatory. However, they do not provide systematic, conclusive,

and widespread evidence that such databases, especially the expanded or 'all inclusive' variety will be proven useful in the fight against crime. (Tracy and Morgan 2000: 645)

It is important instead, as argued by Her Majesty's Inspectorate of Constabulary (HMIC), that the use of DNA is 'carefully, and objectively considered against other policing methods in order to ensure best value' (HMIC 2000: 15). There also remain concerns over the potential for fabrication and error, and issues of discrimination, privacy, and civil liberties.

The NDNAD: efficient and cost-effective?

As detailed in Chapter 2, the DNA database is expected to aid in investigations, with power to exculpate suspects as well as incriminate, leading to swifter, cost-effective policing (Martin *et al.* 2001: 228). In 1998 the US National Institute of Justice claimed 'great success' for the UK's forensic DNA testing arrangements, particularly the use of mass-intelligence screenings and the use of DNA as a 'primary investigative tool', which was reported to have 'reduced overall law enforcement costs by eliminating extensive traditional police investigations in some cases' (NIJ 1998: 6). Meanwhile, the Home Office also claims great success for the domestic national database, stating that there is more than a 49 per cent chance of DNA found at a crime scene being matched with a criminal justice sample on the database (Home Office Forensic Science and Pathology Unit 2006).

It was claimed by ACPO that by January 2001, there had been 134,812 'hits' on the DNA database, 'leading to thousands of people being convicted of charges ranging from burglary and car crime to murder'.[28] The picture was confusing however, with a HMIC report in 2002 stating that there had been over 70,000 identifications made over the life of the database (HMIC 2002: 18). There clearly needed to be clarification over what constituted a 'hit' and what exactly is a 'match' if these were going to be justifying criteria of the database. This problem was addressed in the first annual report of the NDNAD, explaining that 'pairwise' comparisons 'did not ... relate in any meaningful way to the number of detections being reported by

---

28   Ben Gunn of ACPO, in BBN News Online 'A Database Too Far?', 19 January 2001.

the police'.[29] The confusion led to the introduction of a new system of match declaration, with statistics now based upon the number of crime scenes for which one or more suspects was nominated, a more meaningful approach to measuring the 'success' of the database. Using these criteria, in 2004–05, 40,169 crime scenes were associated with one or more suspects, and 4,500 crime scenes were linked.

Of course, there exist other important considerations when accepting such 'matches' as indicators of success, for 'match' statistics are 'misleading in some crucial respects' (Saul 2001: 93). Such 'matches' do not represent convictions, or even arrests made (see Chapter 2), they simply denote the presence of someone at a crime scene *at some point in time*. In effect, particularly at scenes that may be public areas, 'a match may not mean very much' (Saul 2001: 93). Even ignoring the potential for DNA evidence to be planted (cigarette butts or apple cores, for example, can easily be moved to a crime scene), crucially in serious violent crimes, most often 'even a genuine match is only evidence as to a criminal act (*actus reus*) and does not indicate intention (*mens rea*) which must be proved in the ordinary manner' (Saul 2001: 93). In response, the Home Office now stresses the number of 'detections' as well as 'matches' (see Chapter 2 for more details on criminal detections using the NDNAD).

As well as problems of defining and interpreting 'success' claimed by partial parties, cost-benefit analyses may throw into doubt the efficacy of a national DNA database in the fight against crime. Unfortunately, the only real attempt to critically examine cost-benefits has been done in the USA, and it may be unlikely that a similar exercise will be undertaken in the UK (at least not publicly), given the political importance in proving that the sums of money spent on the database have been, and continue to be, worthwhile. Reports from the Home Office have reported the 'achievements' of the NDNAD – although their very own data show that in the year 2004–05 the NDNAD only assisted in detecting 0.34 per cent of crimes recorded by the police, and of these in 42 per cent of the cases the police already had the suspects' name so these cases may have been cleared up even without the NDNAD – so these cannot be counted as detections that would not have happened otherwise. Considerations then of the heavy investment in the NDNAD and the ongoing 7 per cent of police budgets that the NDNAD costs – for a

---

29 *National DNA Database Annual Report 2002–3*, available at www.fss.gov. uk, p. 13.

return of less than 0.34 per cent detection rate may raise question marks over cost–benefits. Could buying more police cars, providing more computing power, and so on have perhaps resulted in greater benefits in terms of detections?

It may be that 'the use of DNA identification is hence being grossly oversold; for instance, the identity of the perpetrator is not an issue in some violent crime and much crime leaves no identifying tissues behind' (Bereano 1992: 121). It remains the case that in the majority of serious (particularly sexual) crime, the perpetrator is already known to the victim, meaning that DNA identification is of use only if the suspect contends mistaken identity, and is not used to 'detect' the suspect. However, DNA can abbreviate lengthy investigations in serious crimes, which can be 'costly' not just in financial terms, but in damaging public confidence in policing and adding to the fear of crime. There is an attendant danger however, that such databases may have a deleterious effect upon police investigation expertise, with an over-reliance or dependence on DNA discouraging a search for other independent evidence, with an investigation stopping at the point of DNA testing (Easton 1991: 28). Indeed, this was a specific concern raised by several interviewees.

In their analysis of DNA databases in the USA, Tracy and Morgan (2000: 665) used crime and prosecution statistics to demonstrate the lack of impact DNA databases would have, and do have, on the overall level of crime and the most voluminous types of property crime, despite the claims made for databases:

> The use of DNA has been touted as one of the most effective tools our law enforcement agencies have ever had to fight crime. It is also claimed that DNA databases might diminish the cost of policing, investigation, and prosecuting criminal cases. These and other benefits make the expense seem more than worthwhile despite DNA mining's limited direct effect on crime-solving so far.

For DNA 'mining expeditions' (speculative searches on the database) to be successful depends upon three prerequisites: a criminal has to leave trace evidence at the scene or on a victim containing their DNA; a trained technician (SOCO) must competently gather this evidence; and thirdly, the DNA evidence must be of sufficient quality to permit testing. These three prerequisites rarely occur in all but the most serious of crimes, meaning that the mining of DNA databases will most likely not succeed in realising substantial crime-reduction results (Tracy and Morgan 2000: 655). In response, police authorities are making efforts to change investigative policy to include the collection of physical evidence from volume crimes. However, the sheer 'volume' of property crime precludes the attendance of SOCOs at most crimes, not accounting additionally for the futility of the exercise in the majority of instances.

Such sentiments are borne out by statistics from the UK where, on average, 16 per cent of crime scenes are examined, with 12 per cent of these resulting in a successful DNA sample being loaded onto the NDNAD, meaning less than 0.8 per cent of all recorded crime produces a DNA sample that can be tested (see Chapter 2 for more details on crime detection and the NDNAD). Tracey and Morgan (2000: 646) conclude that in the USA, while the logic behind DNA databases appears convincing, 'when one examines the nature and distribution of crime, the presumed usefulness of DNA databases as a crime control measure may not only be far from obvious or certain, but may turn out to be grossly exaggerated'. As police do not collect 'physical' evidence from most crimes there, and most prosecutors don't rely upon DNA evidence at trial,[30] DNA databases were then only of subsidiary interest in the overwhelming majority of police and prosecutors' work. It is likely then that national DNA testing on a large scale will lack cost-effectiveness in the more general fight against crime (Walker and Cram 1990: 489). This may hold true in the UK, although recent short-term special initiatives have seen the police and FSS targeting burglary with apparent success. The police occasionally acknowledge the limited capability of the technique to cut crime rates across all crime types, but counter that it helps obtain convictions in more serious, but rarer, offences against the person with the cost of DNA profiling absorbed by the large budgets usually accorded to serious inquiries (Walker and Cram 1990: 480).

Supporters also claim other benefits from use of the NDNAD after investigations have been completed. For example, such databases can further 'speed up' justice by supporting the securing of guilty pleas.

---

30 In their analysis, prosecutors rarely used DNA to prosecute charges, using alternate evidence wherever possible, although this may have increased since the research was conducted, and 'problems' prosecutors associated with DNA evidence have been overcome.

The FSS Pathfinder Project found that those cases with strong forensic evidence resulted in a high proportion of guilty pleas.[31] Rudimentary research in West Yorkshire demonstrates that when there is DNA evidence, cases are routinely disposed of without resort to a full trial,[32] however research in Australia found no correlation between guilty pleas and DNA evidence (see Briody 2002; 2004). The notion that guilty pleas are a positive boon to the criminal justice system prevails, with palpably guilty offenders not 'wasting' public time and money on trials where guilt is 'unequivocally' established by DNA evidence. The aim of securing guilty pleas at an early stage in the criminal process is influential in criminal process reform, with the cost of trials and their supposed ineffectiveness at securing convictions used as arguments for the earlier resolution of cases before formal adjudication proceedings.

There are also justifications for the DNA database which invoke the potentially powerful demotivator: deterrence (see Chapter 2). There are clear problems in proving that the database is effective at achieving such aims as deterrence, or speedier arrests, with arguments necessarily remaining hypothetical. It is widely accepted that crime is often linked to social or psychological factors, correlations which evade easy 'technological fixes': 'the existence of new technologies will not serve as a deterrent. The argument that DNA based identification will deter sex offences is purely wishful thinking, not based upon any supporting evidence' (Bereano 1992: 120). It is also known that identity is often not at issue (particularly in sexual offences) because the perpetrator is often known to the victim, making DNA evidence irrelevant in detection, weakening deterrence arguments for the DNA database (Saul 2001: 93). Supporters will contend however, that the value to society of catching a rapist nullifies objections to DNA databases based on cost–benefit or efficiency evaluations. Such arguments are indeed difficult to counter, however, as one interviewee summed up:

---

31 FSS Pathfinder Project, Summer 2002. Despite attempts, the Pathfinder Projects are not available to the public so their methodology and further conclusions remain unknown. This information was derived from the *NDNAD Annual Report 2002–3*, which reported on the Pathfinder Project.

32 Confidential statistical information in personal communication with interviewee 9/L/P, July 2003.

It's a fine balance, depending on where you are starting from as to whether it is beneficial. The potential benefits to a community of catching a rapist are great, but the potential benefits to society as a whole of having a DNA database are proportionally much smaller, you're not comparing apples and apples, you're actually comparing apples and sheep – they are very different matters.[33]

This interviewee returns to the original position: that use of cases where a criminal has been caught by virtue of DNA should not suffice as general justification for the creation of a permanent, large database with potential negative implications for society as a whole. Do we need up to 12 per cent of the population to be on a database, in order to solve less than half a per cent more crimes per year? However, there are also immediate concerns that have important, immediate consequences for individuals, surrounding issues of fabrication, contamination, and error.

Databases and DNA evidence: contamination, fabrication, and error

In 1995, a team of American DNA experts highlighted problems of contamination, fabrication, and misinterpretation as just some of the potential sources of error, writing that:

the potential for error exists at each step in the inferential chain. A reported match may not be a true match if a laboratory errs; a suspect who provides a true match may not be the source of the trace if the match is purely coincidental; the source of a trace may not have been at the crime scene if the real perpetrator deliberately left the suspect's genetic material; and, finally, the source of the trace may have the left the crime scene trace in a way that is consistent with innocence. (Koehler *et al.* 1995: 201)

Such warnings came in the same year as *The Office of the Inspector General Report of 1995* from within the US Department of Justice which identified a multitude of problems with DNA and other forensic evidence, their report including evidence of:

scientifically flawed and inaccurate testimony in leading cases; … improper preparation of laboratory reports; insufficient

---

33   Interviewee 3/L/P

documentation of test results; inadequate record management and retention systems; failures by management to resolve serious and credible allegations of incompetence, to resolve scientific disagreements, to establish and enforce validated procedures and protocols and to making a commitment to pursuing appropriate accreditation; and a flawed staffing structure within the Explosives Unit with examiners failing to possess requisite scientific qualifications ... (Freckleton 2000: 258–9)

Sociological study of forensic scientists also demonstrates that the 'institutional context' within which such scientists work leads to reluctance to question reliability of tests, and in ambiguous situations, interpretive errors are likely to be made (Thompson 1997). Edwards (2005) details ten things that all lawyers should know about possible DNA contamination and laboratory error, outlining some of the more common human errors and problems with forensic DNA testing, including: selective testing; contamination; switching; coincidental matching and others. She advises lawyers that they should always be alert for error in DNA testing and reporting, and that issues such as backlogs at laboratories, as well as poor laboratory standards can make the risk of error higher.

Whilst assertions are made that problems with DNA testing can be overcome with stringent quality controls, 'concerns about tampering with the samples themselves or negligence in their analysis will probably always be a concern' (Stevens 2001: 931). With ever greater reliance placed upon DNA evidence by prosecution authorities, 'there comes the very real risk that evidence of this kind may be fabricated or tampered with in order to meet burgeoning expectations' (Findlay and Grix 2003: 280). The Chairman of Australia and New Zealand's Forensic Laboratories has stated that while people have long suggested it would be easy for police to plant DNA evidence, 'I've always thought it would be easy for a criminal to plant DNA evidence'.[34]

An Australian geneticist has demonstrated the ease with which DNA profiles can be masked using straightforward techniques, kitchen utensils, and instructions available on the internet. Despite his experiments,[35] such concerns have been met with assertions that

---

34 'Shadows of Doubt' (2003) *The Weekend Australian Magazine*, 27–28 September, p. 18.
35 Including one where he took a buccal swab of his own cheek, then 'masked' it with a colleagues' DNA he had 'cooked up'; the laboratory testing the swab then returning the DNA profile of his colleague.

criminals would be too stupid to be able to replicate such results,[36] but such an experiment justifies the lengths which prisoners have been reported to go to (spitting into each other's mouths before buccal swabs) to evade detection or accurate registering of their profile on a DNA database. Indeed, the creator of the PCR (Polymerase Chain Reaction) profiling technique, Kary Mullis, predicted in 1995 that there could be large-scale forgery of DNA.[37] Even if tampered-with, or 'planted' DNA evidence was not successful in implicating an innocent party, a defence team could raise the possibility of deliberate contamination or fabrication to raise a reasonable doubt as to a defendant's guilt.

There need not be any intention to mislead, the FSS conceding that because of the incredible sensitivity of modern DNA testing, there is increased risk of detecting the DNA of more than one person in samples:

> This may be background DNA which is ubiquitous in the environment and cannot be avoided ... It may also be DNA deposited inadvertently by persons attending the scene after an incident has occurred or collecting samples for analysis; or DNA shed by scientists involved in the analysis of the samples or by persons involved in production of the materials used in the analytical process; or DNA accidentally transferred from one item to another. DNA from these sources is referred to as contamination.[38]

During the most recent reinvestigation of the Hanratty case, a scientist reported finding his own DNA profile when testing exhibits, while in another case, a scientist testing for a DNA sample from the back of a postage stamp got the DNA profile of the court attendant who had attached the court exhibit label.[39] A strict chain of custody is required, although even then contamination cannot be ruled out, particularly in revisiting evidence in older cases, a interviewee explaining that testing exhibits from old cases is difficult because of continuity: 'Some defendants may have come into contact with the exhibits

---

36   'Shadows of Doubt' (2003) *The Weekend Australian Magazine*, 27–28 September, p. 16.
37   As above at p. 17.
38   *NDNAD Annual Report 2002–3*, available at www.fss.gov.uk, p. 18.
39   Information derived from private correspondence with Interviewee 6/ P/C.

innocently after the crime for example, they were handed it in the witness box'.[40]

Investigations into instances of contamination in FSS cases have found an additional risk of contamination from personnel involved in the production of the consumables used in the testing procedures (tubes, swabs, etc.). In July 2003, protocols were put in place to minimise the risk of contamination from personnel involved in the production of the consumables used during DNA analysis, following two high profile murder investigations in which casework contamination had occurred, the profiles reported being found to match personnel employed by the manufacturers of the tubes used by the laboratory. Whilst the occurrence of such contamination is deemed to be rare, when it does occur it can result in misleading information, forcing processes to be introduced to consumable production to minimise risk, including the establishment of a Manufacturers Elimination Database (MED) to help identify any contamination risks. Other processes are being put in place to record, and further minimise risks of contamination in the environment (Townsley and Laycock 2004: 13).

The integrity of crime scene samples was highlighted as a problem by HMIC (2000: 83), who reported that 'processes for dealing with DNA sampling and subsequent identifications have been found to be lacking in rigour'. The inspectorate found incorrect form filling; forensic evidence bags left unsealed; inadequate dispatch and delivery security; and inadequate storage of DNA samples (HMIC 2000: 21–22). In addition, the FSS were reported as experiencing a total of 156 security breaches in the year ending June 2002, including 'minor' breaches such as exhibits not being locked away at the end of the working day (Comptroller and Auditor General 2003: 6). HMIC stress that issues concerning accuracy and compliance with the law were not 'a bureaucratic chore' but were essential 'to fostering public confidence in police guardianship of this important database' (2000: 18), arguing that whilst 'administrative' problems were to be expected: 'the extent of those problems is now such that urgent action is required' (2000: 15). Instances of contamination and security breaches demonstrate how easily mistakes can be made. Such instances, in addition to the mistaken 'match' of Mr Easton (detailed in Chapter 1), led one interviewee to disclose doubts: 'I do wonder where it is all going to end, as the Easton case shows, there may always be a

---

40   Interviewee 6/P/C

flaw. So little is known about it even now, it's worrying so much reliance is placed on it.'[41]

There is also potentially a misplaced faith in the accuracy of large databases. In *Nature* in February 2003, an article warned of the high error rate in mitochondrial DNA sequences, claiming that more than half of all published studies of such DNA contain mistakes which may then be compounded in databases. Such concerns are heightened in the case of forensic testing of DNA as the 'control region' most often used in forensic analysis is highly polymorphic (variable), differing between cells of the same person, for instance, which 'erodes the reliability of forensic assays' (Dennis 2003: 773). The FSS estimated that there should be no more than 'one or two' adventitious matches on the NDNAD in the next 5 years; however, they go on to state that such matches do occur more frequently, requiring further analysis and elimination of possible explanations.

In 2003–04, while upgrading some 6,000 SGM profiles to SGM Plus that had 'matched' with crime scene samples, it was reported that just 52 per cent of the original 'matches' were sustained following upgrading, with 19 per cent of previously reported 'matches' being adventitious. In addition, no comparison was made for 29 per cent of the suspect samples as the crime scene samples had subsequently been removed from the database, so indicating that 26 per cent of the original 'matches' at the SGM level had been adventitious. The FSS had previously concluded that analysis has demonstrated that all 'adventitious' matches so far have actually been down to error, though they conceded that adventitious matches will increase in likelihood as the database grows.[42] However, the NDNAD governing board is now recommending the upgrading of all SGM profiles to SGM Plus.[43] In Germany, a man with a violent history was linked via a 'cold' hit to a rape and murder that had occurred whilst he had been confined to a secure mental institution, this 'iron-clad' alibi able to demonstrate the erroneous match (Edwards 2005: 76).

Additionally, multiple false identities appear on the national database, indicating 'a need for more scrupulous attention to detail' (HMIC 2002: vii). Replication on the NDNAD is estimated to run at 10 per cent, though it was hoped (in vain it appears) that this replication would reduce when the Police National Computer (PNC) was linked to the NDNAD in 2001. Recommendations now state that since the

---

41 Interviewee 6/P/C
42 *NDNAD Annual Report 2002–3*, available at fss.gov.uk, p. 15.
43 *NDNAD Annual Report 2003–4*, available at forensic.gov.uk, p. 16.

Criminal Justice Act 2003 and the introduction of LIVESCAN, identity can be confirmed via fingerprints before the taking of samples for the NDNAD; this then stopping replication by preventing the successful use of aliases by arrestees.[44] However, LIVESCAN units remain rare, and problems with accuracy and the PNC are renowned. The Home Office provided funding in 2003–04 to facilitate the reconciling of 100,000 records between the PNC and the NDNAD. By mid-2005, 22,500 of these PNC records had been synchronised with the NDNAD, and 15,000 records on the NDNAD had been amended to match with those on the PNC.[45]

In 2003, it was revealed that police forces were failing to provide accurate information when submitting DNA profiles to the FSS, and that many forces were simply failing to load DNA samples onto the database or remove crime scene profiles once the crime had been cleared, meaning duplicate scene profiles were also a growing problem: 'which may lead to the risk of unlawful arrest for an offence that has already been dispensed with' (Lund 2003: 6). The FSS report that 'load failures' are always investigated, with failures often down to keyboard data entry error and/or misreading of handwritten information. Analysis of erroneous records on the database highlight problems with:

- incorrect data recording at the time of sampling by the police;
- transposition of samples, or the information relating to samples during analysis;
- mis-identification of the STR markers or misrecording of data by supplier;
- clerical mistakes by the custodian when amending/deleting profiles; and
- profiles affected by contributions from DNA unrelated to the offender.[46]

Further automation is being developed to enable data entry via barcode scanning.[47] Improvement in data accuracy is necessary for compliance with Recommendation No. R (87) 15 of the Council of Europe, Principle 3 and 7, which dictates that the storage of personal data should be limited to accurate data.[48]

---

44 *NDNAD Annual Report 2002–3*, available at fss.gov.uk, p. 12.
45 *NDNAD Annual Report 2003–4*, available at forensic.gov.uk, p. 15.
46 *NDNAD Annual Report 2002–3*, available at fss.gov.uk, p. 17.
47 As above at p. 12.
48 Council of Europe Recommendation No. R (97) 1, p. 31.

The problem of data accuracy and the maintenance and utilisation of databases are clearly demonstrated by reference to the PNC. In 1995, with the launch of the PHOENIX database (the core of the PNC), individual police forces became responsible for adding and updating records on the PNC, leading to ongoing problems, particularly with the timeliness of record creation. Five separate reports have detailed problems with the PNC, including one by PITO (Police Information Technology Organisation) in 1996, one by the Home Office Police Research Group, and three by HMIC,[49] one of which concluded that 'the level and nature of errors, omissions and discrepancies found were unacceptable' (HMIC 2000: xvii). The Home Office finally admitted that 'the police records system is seriously inadequate ... this has been the case consistently for a very long period of time ... it is a very bad state of affairs and it is one the government has given a high priority to solving'.[50] In April 2000, ACPO issued Codes of Compliance regarding the timeliness and accuracy of PNC data entry, though this did not immediately raise standards, and another critical report by HMIC followed, describing police performance in this area 'abysmal'. Recent improvements have been made, but, the claim that the NDNAD would be entirely different due to its custodians being the FSS rather than the police holds less sway now that the issuing of 'criminal record certificates' (established by the *Police Act* 1997, part v) were taken over by an agency in March 2002 (the CRB), and the situation has, if anything, worsened, with the quality of data input declining (Thomas 2001: 886).

Reliance upon human data inputting makes correction mechanisms essential, but such mechanisms increase opportunities for fraud.[51] Inaccuracies then raise further problems concerning not just the use of the forensic identification databases in investigations, but also protections against improper disclosure and the security of the data. With identity theft and 'cybercrime' on the rise, data security is a serious issue. Were it possible to design a completely secure system (which appears improbable), there is still the potential for corrupt individuals with legitimate access to compromise the database, 'given

---

49 *The Bichard Inquiry Report* (2004) HC 653 London: The Stationary Office, p. 116.
50 House of Commons, Home Affairs Committee, *Criminal Records Bureau* Second Report (2000–1) HC227, para. 24.
51 See National Research Council of the US National Academy of Sciences 2002: 13.

the very large numbers of people needed to maintain and administer the system'.[52]

Forensic identity databases: some new risks

Despite much optimism, there are limitations to 'technological fixes', as well as social and ethical difficulties arising from the introduction of technology: 'technology's narrowing of focus may come at a cost of failing to see larger systematic contexts, alternatives and longer range consequences' (Marx 2001: 1). The development and acceptance of novel technologies can impact upon future uses and aims (new means generate new needs), in terms of invention, and may in some circumstances, determine ends:

> The push from possibility may lead to a re-definition of, or re-prioritising of need ... For example, with respect to both health and crime control, the new goal of prevention or risk avoidance has now become increasingly important as scientific means have developed, making early identification possible, particularly on a broad aggregate basis. (Marx 2002: 17)

A crime control 'techno-fix' avoids questioning why some individuals break rules, and the addressing of causes of crime: 'technical solutions seek to bypass the need to create consensus and a community in which individuals act responsibly as a result of a voluntary commitment to the rules, not because they have no choice, but only out of fear of reprisals' (Marx 2001: 5). Instrumental approaches to social problems, as seen in panoptic technologies, can serve then to 'oust moral orientation' (Lyon 1991: 614). Technological fixes can potentially have undesirable side effects:

> There are some parallels to iatrogenic medical practices in which one problem is cured, but at a cost of creating another. Technical efforts to ensure conformity may be hindered by conflicting goals, unintended consequences, displacement, lessened equity, complacency, neutralisation, invalidity, escalation, system overload, a negative image of personal dignity and the danger or the means determining, or becoming the ends. (Marx 2001: 1)

---

52   *Ibid.*

Forensic identity databases are not part of a 'crude and obvious totalitarianism', but are 'an "efficient" and "rational" means of reaching socially desirable ends (like dealing with violent crime, drug abuse, missing people and so on)' (Bereano 1992: 122). It is this supposed efficiency and rationality with socially desirable ends that begets public acceptability and legitimacy. Yet such surveillance has become a potent, if indirect, means:

> of affecting life chances and destinies. Technological developments and social processes interact to produce outcomes which, although not necessarily as stark as the rigid class division of early modernity, nevertheless raise analogous questions of fairness, mutuality and appropriate resistance. (Lyon 2003b: 182)

The legitimacy and public acceptance of forensic identification technologies and forensic databases may prove to have been too easily and hastily won. Normative approaches are as yet undeveloped and require urgent formulation, for 'what happens to personal data is a deeply serious question if that data in part actually constitutes who the person is' (Lyon 2003a: 3). As such 'ethics and politics ... cannot responsibly be evaded in any discussion of surveillance and society' (Lyon 2003b: 163). Indeed, surveillance systems, as central to 'risk society', raise questions

> not only of the role of surveillance in constituting modernity, but also how surveillance should be conceived in ethical and political terms. While discourses of privacy have become crucial to legislative and political efforts to deal with the darker face of surveillance, they frequently fail to reveal the extent to which surveillance is the site of larger social contests ... surveillance practices and technologies are becoming a key means of marking and reinforcing social divisions, and thus are an appropriate locus of political activity at several levels. (Lyon 2003b: 166)

Public debate in the UK over forensic surveillance is rarely conducted on an ethical, or normative level.[53] Instead, commentaries tend to focus upon pragmatics, for example in DNA testing issues such as

---

53 This can be contrasted with the USA and Europe where there have been numerous legal articles addressing ethical issues surrounding DNA databases.

laboratory and practitioner quality assurance, as well as the potential for subjectivity in interpretation, and the problematic representation and dissemination of DNA 'match' results, are discussed. Albeit essential concerns, they ignore more wide-reaching and potentially irreversible risks created by the expansion of forensic identity databases, and the routinisation and industrialisation of police powers to take bodily samples. As Maguire-Schultz (1992: 24) warned over a decade ago:

> Convictions about the centrality of the individual, the need to restrain state power, and the preference for some risks over others all have important implications for the controversy over the use of DNA identification evidence. When the risks of using DNA evidence are judged not simply in terms of scientific accuracy or truth value, but in terms of values about the legitimate use of government power to punish actual individuals, significant and special dangers accompany the uncritical adoption of DNA identification techniques.

Such 'risks' include the support lent by forensic science, and in particular DNA profiling, to a criminal justice reform agenda which has seen the dilution of safeguards (i.e. the weakening of suspect or defence rights), increasing the risk of miscarriages of justice in the most obvious conviction of innocent defendants. However, the potential for injustice created by forensic identity databases is far greater than just the punishment of the innocent. There is a wider threat than that directly posed to the individual, for if the treatment of individuals 'is unwarranted by, or disproportionate to, the need to protect the rights of others, then serious damage will be inflicted not only on the individual but on society (all citizens) as a whole' (Walker 1999: 33). Focusing upon the wrongful imposition of state coercive powers against individuals and groups – including the wrongful invasion of privacy (i.e. by surveillance and police investigative techniques) – where 'public interest' or 'community safety' arguments are invoked to justify oppressive powers, the potential for injustice is considerable.

With specific reference to DNA identification, it is argued that the acceptance of DNA technology as 'absolutely accurate' has left us 'struggling with the social implications of this newfound precision' (Garfinkel 2000: 48). One consequence may be the reinforcement of the notion of criminality as having a biological basis, a personal pathology rather than a social pathology, which may support racial stereotypes of criminals. Such arguments are countered by assertions that reliance on 'objective' evidence such as DNA will correct racial profiling tendencies (Elkins 2003: 271). However, there is still significant discrimination occurring in surveillance practices, with racial groups more likely to be 'captured' by surveillance technologies (there are already concerns being expressed about the racial make-up of the NDNAD, with a large proportion of the young, male, black population already being on it) and consequently, more likely to appear on forensic identity databases (of course they are overwhelmingly male, with 98 per cent of subject samples of the NDNAD being male). Such discrimination makes surveillance 'not merely a matter of personal privacy, but of social justice' (Lyon 2003: 1). The issue of discrimination remains problematic however, with opponents leaving open the rebuttal that a compulsory national database (including a regime of newborn screening) or even a 'global' database should be constructed to eradicate problems of discrimination.

Surveillance, civil liberties, and privacy

Fiscal constraints appear to have not curtailed policymaking to date, especially with large-scale IT projects such as LIBRA, for example, which cost millions of pounds and yet ultimately failed. Likewise, normative constraints are not yet proving sufficient to restrain policy which prioritises risk aversion above human rights and justice for all members of society. Other concerns may yet restrain surveillance developments, with the threat to privacy by surveillance described as so 'potent' that 'it is of the utmost importance that its use is regulated both rationally and clearly' (Fitzpatrick and Taylor 2001: 351). In both *Kruslin v. France*,[54] and *Amann v. Switzerland*,[55] the ECtHR held that it was essential 'to have clearly detailed rules on the subject, especially as the technology available for its use is continually becoming more sophisticated' (Fitzpatrick and Taylor 2001: 351).

Control over personal information has become 'an essential feature of civilised society', with most people assuming (wrongly) that, if law abiding, they have a 'right' to enjoy their privacy.[56] Yet it is often the increased demands for anonymity and privacy which has furthered reliance upon 'external, impersonal, distance-mediated, secondary

---

54   *Kruslin v. France* (1990) 12 EHRR 528.
55   *Amann v. Switzerland* App no. 27798/95, Judgement of 16 February 2000.
56   Lyon, D. (2002) 'The Surveillance Society' *The Economist*, 29 April.

technical means and database memories that locate, identify, register, record, classify and validate or generate grounds for suspicion' (Marx 2001: 1). Commentators, including the Human Genetics Commission (2002), highlight civil liberties issues, and shifting relations between citizen and state as pertinent to identity databases as technologies of surveillance and social control. Implications for notions of 'privacy' and 'freedom' are noted: 'perhaps less tangibly, but no less importantly, the accumulation of various technologies of surveillance and control is regarded by some as imposing intolerable constraints on individual privacy and freedom' (Grabosky 1998: 5).

While tensions between privacy and law enforcement objectives are growing, 'overkill' arguments are increasingly being aired (Fox 2001: 261) that surveillance can:

> distort the relationship between citizens and police by producing an asymmetry of knowledge and consequent imbalances of power. Reliance on surveillance techniques for law enforcement inevitably results in a situation of overkill ... (more and more surveillance to counteract criminal intelligence to get round police techniques) ... the privacy of the majority being sacrificed in the process.[57]

As Sedley LJ noted in *Marper* at the Court of Appeal, in a majoritarian democracy, when weighing the rights of suspects and society, the 'individual will always lose'.[58] The rights of the majority are most often invoked however, by politicians and professionals dismissing concern about the civil liberties of those caught in the control net, claiming it is; 'the rights and liberties of potential victims with which they are concerned' (Hudson 2003: 69).

The growth of surveillance is often framed in terms of 'signalling the death of privacy' (see Garfinkel 2000; Sykes 2000; Whitaker 1999). However, as Fox (2001: 261) points out, the concept of privacy is complex, involving 'a collection of related interests and expectations, rather than a single coherent idea'. Privacy may be considered an abstract and contentious notion, although there are several agreed dimensions to the concept, including; privacy of the person (bodily privacy); privacy of personal behaviour; privacy of

---

57   New South Wales Privacy Committee (1996–7) (NSW Government), p. 15.

58   *R. (on the application of S)* v. *Chief Constable of South Yorkshire* [2002] EWCA Civ 1275; [2003] Crim. LR 39 (CA).

personal communications; and privacy of personal data.[59] Westin (1967: 12), defined privacy as 'the claim of individuals, groups or institutions to determine for themselves, when, how, and to what extent information about them is communicated to others'. Privacy today is often considered in relation to modern technological developments that have meant there is now virtually no limit to the amount of information able to be captured and recorded (forever), in addition to an almost limitless scope for analysis of such data. Indeed, technology is only limited by human ingenuity, and may not only be enhancing or eroding privacy – but forcing a rethink on what is meant by privacy (Austin 2003).

Max Weber, seeing surveillance as a necessary accompaniment to modernisation, rationalisation, and bureaucratisation, regarded it as trapping people 'in an "iron cage" of rules and procedures that destroyed initiative and individuality' (Ball and Webster 2003: 11). Ball and Webster (2003: 15) stress that 'a search to have all revealed to the surveillance gaze is a threatening prospect for one's very soul'. Galligan (1998b: 88) similarly links a lack of privacy to, ultimately, the destruction of 'personality':

> privacy is important because it protects personal identity and autonomy. Without a zone of privacy, identity, autonomy, personality, cannot exist. This is easily shown: suppose that your every action could be monitored, that every thought, urge and desire could be known and recorded, to be used for any purposes by a stranger. Identity and autonomy, let us use the general term personality, under such conditions would be seriously distorted if not destroyed. It follows that a zone of privacy is essential to personality.

Piessl (2003: 22) explains that the loss of privacy then can have an 'inhibiting effect', or lead to a loss of autonomy with individuals not exhibiting their 'own' behaviour, but that which they believe is expected. He has called this impact, the 'mainstreaming' of citizen's behaviour (2003: 22). Mill also famously argued that liberty was essential for human flourishing, implying that 'any restriction of liberty is likely to be inimical rather than beneficial to general welfare' (Hudson 2003: 15).

---

59 Clarke, R. (1997) 'Introduction to Dataveillance and Information Privacy' at www.anu.edu.au/people/Roger.Clarke?DV?Intro.html.

Concerns over potential negative consequences of surveillance then include the creation of: 'an abiding sense of communal unease in which awareness of such scrutiny tends to chill the exercise of accepted civic rights, such as freedom of movement, association, assembly and speech. Surveillance of citizens inhibits full participation in democratic society' (Fox 2001: 261). Nguyen (2002: A.26) argues that the 'omniprescence' of the 'watchers' can have a 'chilling effect', in line with Foucault's description of the panoptican, where inmates could not be sure if they were being watched or not, only that they *could* be watched, as a result of which their behaviour was deterred and conformity was thus coerced. Thus Nguyen (2002: A.27) argues that it does not matter whether citizens are actually watched, but that 'the mere perception that they are is erosive of privacy'.

While privacy is 'essential for the well-being of the individual', it also then has significance for public order: 'the restraints imposed on government to pry into the lives of the citizen go to the essence of a democratic state' (Westin 1967: 427–8). A maximum surveillance, or 'transparent' society 'would be more orderly, but likely less creative, dynamic and free ... A social order based primarily on technical fixes is likely to be as fragile over time as one based primarily on overt repression' (Marx 2001: 4). Diminishing individual rights such as privacy can foster the diminishment of rights of citizens as a whole, which leads in turn to people becoming inhibited in their thought and actions until democracy suffers as a result: 'a subtle shift in the delicate balance between individual rights and the interests of the state will necessarily occur' (Peck 2001: 460). Austin (2003: 143) also warns that a corrupt government could use information to 'weed out ... undesirables', with prevention the best cure: 'the best remedy against this is to prevent the information gathering in the first place, even by a relatively benign administration'. A position that Peterson (2000: 1237–8) adopts when arguing against database expansion:

> Allowing the government to maintain a database of every individual's genetic information creates, at the very least, a government that knows more about its citizens. Even if the information is limited to identifying fingerprints, genetic or traditional, without more intrusion into the private thoughts and minds of individuals, there is still something ominous and oppressive about an all-knowing state. The inherent danger to our conception of ourselves as a free and autonomous society requires that further expansion of the preventative

state, represented by the creation of a universal database, be vigorously opposed.

However, evoking privacy to counter the spread of state surveillance is problematic; if surveillance is accepted, even expected, it is difficult to characterise as an invasion of privacy (Austin 2003: 129). Additionally, while privacy has been recognised by human rights declarations, this recognition is qualified by interests of national security, public safety, or the prevention of crime. Indeed, Etzioni (1999: 4) argues that privacy rights in the USA have been protected at the expense of other important values: 'we need to treat privacy as an individual right that has to be balanced with concern for the common good – or as one good among others, without *a priori* privileging any of them'. Interests in protecting differing dimensions of privacy must then be weighed; 'the balance between freedom and security in a democratic society is not one which can be struck lightly' (Grabosky 1998: 5).

In the UK, the law permits monitoring of individuals, such powers allowing the police (among others) 'to transcend space, and to prod deeper and more intensively into targeted persons and organisations. They also allow for time to be transcended, because information can be registered and stored indefinitely for any later occasion when it may come in handy' (Ericson and Shearing 1986: 141). Such moves are accompanied by:

> demands for better definition of the means of controlling potential misuse of the monitoring powers and a clearer enunciation of those civil liberties and human rights standards that are relied upon to counter-balance the view that, in fighting crime, the ends can always justify the means. (Fox 2001: 262)

The use of police surveillance has been treated individually by the courts, approaching each case with the reliability of evidence, and proportionality in mind (Taylor 2003). In *Jersild* v. *Denmark*, the ECtHR stated that justifications proffered by states for interference must be 'relevant and sufficient'; means employed must be 'proportionate to the legitimate aim pursued'; and a less intrusive alternative unavailable.[60] Interference must also be based upon relevant considerations and not arbitrary.[61] In considering each case therefore, the courts must

---

60 *Jersild* v. *Denmark* (1995) 10 EHRR 1, para. 31.
61 *W* v. *UK* (1988) 10 EHRR 29.

answer 'questions of balance between competing interests and issues of proportionality'.[62] However, proportionality calculations are increasingly weighted in favour of the police who can call upon greater powers to tackle organised crime, as well as terrorism and 'anti-social behaviour'. Indeed, the 'fight' against specific crime-types are becoming institutionalised, with targeted 'police units', such as the National High-tech Crime Unit and the Serious Organised Crime Agency (SOCA), who can then co-opt other agencies and the private sector.

The collection and utilisation of personal data, and the use of identity databases, raises issues then about disclosure and data protection as it pertains to law enforcement agencies. Many interviewees were concerned about the sharing of information, particularly if information held could be inaccurate, for example one interviewee claimed:

> There is a great amount of sharing between agencies with greater dissemination of databases, yet there is no such thing as the perfect database and that imperfect information is then disseminated. There is no way of auditing these databases to see if the information they hold is actually correct. My fear is that, with the inaccuracies on the DNA database, it will be very hard once that information is shared between public bodies, for people to check whether there is false information about them being held. Any inaccuracy on a DNA database could potentially affect the whole record.[63]

Although concerns were tempered by the realistic appraisal that by no means everyone that appears to be aware, or concerned about, personal information gathering and sharing:

> There is no doubt that information about each of us is being collected to a degree that we barely understand, information is held about us by public and private bodies. Whether people are bothered about it is another matter. Most people don't seem to be. We sign away lots of our privacy rights every time we take out our Nectar cards.[64]

---

62   *R v. DPP ex parte Kebilene* [1999] 3 WLR 972 at 994.

63   Interviewee 1/P/C

64   Interviewee 1/P/C

Attention necessarily turns then to provisions for the sharing of information between agencies and the legal protection of personal data.

Police disclosure, information sharing, and data protection

Fingerprint records and DNA profiles are held electronically as a digital record and as such, are required to be stored in compliance with the *Data Protection Act* 1998 (Starmer *et al.* 2001: 85). The *DPA* is a strict regulatory regime founded upon eight principles:

1 Personal data must be processed fairly and lawfully.
2 Personal data must be obtained only for specific and lawful purposes and not be processed in any manner incompatible with those purposes.
3 Personal data must be adequate, relevant and not excessive in relation to those purposes.
4 Personal data must be accurate and kept up to date; data is inaccurate if it is misleading to any matter of fact.
5 Personal data must not be kept for longer than is necessary for the specified purpose.
6 Personal data must be processed in accordance with the rights of the subject under the Act.
7 Appropriate technical measures must be taken against unlawful processing or loss.
8 Personal data must not be transferred to any area outside of the EU which does not have the equivalent data protection.

Police are subject to this regime, but there exist statutory exceptions for law enforcement purposes; for example, exempting police from the 'fair and lawful' processing provision, which serves to nullify much of the protection offered by the scheme. This police exemption was considered by one interviewee as just one of the problems with the *DPA*:

> The police are exempt from the *DPA* and the police can obtain information from other bodies who would normally be subject to the *DPA* – which can all be covered by the exemption for the prevention and detection of crime. The *DPA* is always put up as being a great protection, but it has lots of problems. For a start, to make a subject access request, you need to know that there is a need for you to make a request. The second problem is that

the *DPA* is run by the Information Commissioners office, which is not only now to have responsibility for the *DPA*, but also the *Freedom of Information Act*. They are just unable to properly police these, the office doesn't have the resources. Anyone who thinks the *DPA* is going to be of some help, is optimistic.[65]

The eight principle of the *DPA* is crucial as DNA databases can be used by international police forces (Alldridge *et al.* 1995: 281). As an interviewee pointed out, sharing between countries also nullifies much regulation and protection:

You have to consider also the lack of privacy laws and human rights legislation and so forth in other countries where this information may be sent. Privacy laws only apply to the people in the country – the American or French have strong privacy laws but they only apply to details of their citizens. It may not apply to information sent from outside the jurisdiction. So while the information at home may be closely regulated, that regulation may fall by the wayside if it gets sent internationally and will be left without any protection.[66]

Additionally, the police gained broad powers to exchange information with other agencies under the *Crime and Disorder Act* 1998, s. 115 providing for any person normally prohibited from disclosing information the power to disclose for the purposes of the Act 'in any case where the disclosure is necessary or expedient'. This could be to local authorities, probation, or health service, although the power is subject to the data protection regime and the common law. This power is wide, relating to 'any provision' within the Act, which itself is comprehensive, and leaves open to judgement what is 'necessary or expedient' ((Raab 2003: 49). In April 2001, Multi-Agency Protection Arrangements (MAPPA) were introduced by virtue of the requirement in s. 67 of the *Courts Services Act* 2000 that each police area must: '… establish arrangements for the purposes of assessing and managing the risks posed in that area by … relevant sexual and violent offenders, and other persons who are considered by (them) to be persons who may cause serious harm to the public.' 'Risk management plans' are agreed by a Multi-Agency Public Protection

---

65   Interviewee 1/P/C
66   Interviewee 2/P/C

Panel (MAPPP) who can disclose information about offenders to schools, voluntary groups and others,[67] creating concern:

> The premise of legislation is that information on us should be shared between public bodies, for reasons such as health and safety, crime prevention etc. What we say is that the premise should be that there should not be sharing unless there is reason to do so, the opposite of the government premise (that sharing should be allowed except under special circumstances). The problem then is that a national DNA database can be passed from public body to public body and we will not know about it or be able to scrutinise whether it is being done properly.[68]

In the absence of statutory provisions, wider disclosure (to non-policing authorities, the media, or public) must be justified as falling within one of the *DPA* exemptions. In *Hellewell* v. *Chief Constable of Derbyshire*[69] the police, in giving photographs of known troublemakers to local shopkeepers, were justified in breaching confidentiality for the purposes of crime prevention. Similarly, where a caravan park owner was provided with the details of two paedophiles, police disclosure was approved, but only where there was a 'pressing need'.[70] This was a lesser standard than laid down in Council of Europe Recommendation R (87) 15 covering data protection in the police sector, which states that there should only be disclosure where it is clearly in the subject's interest, or to prevent serious or imminent danger (Starmer *et al.* 2001: 92). A more developed standard was espoused in *R* v. *Local Police Authority in the Midlands, ex parte LM*,[71] where it was held that power to disclose information existed when there was a genuine and reasonable belief in the necessity to disclose for the protection of children; there was a pressing need; and it was in the public interest (Starmer *et al.* 2001: 92).

In *Woolgar* v. *Chief Constable of Sussex*[72] the court was asked whether the police could pass on information obtained during interview, in

---

67 See Chapter 1 of Home Office (2003).
68 Interviewee 1/P/C
69 *Hellewell* v. *Chief Constable of Derbyshire* [1995] 1 WLR 804.
70 *R* v. *Chief Constable of North Wales, ex parte Thorpe* [1998] 3 WLR 57.
71 *R* v. *Local Police Authority in the Midlands, ex parte LM* [2000] 1 FCR 736.
72 *Woolgar* v. *Chief Constable of Sussex* [1999] 3 All ER 604.

this case to the UK Central Council for Nursing. Police investigations into a death at a nursing home involved the arrest of the matron, the matter also giving rise to a UKCCN investigation, during which the police were asked for details of their inquiries. Appealing the dismissal of an application for an injunction to prevent disclosure, the matron contended that the information obtained during police interviews must be confidential, or interviewees would cease to offer information if this was then be disclosed to other bodies for use against them in non-criminal proceedings. As observed in *Marcel* v. *MPC*[73] a presumption in favour of confidentiality is important due to the police investigative function and the prosecution of crime, but this may also entail an entitlement to disclose matters to 'other public authorities'.[74] Woolgar's appeal was dismissed, stating that where a regulatory body inquires into a matter of public concern, the police are entitled to release information that they are satisfied is pertinent.

The ECtHR held in *Leander* v. *Sweden*[75] that disclosure of police files to prospective employers can be justified on the grounds of national security. However, the principle of proportionality requires each case to be judged individually with a blanket policy of disclosure difficult to justify (Starmer *et al.* 2001: 91). In *R* v. *DVLA, ex parte Pearson*[76] keeping details of a conviction for drink-driving, although spent under the *Rehabilitation of Offenders Act* 1974, was also justified under Article 8(2) and did not then interfere with Pearson's right to a private life, despite his conviction for drink-driving preventing him from gaining employment as a heavy-goods vehicle driver. However, disclosure to an employer under s. 115 of the *Police Act* 1997 (the Enhanced Disclosure regime) was successfully judicially reviewed in *X* v. *Chief Constable of the West Midlands*.[77] Justice Wall concluded that the discretion to disclose had to be exercised in accordance with common law principles of fairness as set out in *ex parte Thorpe*[78] and *ex parte LM*.[79] This requires that job applicants be given opportunity

---

73   *Marcel* v. *MPC* [1992] Ch 22.
74   *Journal of Criminal Law* (2000) 64(1): 34.
75   *Leander* v. *Sweden* (1987) 9 EHRR 433.
76   *R* v. *DVLA, ex parte Pearson* [2002] EWHC Admin 2482.
77   *X* v. *Chief Constable of the West Midlands* [2004] EWHC (Admin) 61.
78   *Ex parte Thorpe* [1996] QB 396.
79   *Ex parte LM* [2000] 1 FLR 612.

to make representations prior to disclosure, a conclusion based upon the severity of the consequences of disclosure for the applicant.

Whilst subject to appeal, this ruling may provoke debates between job applicants, lawyers, and police in all Enhanced Disclosure cases, with practical implications.[80] However, the police are still permitted to disclose material and information, although they retain discretion which can be exercised if they do not believe the information is relevant to a matter of public interest. Disclosure is limited to that required for the purposes of the inquiry, and the police must balance rival claims, confidentiality rights of suspects and the public interest. Refusal to disclose can be challenged in the courts, just as the reasonableness of disclosure can be challenged, the courts only interfering if a defendant can demonstrate the police decision was unreasonable. The court addressing whether 'the state, backed by compulsory power, may require information for one purpose and then allow it to be used for another'.[81]

The concept of 'proportionality' however, in a risk society prepared to weight 'balancing acts' in favour of risk aversion, increasingly holds little power to protect against encroachment of surveillance and social control techniques on human rights, particularly when evidence obtained through surveillance breaching human rights is often admissible at trial (Tracy and Morgan 2000). Ethical and normative debates over expansion of forensic identity databases are complicated by lack of consensus upon the parameters of 'privacy', yet justification for surveillance powers for law enforcement and social control agencies are, by contrast, easily found within the search for security and safety. However, problems with raising moral or ethical objections to surveillance expansion do not entail a reliance upon more pragmatic concerns, with practical issues also readily ignored or again 'justifiable'.

Expansionism: comprehensive databases and discrimination

Calls for databases comprising the DNA of all citizens have been widespread, gaining support from different groups, including police, legal scholars, and geneticists. Support cannot be assumed however, with research in Spain finding that 57.42 per cent of the public

---

80   *The Bichard Inquiry Report* (2004) HC 653. London: The Stationary Office, p. 150.

81   *Journal of Criminal Law* (2000) 64(1): 34.

opposed a comprehensive national forensic DNA database (Gamero et al. 2003: 775). In the USA a Judge stated:

> We would be appalled, I hope, if the state mandated non-consensual blood tests of the public at large for the purposes of developing a comprehensive ... DNA databank. The Fourth Amendment ... would mean little indeed if it did not protect citizens from such oppressive government behaviour.[82]

Attitudes to expansion of the NDNAD can be mixed, with one police interviewee pointing out false hopes raised, as well as persuasive arguments against expansion:

> The logic presumably is that wherever we get DNA, because we have everyone on the database, we are bound to hit upon the individual. I have serious doubts about that. We have millions in this country travelling in and out, we haven't got their DNA. If they commit a crime then we won't get a hit. I don't think the argument stands up to proof, it is accepted that even in the census there is a shortfall. There are people who don't fill in forms or are here illegally etc. There are enough people in the country not accountable which makes the logic of the argument fall down. Also, even if you started today to take samples of newborns, it's going to take 12 years before you start getting the youngest criminals on, and 23 before you get most criminals on. It's a very long-term proposal. It would also take a very long time to pass it into law. You would have people objecting on moral grounds with police having to violently take their DNA. What government is going to go through that and what police service would do it? I don't want to kill civil liberties, the police service is here to protect civil liberties, not encroach upon them. It would also cost thousands of millions of pounds. A huge proportion of the population also never come into contact with the police, so you will have millions of DNA profiles that are never of any use whatsoever. It's pie in the sky. And the general public will only support the database as long as it is seen as a tool to tackle criminals. It will lose support as soon as they see it attacking civil liberties. It isn't valid or worthwhile.[83]

---

82 *State* v. *Olivas*, 856 P.2d 1076, 1094 (Wash. 1993) (Utter, J. concurring).
83 Interviewee 2/L/P

Indeed, the police DNA elimination database itself, while obligatory for new officers, has not seen full cooperation from other officers:

Probationers have to be on a police database – but for older officers, it's voluntary. There are lots of reasons why there hasn't been 100 per cent consent to DNA samples to go on the police elimination database. There's lots of misunderstanding – could they discover I have a drug problem? Could they use it for paternity testing? There are lots of worries about the CSA [Child Support Agency], as well as various issues about the information being sold on. A lot of officers just need talking through it though there are also some cultural and religious issues. For some people, it will just be against their principles.[84]

Many interviewees did believe however, that further expansion of the NDNAD was possible, with progress towards comprehensiveness depending upon political persuasion and public opinion:

[It's] whether the government of the time can sell it. Whether the public believe it is there for positive reasons or whether it can be used for negative reasons. Such as, if they do decide to finance the system by selling the information, or if they do research on it and the security of the information. People are always concerned that there are no guarantees, we've all seen sci-films about cloning etc., it depends on the picture that's sold to the public and the security of the information.[85]

Not all interviewees were satisfied with public consultation and debate, concerned that public opinion about law reform is not informed by a true appraisal of the situation regarding personal information retention:

Changes to *PACE* aren't debated enough and there isn't enough consultation on it. If they want to create a database then there needs to be a proper debate on it. There hasn't been a proper debate as yet. It's being legislated by stealth instead of being properly discussed. What seem like small changes at the time can end up being big changes that the public were unaware of

---

84 Interviewee 3/F/S
85 Interviewee 9/L/P

at the time. You can develop a DNA database without people realising. If people understood the amount of information kept about them and the way it could be used, then they might be more worried.[86]

Another interviewee claimed that the public were not simply ill-informed, but most often were ignorant even that there were potentially wider issues to be considered:

> There hasn't been enough debate about the NDNAD. People's opinions are very much informed by what they read in the media, unless they take it upon themselves to find about these things, then we are not well informed about the creation of DNA databases. DNA stories come up when DNA helps to solve a murder, and therefore it's portrayed as DNA is good, and by extrapolation, a DNA database is good so we should have a national DNA database. You can't really blame the media as it is their duty to report the news and this isn't a subject which excites the public very much. Privacy and DNA databases are not subjects which seem to attract a lot of public attention. As yet it hasn't really engaged the public imagination. Like the ID card, until the card is actually introduced, people really aren't that interested.[87]

One interviewee was clear in dividing wider issues concerning uses for DNA from forensic uses, with problems for a comprehensive database only occurring with alternative uses:

> The NDNAD will carry on growing. What is the problem with having everyone on the database? I can see a problem perhaps with keeping samples, but I can't see a problem from the criminal point of view. I can see a problem from a society point of view if they look at your DNA from birth and say 'you're a dead loss' because you are predisposed to cancer. How do you stop insurance companies wanting to have a look, they will certainly be interested. I'm in favour of having a very wide database with regards to crime; it would save time and would

---

86   Interviewee 2/P/C
87   Interviewee 1/P/C

result in so much better justice if they could just get a sample and then plug it into the system and 'bingo!'.[88]

An interviewee was undecided as to how soon we might see a comprehensive database, viewing it as a debate that could be won by expansionist arguments:

There is no doubt that the government want a NDNAD to effectively hold information about all of us. I don't think as yet they will go as far as taking DNA samples at birth. I don't think that is going to happen for a while, but it may happen in the next few years. The trouble is they can find justifications for anything. There is no doubt that the taking of DNA can have uses in terms of crime control and hereditary diseases. Once you have justified it, it's easy to say, OK it doesn't matter. Personally I don't think that a national DNA database is a desirable thing.[89]

While again personally against a comprehensive database, one interviewee was clear that it was a parliamentary decision to be taken, rather than one for the courts:

I think parliament ought to make a clear decision as to whether we are going to have a [comprehensive] national DNA database or not. It shouldn't be a decision taken by the courts, parliament should say they are going to establish a DNA database by taking a DNA sample of all newborns and keeping the DNA of all those tested, that is a decision for parliament. If parliament were to vote on it I would have real reservations about voting in favour of a national DNA database.[90]

Other interviewees were convinced that expansion would ultimately depend upon perceptions of how the database is used, and whether it will impact on them personally:

If the government suddenly decides it's a good income generator to sell this information to whatever organisations, it could have a massive impact on how they view the system. At the moment, people think it's a very good idea to have criminals on it, but if

---

88   Interviewee 8/L/P
89   Interviewee 1/P/C
90   Interviewee 3/L/P

you stop and ask if they would mind being on it, people with no intention of committing a crime or have nothing to fear from their past, how they actually feel about everyone being on the database or babies being put on from birth, you start to find opinions start to vary … It'll depend if people pick up on this issue – like Alder Hey, the keeping of tissues became an issue when they discovered the practice by accident. It'll be up to people to react.[91]

Concerns about expansion and a comprehensive database were expressed then in terms of personal impacts and 'function creep':

The only potential drawback I can see is if it starts to spill over into other areas and I can see huge problems there. The biggest problem is with insurance where certain segments of society will become uninsurable and that will have huge social problems … I would get very hot under the collar if I thought they were analysing my DNA and I couldn't get insurance and I couldn't get insurance for my family – that would be socially unacceptable.[92]

Another interviewee did believe however, that there were potentially strong arguments for DNA testing at birth which could gain public support:

There is a strong lobby for DNA testing at birth from different areas. The debate about taking everyone's DNA is a tricky one and I wouldn't necessarily advocate that. Having said that, if you look at the point of view of identifying people, such as missing people, then there is a strong argument. Parents want their children profiled in case anything happens. It's quite an emotive issue. There needs to be an open discussion, you have got to take the public with you on this.[93]

Alternative arguments for making forensic databases comprehensive are based on the premise that forensic databases are presently 'discriminatory in that only suspects and those previously convicted

---

91 Interviewee 3/F/S
92 Interviewee 8/L/P
93 Interviewee 1/L/P

are in danger of falling victim to a false match. A universal database would be equally fair or unfair to everyone' (Evison 2002: 359). Many see the need to rid databases of racial skewing or discrimination as justification for submitting all citizens to sampling:

> The logical response to concerns (about discrimination) is to make the database truly representative by taking samples from the general population, to be extended in time to cover the entire population ... A truly national DNA database will aid the crusade and we have yet to locate any convincing argument based on civil liberties that can be set against it. (Mahendra 2002: 1405)

Sir Alec Jeffreys has called for the UK to have a comprehensive DNA database, although tempered by his belief that evidence secured from such a database should only be considered indicative – not conclusive – and should not be able to convict suspects. Sir Jeffreys has described the NDNAD as 'highly discriminatory', with 32 per cent of black males in the UK on the database, and only 8 per cent of white males. Sir Jeffreys has also expressed concern that the DNA database has been expanded to suspects, which opens the system to discrimination, arguing instead that there should be two databases running in parallel, one for convicted criminals, the other for the whole population (not owned by the police), thus solving discrimination concerns.[94] However, arguments that a comprehensive database will solve the discrimination 'problem' are flawed, for establishing such a database does not preclude the discriminatory use or application of the database.

In 2001, three legal scholars on the US National Commission for the Future of DNA Evidence, advocated an all-inclusive database for the USA, arguing that making the database universal would eliminate the racial skewing of present DNA databases:

> The Bureau of Justice statistics reports that a black man is six times more likely to be imprisoned during his lifetime than a white man ... Whatever the reasons, it seems clear to many that racial minorities are unfairly over represented among arrestees and convicts. Given this, the construction of huge convict or

---

94 Bratby (2003); see also interview with Prof. Jeffreys in *The Observer*, 8 August 2003, p. 19.

arrestee DNA databases could exacerbate the racial divisions that plague us. (Smith *et al.* 2001: 15A)

In Operation Minstead in South London (see Chapter 2) police officers were required to stop 'light-skinned' black males from 25–40 who were between 5 foot 8 inches and 6 foot tall, and request DNA samples. If those stopped were then to refuse, they could be arrested and their samples legally taken without consent. Officers were told that people who 'gave them concern' should be stopped and their samples taken.[95]

In Michigan, the Commission on Genetic Privacy proposed permanently storing blood samples of newborns collected for health purposes, because the samples 'are a "valuable resource" for law enforcement and scientific research' (Saul 2001: 89). Similarly in Australia there have been calls for a national inclusive database, to be generated from newborn screens, with the practice of taking blood spots (Guthrie cards) having been in operation since the 1960s (Saul 2001: 89). Guthrie cards are already in use for identifying corpses, however, newborn screen databases raise questions over ownership of the data, and the circumstances in which they can be seized and used by the police. In Western Australia, the police seized Guthrie cards for use in an incest prosecution, purposes for which consent was never obtained, but then newborns are not in a good position to give consent (Boyes 1999: 152).

DNA testing at birth not only raises issues concerning consent, but also 'makes social engineering on a genetic basis a real possibility'.[96] Newborn screening can provide opportunity for future social control techniques when complete genetic profiles can be obtained, Boyes (1999: 150) warns that 'it is this latter context that gives the hegemony of scientific truth claims the potential to define the "normal" in human terms'. Such arguments may not be raised in public debate however, if the creation of newborn screening databases are couched in medical terms, with benefits to the health of the individual, and society, with databases portrayed as an expansion of existing programmes, including conventional medical record-keeping (Boyes 1999: 152).

---

95 Quershi, F. (2005) 'Worries over DNA and racial profiling' Institute of Race Relations, available at www.irr.org.uk, accessed 13 June 2005.

96 The NSW Council for Civil Liberties (2000) 'Policy on DNA', Civil Liberty, 186: 15.

The benefits of comprehensive identity databases in eliminating discrimination may perhaps be overstated, with voluminous data being necessarily categorised. Such categories could then lead to discrimination, with people 'suspect' by virtue of their membership of a 'suspicious' category, or sharing a category with a suspect. This is necessarily the result of the mechanical application of surveillance: 'modern instrumentality, bolstered by bureaucratic organisation, is today electronically extended. For example, we become police computer "suspects" or commercial surveillance targets because of the categories into which we fall, irrespective of our actions or intentions' (Lyon 1991: 614). New surveillance technologies apply not just to 'suspects' in the conventionally understood sense:

> In broadening the range of suspects the term 'a suspected person' takes on a different meaning. In a striking innovation, surveillance is also applied to contexts (geographical places and spaces, particular time periods, networks, systems and categories of person), not just to a particular person whose identity is known beforehand. (Marx 2002: 10)

Categorising is tasked with identifying threats to order, stretching from 'disaffected and troublesome young men to organised criminals ... Categorical suspicion encompasses all the policing dimensions of surveillance, and few dispute its necessity, though many are concerned about its boundaries and intrusions into the civil liberties of citizens' (Ball and Webster 2003: 7–8). Categorical suspicion can have tangible consequences for some:

> At the margins of criminal justice, in the wider control system, the distinction between offender and suspect has been erased altogether for some sorts of people. The surveillance gaze operates on the basis of suspicion, but categorical suspicion can have consequences beyond (mere) surveillance. People can be and are excluded from shopping malls, made subject to curfews, coercively recruited to behavioural programmes, all because of who they are and what they look like. (Hudson 2003: 69)

There is the possibility of being falsely implicated by categorical suspicion: 'the computer matching of name lists generates categories of persons likely to violate some rule. One's data image could thus be tarnished without a basis in fact' (Lyon 2003b: 168). Such results of mass data collection erode 'individualised suspicion' (Marx 2002:

17). Ericson and Haggerty describe this as the 'decline of innocence': 'coercive control gives way to contingent categorisation. Knowledge of risk is more important than moral culpability and punishment. Innocence declines, and everyone is assumed to be "guilty" until the risk communication system reveals otherwise.' Searching identity databases can then be characterised as 'fishing expeditions', where everyone is assumed guilty 'until evidence (lack of a file in a database) proves otherwise' (Nguyen 2002: (VI) B36). In a prescient comment in 1993, Annas foresaw the databasing of DNA and its potential societal impacts:

> It could be seen as reasonable at some point in the future to have the FBI store DNA fingerprints (just as the FBI now has a large proportion of the population's fingerprints) to make the job of law enforcement easier. The central problem is that this treats everyone in the United States (whose DNA is on file) as a crime suspect, making us into a 'nation of suspects' and radically alters the relationship between the citizen and government.

Debate concerning the expansion of identity databases then, can be framed as a conflict between state surveillance power and individual privacy, the use of information to effect social control and the creation of a 'suspect society'.

(In)security and (un)certainty

Criminal justice policies often reflect deep-seated, 'emotional and symbolic concerns' (Young 1999: 78), with the rapid growth of forensic identity databases fuelled by fears about crime, but also, the possibility of 'vanquishing the age-old foe of uncertainty' (Maguire-Shultz 1992: 19). Interest in genetic explanations for disease and even maladaptive or deviant behaviours not only reflects the high status of science, but is a response 'to the stresses and strains of an increasingly secularised, complex, and seemingly chaotic society. Biological explanations often appear to be more objective and less ambiguous than environmental or social ones' (Nelkin and Lindee 1995: 16). Forensic science has been seized upon as providing 'an especially pure and objective form of evidence [with] the capacity to give universally accepted, clear-cut answers leaving no doubt' (Walker 1999: 126). However, there is a case to be made that the modern 'existential uncertainty' which has led to the search for 'safety' guarantors, can be a self-fulfilling prophecy, 'reinforcing and exacerbating the conditions that gave rise to it in the first place' (Newburn 2001: 842). Security technologies may stimulate insecurity and thus have an inbuilt 'inflationary logic' with their implementation increasing demands for protection: 'Although security hardware is "sold" on the basis that via deterrence it increases safety ... the very visibility of such hardware is a regular reminder of "insecurity"' (Newburn 2001: 842). Whilst forensic identity databases may not be considered security 'hardware' in the same way as CCTV, for example, it is undeniable that they are security technologies and have entered the public consciousness.

With individuals ever mindful of risk, crime awareness 'institutionalised' (Garland 2001), and technologies of security either visible or having a high media profile, there is almost limitless public and political enthusiasm for new and improved strategies to tackle crime and criminals. The pursuit of security, both on a personal and a societal level, creates a 'market' in public policy with the demand for improved quality of life responded to: 'It is not so much that modernity has failed to keep its promise to provide a risk-free society as that late modernity has taken seriously this promise, has demanded more and realised the greater difficulty of its accomplishment' (Fitzpatrick and Taylor 2001: 78). It may also be realised, if only by a minority, that, 'if high levels of objective personal security are obtainable only at the cost of living in a "fortress society" with significant limitations on freedom of movement and civil liberties, then that cost may be too high' (Zedner 2000: 203). Or, as one interviewee remarked: 'The DNA database is not going to make people feel safer, but people are increasingly scared so think they want it. It won't address their real concerns though.'[97] Indeed the utility of DNA databases in the general fight against crime was claimed to have been overstated by one interviewee: 'it is marginal in the whole fight against crime really. It can have an impact on convictions where identity is an issue, but this isn't clearing up crime as a whole.'[98]

Another interviewee referred to the potential negative impacts falling upon individuals, which may be overlooked, or 'factored in' by society in the quest for safety:

It's the individuals who will suffer, society as a whole may well benefit. There might be a feeling that the trade-off between privacy and safety is worth it, that for the sake of giving up

---

97   Interviewee 2/P/C
98   Interviewee 2/P/C

our privacy we gain a safe society. If you take a utilitarian view and it impacts on a small number of people negatively but a lot of people positively, then it could be a good thing. But I think this is wrong, I think that is misguided and we shouldn't put so much faith in the state. I don't believe the government are evil, I don't believe the government intend to infringe on our rights as a matter of course, but it does happen and it tends to be those who are most disenfranchised and disadvantaged and vulnerable who will suffer the greatest. It is those people who should be protected.[99]

Whether safety or security is achievable or desirable (it is questionable whether it is either), it is pursued fervently today, as Zedner (2000: 201) explains, security '(with its fashionable analogue "community safety") attracts increasing attention from national governments as an area in which they can offer citizens evidence of their continuing power and effectiveness. It furnishes the conceptual framework within which contemporary governments promise to deliver social order.' As a Home Secretary stated: 'If there is one single expectation of government which we share throughout our lives, it is security and protection. This is one of the most basic functions of all forms of government throughout the ages'.[100] The pursuit of security has ramifications for individuals and society, with the focus of attention turning from individuals, to an entire 'target population of potential wrongdoers' (Zedner 2000: 202). This has led to a disconnect between crime and punishment: 'The previously necessary connection of punishment to an actual act is in danger of being lost, with the demarcation between offenders, potential offenders and suspects being blurred' (Hudson 2001: 151). Identities are stored until suspicion is cast upon them, when they can be presumed guilty until the data proves them innocent, or they are able to successfully contest an allegation. Further, the realignment of the criminal justice system to deal with the new priorities of safety, security, and risk avoidance, mean that 'suspects' (presumed guilty), can be denied basic protections and a commitment to just (i.e. 'fair') processes:

'Justice' is now very much less important than 'risk' as a preoccupation of criminal justice/law and order policy; the

---

99   Interviewee 1/P/C
100   See Foreword in Home Office 2001.

politics of safety have overwhelmed attachment to justice ... If someone, or some category of persons, is categorized as a risk to public safety, there seems to remain scarcely any sense that they are nonetheless owed justice. (Hudson 2001: 144)

The attainment of security then involves identifying and excluding those that constitute the 'threatening' population (Zedner 2000: 203. The emphasis on risk aversion leads to a desire for panoptic vision that can anticipate, so necessarily 'the concern is with categorical suspicion rather than with a specific suspect, as everyone is subject to scrutiny and analysis to see if their data traces can be matched or profiled to confirm suspicions' (Ericson and Shearing 1986: 148). This process is based upon another presumption: that new security technologies have 'the ability to produce hard facts to capture and convict hard criminals' (Ericson and Shearing 1986: 148). However, technology does not necessarily work in such an efficient and exact manner, and is made operational by fallible humans. Furthermore, 'hard facts' must be presented in a courtroom, where adversarial practices mean that 'facts' are open to debate and may or may not be relied upon when reaching decisions. This lets uncertainty back into the equation, though attempts are continually being made through reform to remove this residual uncertainty from the criminal process. Such efforts have included the introduction of inquisitorial procedures and greater reliance upon scientific ('objective') evidence, taking place within a culture of increased efficiency, with convictions to be effectively secured, as cheaply and swiftly as possible. Such 'modernisation' is informed by a conception of justice as 'truth', with the focus of the criminal process shifted from the public trial, to earlier decision-making junctures, making it essential for scholars of miscarriages of justice to broaden their focus of attention to the endangerment of innocence in risk society.

Forensic identity databases: current problems, future risks

The problems highlighted and cautions regarding claims made for forensic identification databases do not consider other risks surrounding such databases: 'the anxiety about what future uses might be made of retained material; ... In a system devoid of independent organisations safeguarding access, use, research etc., (as was recommended by the Phillips Commission in 1993 CM 2263: 16), these are significant public concerns' (Barsby and Ormerod 2003). Uses may be found for DNA profiles, the information contained in DNA samples being 'more compendious than is required for the purposes of criminal investigation' (Walker and Cram 1990: 489), raising important questions: 'donors have no guarantee that their samples won't be used for other purposes other than crime detection, and must rely on the integrity of the FSS (or any other future guardian) to ensure that they are not misused' (Redmayne 1998: 441). There is potential that research using stored DNA profiles could lead to a situation where 'genetic information could be improperly used to red-flag individuals with specific traits that may be considered undesirable' (Herrara and Tracey 1992: 246). There are always risks attached to the pursuit of preventative policing measures: 'the consequences for those wrongly categorised as a risk, or whose label is maintained though no longer valid, are significant once the "profile" is loaded into databases that never forget' (Fox 2001: 258). Such concerns are pertinent to the NDNAD, with those whose profiles are kept at risk of being implicated in crimes for as long as their profile remains stored.

The notion of 'function creep' where 'previously authorised arrangements ... are now being applied to purposes and targets beyond those envisaged at the time of installation' (Fox 2001: 261), can already seen to have occurred with the NDNAD where the intention of keeping profiles permanently as an intelligence and research tool, and for profiles to be the basis of prosecutions, runs contrary to original promises for profiles to be limited to assisting in the investigation of serious crimes. As Marx[101] warns: 'once DNA analysis comes to be seen as a familiar and benign crime control tactic, the way will be paved for more controversial uses'. Sir Alec Jeffreys warns of the dubious ethics of current research, particularly into 'DNA Identikits', whereby physique and ethnic origins can be determined from DNA, research he labels 'hocus-pocus', although such work is already reaping 'results' with the racial origins and family ancestry of suspects being used for investigative purposes (see Chapter 6).[102] Such expansion and 'function creep' may prove irresistible 'in an age where information is power and more is almost always better, the dynamic of system expansion is very powerful' (Gordon 1986–7: 496). As Casey warns:

---

101 Marx, G. (1998) 'DNA Fingerprints may one day be our national ID card', *Wall Street Journal*, 20 April.
102 Prof. Alec Jeffreys in 'Inventor Warns over abuse of DNA Data', *The Observer*, 8 August 2003, p. 3.

Scientific progress continues to advance rapidly as society scrambles to keep apace. But no one can anticipate some of the ways current and ever more powerful future DNA technologies will be put to use, nor their unintended and potentially controversial or adverse effects.[103]

As the science of genomics develops, increasing numbers of 'problems' are being given a genetic basis, thereby enabling the mounting of 'rational and efficient arguments … to extend DNA libraries and use them to combat new problems that will be defined as "genetic" (e.g. alcoholism, schizophrenia, criminality, and homosexuality)' (Bereano 1992: 124). It is this qualitative difference between DNA and other biometric identifiers (i.e. fingerprints or iris scans) that raises ethical questions and could lead to misuse:

Most notably, genetic information has an ability to predict. Secondly, it divulges information about other people, those who are genetically related. Thirdly, one's genetic characteristics cannot be altered. Lastly, one's genetic make-up is regarded as the essence of one's identity, and this perhaps is the most clearly culturally inscribed aspect of genetic information. (Boyes 1999: 148)

Further, as one interviewee explained:

You've reached a point where the state can know more about you than you do. The state can always find out stuff about you, but in a sense you also know those things as well. With DNA though, the state can know things about you that you don't. People have yet to accept just how much you can know about a person from their DNA … the consequences of the state having access to that information, for the purposes of solving crime is unknown … it is worrying to think the state could have that detailed knowledge. There are things that you can know about people from their DNA that the state doesn't need to know, or shouldn't have the ability to find out, simply for solving crime.[104]

---

103 See Casey (1999) at http://www.ornl.gov/sci/techresources/Human_
    Genome/publicat/judicature/article3.html.
104 Interviewee 2/P/C

Additionally, there are concerns over the populating of the databases and discrimination. Despite recent legal rulings that police powers are compatible with human rights,[105] police can arrest suspects on flimsy evidence (with 'reasonable suspicion' justifying arrest) and subsequently release the suspect with no charges brought (43 per cent of arrests result in no further action being taken), thus enabling police to collect and retain the fingerprints and DNA of whomsoever they so choose: 'This ... arouses fears of the police being able to create (and perpetuate) a category of usual suspects, and for the police to decide who are those free of any taint of suspicion whose samples should be destroyed' (Barsby and Ormerod 2003: 41). In such a situation, the perennial problem of policing based upon stereotypes is raised. It is known that the police, for obvious reasons, do not arrest a representative cross-section of society, so forensic identity databases will continue to be biased in favour of those regularly arrested; in other words young males, often from ethnic minorities. Indeed, the racial bias of a DNA database is one of the main objections to the growth of such databases in the USA, with their arrestee population skewed racially (though not necessarily their criminal population); the impact of a racially skewed DNA database will exacerbate the racial bias already present in the criminal process.

Despite concerns and problems detailed, forensic identity databases appear to have widespread support, most likely due in part to a lack of critical attention to the implications of growing reliance upon forensic identity databases: 'societal pressures to solve crime creates incentives to push forensic DNA technology as far, and as fast, as possible ... And yet, state laws currently fail to address the myriad social, individual, and legal issues that DNA technology presents' (Hibbert 1999: 825). The development and expansion of such databases should be understood in this wider context of social policy and criminal justice reform. Placing such identity databases within the discourse of the risk society, considering its panoptic qualities and potential as a disciplinary institution will lead to a fuller understanding of its implications for justice.

Forensic identity databases form another information resource with which police attempt to meet the informational demands of institutional networks and find the ultimate resource for combating crime. Fingerprint and DNA databases then can be viewed as devices

---

105 *R* v. *Chief Constable of South Yorkshire Police (Interviewee) ex parte LS (Appellant) R* v. *Chief Constable of South Yorkshire Police (Interviewee) ex parte Marper* (FC)(Appellant) (2004) UKHL 39.

to perfect data gathering and intelligence, with which to control a 'risky' population: the criminal, or the suspect. This corresponds with statements asserting that police attention should turn from 'crimes' to 'criminals':

> the operational thrust of policing now emphasises the investigation of criminals as well as the traditional focus on crimes. This approach is heavily dependent on the gathering and analysis of intelligence. Technical support has a pivotal role as a cost-effective means of gathering intelligence and evidence. (HMIC 2000: 53)

There is powerful incentive then to expand and develop identity databases: 'such a program would also fit with the actuarial mind-set – the faith in facts, the need for economic efficiency, and the tendency to reduce complex social problems to manageable and measurable dimensions' (Nelkin 1989: 17). However, this reduction of complex social phenomena, and the application of 'technological fixes' to the problem of crime and criminal investigation, is more problematic than often considered. Technological developments can produce risks or unintended consequences, thus necessitating constant vigilance and reflexivity. An account of potential 'new risks' is then required, to inform the formation of a (hitherto missing) normative, ethical position on the expansion and utilisation of forensic identity databases.

Conclusion: the endangerment of innocence in the pursuit of security

Late-modern society's risk aversion leads to the relentless pursuit of technologies with which to achieve security, safety, and certainty, which 'attracts substantial funds, both public and private, and serves to justify draconian intrusions on personal freedom' (Zedner 2000: 201). It is the consequences of draconian intrusions on freedom that this chapter highlights, leading to a conclusion similar to that reached by Fitzpatrick (2002: 372):

> The endless refrain that the innocent have nothing to fear is the usual Orwellian means of neutering the civil liberties argument that the proper distinction is not between the innocent and the guilty (as if innocence were an ontological category and

not a legal one!), but between the relatively powerless and the relatively powerful. In fact, the relatively powerless do have something to fear whenever the presumption of innocence shifts towards a presumption of guilt. Yet, in denying this what the Orwellian refrain does is to employ an actuarial logic where individuals are required to obey the norms that define them as moral/insiders rather than immoral/outsiders. Yet, since there is no system that is immune to abuse and errors 'the innocent' do have something to fear and only a naïve technological determinism can pretend otherwise.

Technological development has created privacy issues not previously considered, making it necessary 'to sharpen and deepen our understanding of traditional concerns regarding privacy in order to respond to these new situations' (Austin 2003: 164). Such a response may clarify often confused and contradictory approaches, helping the articulation of privacy arguments, and ending the use of the term 'privacy' as a 'catch-all' to express a variety of concerns (Marx 1998: 2). Such a goal may be impossible when privacy is defined as inherently personal, with a lack of consensus over the intimacy of different information making it 'very difficult to collectively agree on the legitimate boundaries of the privacy bubble' (Stalder 2002: 121). Indeed, some propose that to achieve a proper valuation of privacy in policy debates, privacy needs to be considered a social or societal value:

> framing privacy as an individual right (value, interest) had a weak impact on congressional policy-making on technological threats to privacy ... [enabling] those with competing concerns ... to eventually shape privacy legislation by invoking social interests, that is, by asking that 'individual' privacy interests be balanced with interests that served the public good such as effective law enforcement ... (Margulis 2003: 249)

In implementing technologies to avert risk, there are new risks created, including the casting of all citizens as 'suspects'; 'the technology of DNA typing can easily lead to increased social control by powerful elites over *potentially* "unruly" citizens' (Bereano 1992: 121). The expansion of identity databases has serious implications for privacy and civil liberties, and their logic is endangering innocence, with the creation of a 'suspect society'. As an interviewee remarked, 'However you dress it up, the creation of a national DNA database, is to treat every person as a suspect'.[106] In this suspect society, principles of justice as fairness are endangered by an 'excessive concern with safety: fear of crime and fear of terrorism are rational fears, but are heightened to the point where they overwhelm our care for liberty and justice. Contemporary Britain furnishes plenty of examples of fears overwhelming concern for justice' (Hudson 2003: x). Perhaps the novelty of such concerns is exaggerated, as Rule (1974: 339) warned thirty years ago, that 'clienteles of [surveillance systems] are apt to see the unpleasant results of mass surveillance as directed against a deviant minority of others, rather than at themselves'. Yet there is evidence that the priorities of the risk society are now accelerating the attainment of 'total surveillance' in the proliferation of identity databases, and creation of a 'suspect society' where the presumption of innocence is bereft of substance. The tyranny of technology is thus being increasingly realised within the criminal process.

---

106   Interviewee 1/P/C

Chapter 5

Forensic identification in other jurisdictions

There are very few international, or even European reviews of the laws surrounding fingerprinting or DNA sampling in jurisdictions outside of England and Wales. This is not surprising considering the challenge in 'mapping' fingerprint and DNA databases around the world, which vary greatly and change constantly, making it near impossible at any point in time to accurately record the various enabling laws for forensic sampling and retention of samples and profiles. Data on fingerprint usage and databases is near impossible to gather without massive research resources, while DNA database information is more readily available, by virtue of its relative novelty and also the greater interest in DNA developments internationally. In making an attempt to 'map' the European situation relating to forensic DNA sampling, Williams and Johnson conclude that: 'legal, financial, operational and political considerations have meant that the proportion of the population whose DNA profiles are currently held on criminal intelligence databases differs greatly from state to state'.[1]

One thing that is clear is that no country has, or appears to ever countenance, reducing its use of forensic identification evidence, including DNA: 'No country has yet ever reduced its established forensic DNA collection or sought to curtail its uses once it has been

---

1 Williams, R. and Johnson. P. (2005) *Forensic DNA Databasing: A European Perspective*. Interim Report. The Wellcome Trust available at www.dur.ac.uk/p.j.johnson.

embedded successfully into its criminal justice system.'[2] Quite the opposite; most countries are continuing to expand their fingerprint and DNA capabilities, including the scope of their domestic databases and involving cooperation with other countries. Yet literature concerning forensic fingerprinting and DNA analysis has still focused on scientific and technological issues with other issues, such as legal or ethical considerations largely absent. This chapter takes a cursory look at the situation in a selection of European and other countries, including a brief look at pan-European developments and Interpol use of DNA data.

Europe

The UK was first to establish a forensic DNA database (with separate databases for England and Wales, and Scotland), around the same time as the Netherlands, but by 1998 a further five European nations (Austria, Germany, Slovenia, Cyprus and the Netherlands) had also established DNA databases. France also commenced a DNA database at this time, although it was very limited in scope. Finland and Norway introduced DNA databases in 1999, with Belgium, Denmark, Spain and Switzerland following in 2000 (Martin *et al.* 2001). In 2001 the Czech Republic, Italy, Portugal and Sweden established databases, followed by Lithuania and Greece in 2002, Hungary in 2003, and Slovakia and Estonia in 2004. To date, in Europe, only Latvia, Luxembourg, Malta, and Poland are yet to establish DNA databases.

The organisational arrangements and legal requirements of the databases differ from country and country, with some European DNA databases being operated and governed by the police themselves (as in the Czech Republic, France, Greece, Latvia and Scotland) all from police laboratories.[3] Plotting the variation in regulations is a lengthy procedure and ascertaining the 'success' or otherwise of the databases is also very hard to establish, with 'hits' being poorly reported or definitions differing, making comparison problematic. Those reports available of database size and 'success' rate also do not tally, leading to confusion over the accuracy of data. What is clear is the huge variation in scope, size and 'hit' rates of the different databases. The following information then is unavoidably erratic, and will simply plot the situation as it stands at the end of 2005.

---

2 As above at p. 16.
3 As above at p. 96.

Ireland

Ireland has been one of the last European countries to entertain the idea of a DNA database, with recommendations for the creation of a database still remaining in the preliminary stages of adoption. It is envisaged however that legislation for a DNA database will be passed in 2006, following a favourable report from the Irish Law Reform Commission in late 2005,[4] and continued pressure from police, with Garda Commissioner Noel Conroy publicly calling again for a national DNA database for Ireland in April 2005.

The first Irish contested case involving DNA was in 1995, in the case of *DPP* v. *Lawlor*, which resulted in a guilty verdict (O'Donnell 1997: 65). Subsequently, the successful detection of a crime from 1979 again highlighted the benefits of a national DNA database. Phyllis Murphy of Kildare was found strangled in 1979, 28 days after having been abducted. DNA left at the crime scene was recently matched with that of a man from Kildare, who was found guilty of the murder, 23 years after the crime.[5] The police now claim that the lack of a DNA database is hampering criminal detection efforts.

The use of DNA evidence at trial has also proved problematic in Irish courts, with the bulk of Irish cases with DNA as a component part to date having been dealt with by way of a guilty plea (O'Donnell 1997: 64). Up until 1997, only six trials with DNA evidence reached the Irish criminal courts. In two of these cases, the DNA was not admitted due to an inability to prove the required chain of evidence. In another case, the jury was discharged prior to the DNA evidence being admitted, and in a further case the DNA evidence was not admitted in a sexual case as the issue of intercourse was not at issue. A trial in 2003 led to a judge-directed acquittal when the only prosecution evidence presented was DNA evidence. The judge ordered the acquittal on murder and firearms charges, following the defence's submission that with no corroborative evidence the jury should not be permitted to convict.[6]

Germany

In Germany plans for a central DNA database for sex offenders followed a series of unsolved sex killings of children over the course

---

4 'Testing time for DNA', *Irish Independent*, 13 June 2005.
5 *Ibid.*
6 'Murder case jury directed to acquit the accused.' *Irish Independent*, 15 October 2003.

of a few months. Germany had previously resisted creating a DNA database because of concerns over privacy and data protection. Then in 1998 a murder in Lower Saxony prompted the police to request saliva samples from all of the 18,000 men between 18 and 30 in the region, causing a spokesman for the Ministry of the Interior to claim that Germany could no longer afford to do without a DNA database (Schiermeier 1998: 749).

The Forensic Science Institute of Germany, operating as 16 separate federal services for each of the criminal investigation authorities and a federal service, carries out most forensic work in Germany, but some forensic DNA analysis can also be undertaken by university institutes of legal medicine as well as private laboratories, who can offer analyses of samples for database purposes. Forensic DNA analysis commenced in 1987 after the formation of a working group evaluating the implementation of the method in Germany, establishing uniform techniques in 1989, until in 1990 advanced laboratories commenced PCR (Polymerase Chain Reaction) based analysis and in 1992 the STR (Short Tandem Repear) technique was introduced. A decision of the Supreme Court in 1990 ruled that DNA analysis was generally acceptable as evidence in criminal trials, although in 1997 the law of court procedures regulated the use of DNA in criminal cases, stating that DNA analysis may only be carried out by order of a judge in a written form, with the expert carrying out the analysis to be denoted. Samples from suspects or witnesses are only to be used in the case for which the samples have been taken, and destroyed when no longer required for that case; samples must be analysed anonymously; and the laboratory performing the analysis must be working separately from the investigating agency, although the law enforcement agencies in Germany are assumed to be independent.[7]

Using these laws of court procedure as a basis, in April 1998 a national DNA database was officially established, with crime scene stains being profiled and placed on the database and individuals only being profiled when under investigation as a suspect in a relevant case; a case of 'substantial significance'. Such restrictions were lifted in September 1998, when the law of court procedures permitted, under certain circumstances, for the taking and analysing of DNA from suspects even when not relevant to a particular case, as well as from convicted offenders. Under s. 81(a) of the StPO (the

---

7 Schmitter, H. (1999) 'Situation of DNA – Analysis in Germany', Paper presented at the *First International DNA Users Conference*, Lyons, 24–26 November.

Code of Criminal Procedure) blood samples may be taken from a suspect without consent, by a Doctor, upon authorisation of the judge.

The Federal Constitutional Court (FCC) ruled on three cases in January 2001, which tested the constitutionality of the ordering of genetic testing of suspects and the inclusion of DNA samples on a database. Three appellants contested the law, arguing that it infringed their privacy and the right to self-determination over personal information. The Court held that there was a compelling public interest in constructing DNA databases to facilitate future criminal investigations, which justified any interference. However, the Court did rule that there must be justification on an individual basis, dependent upon a careful prognosis of future risk, for inclusion on a DNA database. This requires the courts to consider how each case meets the prerequisites for inclusion, and simply stating that future offending cannot be ruled out does not satisfy the requirements (Beulke 2005: 115).

Switzerland

On 1 July 2000 the Swiss Federal Council (the government of Switzerland) set the legal ordnance for the DNA Profile Information System, which has been operational since August 2000 (Stehler *et al.* 2003: 777). In Switzerland, the local police take a buccal swab of every person who is suspected of having committed a crime according to the crime catalogue (Strehler *et al.* 2003: 780). Approximately 1,000 DNA profiles are entered monthly – and by August 2001, 8,974 profiles from suspects and 1,039 crime scene stains were stored. One of Switzerland's most remarkable cases was a person, who was repeatedly throwing bicycles from a bridge over a highway causing serious accidents, caught from a buccal swab taken from a burglary suspect which resulted in a 'hit' which identified the mentally ill person as being the bike-thrower (Strehler *et al.* 2003: 780).

Austria

A national DNA database for Austria was piloted in October 1997, run by the Department of the Interior, with forensic DNA analysis performed by the Institute of Legal Medicine at the University of Innsbruck. In September 1999, legislation was enacted concerning the DNA database (which had been commenced under the *Sicherheitspolizeigesetz – Security Police Act*), which was revised in 2004. Suspects of serious crime (including burglary) can be sampled as well as convicted offenders. To November 1999 more than 20,000 mouth swabs were analysed, as well as 3,000 crime scene stains, with more than 380 crime stains linked to suspects, including four murders, 22 rapes and more than 300 burglaries.[8]

The Netherlands

Forensic testing in the Netherlands came into use in 1989, with the Dutch Supreme Court admitting exculpatory DNA evidence in a case in 1990 (Kloosterman and Janssen 1997), although the use of incriminatory DNA evidence in the courts was restricted. On 8 November 1993, legislation was passed which amended the Dutch Code of Criminal Procedure to enable forensic DNA testing and databasing, permitting the use of force to obtain a DNA sample from non-consenting suspects, the results of which can be used as proof of guilt. The Dutch DNA database is held by the DFSL (Dutch Forensic Science Laboratory) and is subject to the Dutch *Registration of Persons Act*.[9]

The DNA database was not operational until 1997, and, as was the case in England and Wales originally, a blood sample, buccal sample or plucked hair in the Netherlands are considered intimate samples, so attracting strict legal regulation. Suspects can be legally forced (with physical force if required) to submit to DNA testing if they are a suspect in a crime where preventative custody is permitted. Authorisation is required by a prosecutor or investigating judge, who must consider whether the test will assist in the resolution of the case. DNA profiles of suspects remain on a database upon conviction, if acquitted they are removed. If stored, DNA profiles can be retained for variable time periods, such as 20 years for those sentenced for between four and six years of imprisonment and 30 years for those serving a sentence of more than six years. The sample is retained as well as the profile.[10]

Only an investigating judge can require a sample from a suspect if they refuse to consent to sampling, and a sample can only then be

---

8 Scheithauer, R. (1999) 'The Austrian National DNA Database', Paper presented at the *First International DNA Users Conference*, Lyons, 24–26 November.

9 Janssen, H. (1999) 'The DNA database in The Netherlands', Paper presented at the *First International DNA Users Conference*, Lyons, 24–26 November.

10 See www.DNAsporen.nl for further details.

required if the crime concerned attracts a sentence of eight years or more. Other serious crimes with penalties of greater than six years can also command a warrant, but it is necessary for the facts and circumstances to indicate serious charges and that DNA is required to establish the truth. This last criterion – that the DNA is necessary in the pursuit of the truth is due to be dropped in new legislation, as will be the requirement of the crime attracting an eight year sentence, with proposals to drop this to four years. Presently, the law presents problems when a suspect confesses to a crime, as the investigating judge can then no longer require a DNA sample (as it will not determine the case). As a result, some serious offenders can evade being placed on the DNA database by confessing. An investigating judge can also order a DNA sample to be taken for possible testing in connection with any other offences, with the police or employees of the DNA laboratory not able to search DNA profiles against the database without explicit permission from the investigating judge, or a prosecutor.

At present the database does not retain profiles from victims or suspects not charged or acquitted, though it is hoped that the database will be expanded in the future. Such changes are largely in response to the problem encountered in England and Wales, with 'hits' being reported with profiles that were being illegally retained on the database as their removal had not been secured. This evidence is not permitted in court as it is unlawful. In light of the limitations placed upon the use of the database, two studies were carried out, to stress the potential of the database and pressure politicians to relax the law regulating its use. In 1998 two police forces in the Netherlands initiated a pilot study on DNA and burglary, a crime normally carrying less than an eight year sentence (so not normally attracting compulsory DNA sampling). During the study, stains from burglaries were analysed and by the end of December 1998, 562 burglary investigations had resulted in 391 profiles, with 23 cases having an identifiable suspect. However, only five of these suspects would have been sampled under the current law.

The second study related to the search for a serial rapist in Utrecht, the fourth largest city in the Netherlands. Between 1995 and 1996, 18 rapes and attempted rapes took place, with semen stains existing in two of the cases providing a DNA profile. By 1998 25 suspects had been sampled, without a result, with public pressure requiring that a large investigation was sustained, which included investigating a large number of rapes from within and outside the region. However, the prior rape cases that had suspects could not be analysed lawfully, forcing stain-to-stain testing only to be carried out. The search then led to the first 'mass screen' in the Netherlands, with 104 individuals being asked for samples (86 cooperated, 9 refused and 9 could not be located). A suspect was not located but the results showed dramatically how rapists could easily be linked to other rapes through speculative searching on the database. As a result of these studies, pressure has been successfully brought to bear on the government, with the database expected to be expanded, with the use of DNA in criminal investigations expected to become more prominent (van der Beek and Tullener 2004).

Belgium

Belgian law on the use of forensic DNA analysis was published on 20 May 1999, although practical details were later clarified by a Royal Decree. The Public Prosecutor (*Procureur du Roi*) can request a suspect to provide a DNA sample for analysis, provided that fully informed written consent has been obtained, with the volunteer informed that if their profile matches that of a crime stain, their profile may then also be linked with other crime stains stored on the national database. An Examining Magistrate (*Juge d'Instruction*) can force a person to provide a reference sample, with the reason for the refusal being documented. This situation can only arise however, if: the case under investigation is a serious offence punishable by imprisonment of five years or more; the magistrate has indication that the person is directly linked to the crime; and at least one biological stain has been collected. Crime scene stains are entered onto the 'Criminalistics' database, with profiles deleted upon request of the Public Prosecutor when they are no longer considered useful, with identified profiles deleted upon completion of the case (unidentified samples are deleted after 30 years). The national convicted offender DNA database contains profiles from persons convicted of serious crimes for which they have been sentenced to imprisonment. Consent from convicted offenders is not required, and speculative searching may be undertaken. Profiles are deleted ten years after the death of the donor. Profiles of suspects not charged or acquitted are not stored on any database.[11]

---

11 van Renterghem, P. (1999) 'Update on the Belgian DNA legislation', Paper presented at the *First International DNA Users Conference*, Lyons, 24–26 November.

France

In France, forensic DNA technology has 'aroused at once ... a mixture of ethical concerns, suspicion, and interest among the scientific and legal communities' (Mangin 1997: 67). The controversy prompted a

> long and passionate debate between scientists and lawyers involving the publication of two official reports at the request of the French Prime Minister; two parliamentary committee evaluations; a recommendation of both Bar and Medical councils; a statement of the National Consultative Committee on Bioethics; and finally, the adoption by Parliament in July 1994 of a law related to the respect of the human body with reference to DNA fingerprinting. (Mangin 1997: 67)

This meant that in France consent was always required for a sample, the human body being 'inviolable'; a direct application of the 1789 *Declaration of Human Rights* which is incorporated as preamble in the French Constitution, although refusal can be used as evidence against a suspect. The French DNA database (the *Fichier National Automatise des Empreintes Genetiques*) therefore is very limited in scope, containing only a small number of profiles from convicted individuals and there is no suspect database. However, indications are that France is relaxing its stance on sampling, with 1,300 prison inmates being sampled in 2003 for inclusion on the national DNA database. It has also more recently become legal in France to take DNA samples of suspects.[12]

Pan-European developments

In June 1997 (and again in June 2001) a political decision was made to plan for a pan-European DNA database for offenders convicted of the sexual abuse of children, forcing the consideration of standardisation of DNA profiling techniques and technologies (Scheider and Martin 2001: 232). In 2001, a European Standard was set and adopted by a Council Resolution of 25 June 2001 (Corte-Real 2004: 143–4). However, national views of civil rights and human dignity issues differ across the European countries, making true harmonisation of all the

---

12 'DNA Samples Taken In French Prisons To Create National Database.' BBC Monitoring International Reports, 20 October 2003.

databases complex as they all include different submission criteria and retention rules (Schneider and Martin 2001: 233). With there being such variety in the laws regulating DNA techniques, sampling and storage in European countries, it is perhaps not surprising that to date a pan-European DNA database remains a remote possibility. Developments and information about potential developments both remain limited.[13] International cooperation has to date centred around the European DNA Profiling Group (EDNAP) and the European Network of Forensic Science Institutes (ENFSI).

The EDNAP was formed in 1988, with the aim of establishing systematic procedures to facilitate data-sharing across Europe, publishing papers on scientific and technological harmonisation.[14] In contrast, very little has been done on a judicial level to bring about the harmonisation required for a pan-European database, or effective sharing of DNA data. European countries still all retain national legislation, which would often prohibit sharing of data as the information would be unlawful in the country providing the information, thus preventing effective cooperation in criminal investigations.[15] In addition, the ENFSI started in 1993 with 11 member state laboratories, rising to 50 laboratories from 32 countries by 2004. The Network works in three key areas: the Expert Working Group Committee (EWGC); the Quality and Competence Committee (QCC); and the European Academy of Forensic Science (EAFS). ENFSI also collaborates with the EU Police Cooperation Working Group (EU-PCWG), with representatives from each member state meeting to consider matters of policy relating to international police cooperation. ENFSI has an advisory role to the EU-PCWG and works to harmonise forensic science across international boundaries.

There have been increased attempts in recent years however to provide for cross-border cooperation throughout Europe. The SCHENGEN information system (SIS) for example, is a computerised network which allows all police stations and consular agents from Schengen group members states to access data on specific individuals, vehicles, and property. The members states provide information

---

13 See Williams, R. and Johnson, P. (2005) *Forensic DNA Databasing: A European Perspective.* Interim Report. The Wellcome Trust, available at www.dur.ac.uk/p.j.johnson.

14 As above at p. 19.

15 Janssen, H. (1999) 'The DNA database in The Netherlands', Paper presented at the *First International DNA Users Conference*, Lyons 24–26 November.

through their national networks which are connected to a central system. In addition, the SIRENE system – scheduled to go live in 2006 – will provide full access to the SCHENGEN information system from each members state's national police computers.

Europol, established in 1999, supports the functions of law enforcement agencies of all the countries of the EU by gathering and analysing information and intelligence, particulary relating to cross-border issues such as immigration, vehicle trafficking, child pornography, forgery, terrorism and money laundering (Fereday 2004). It is also allowed to collect and store 53 specific types of data relating to individual suspects, including information about 'racial origin, religious or other beliefs, sexual life, political opinions or membership of movements and organisations that are not prohibited by law'. Other categories include 'personal details' (14 types of data); 'physical appearance' (two types); 'identification means' (five types including DNA and fingerprints); 'occupation and related qualifications' (five types); 'economic and financial information' (eight types); and 'behavioural data' (eight types)[16] Williams and Johnson (2005) p. 109 – but again, differences between country's laws means Europol may use data in a way that is illegal in its home country. The best example of a successful pan-European database then remains that of Eurodac.

Eurodac

Council Regulation No 2725/2000 of 11 December 2000 established the first pan-European AFIS (Automatic Fingerprint Identification System), 'Eurodac', created as part of the development of a common asylum policy for all member states, by preventing duplication of asylum applications.[17] The regulation applied strict, harmonised rules regarding the storage, comparison, and erasure of fingerprints. Eurodac is a system for the comparison of fingerprints of all asylum applicants and illegal immigrants, to facilitate the Dublin Convention of 15 June 1990, which stated that all refugees must apply for asylum in the first European member country in which they land, and

---

16 See Williams and Johnson (2005) see footnote 13.

17 Council Regulation (EC) No 407/2002 of 28 February 2002 laying down certain rules to implement Regulation (EC) No 2725/2000 concerning the establishment of 'Eurodac' for the comparison of fingerprints for the effective application of the Dublin Convention [Official Journal L 62, 5.3.2002].

prohibited multiple applications being lodged in different European countries. Member states were having difficulties identifying aliens who may have already lodged an application in another member country. By taking all applicants' fingerprints it should be possible then to determine the state responsible for examining the asylum application. Eurodac exists as central computerised database with electronic data transmission capabilities, within a central unit in the European Commission. Details stored include not just the individual's fingerprints, but their member state of origin, the place and date of their asylum application, sex, and a reference number. This is collected for anyone aged over 14 and stored for ten years, unless the individual obtains citizenship of a member state. Data relating to foreign nationals apprehended attempting to cross an external border irregularly are kept for two years from the date on which the fingerprints were taken. Data are immediately erased before the end of the two years if the foreign national receives a residence permit, or leaves the territory of the member states.

National supervisory bodies oversee the operation of Eurodac, in addition to a central independent joint supervisory authority, with responsibility for monitoring the activities of the central unit to ensure the rights of data subjects are respected. Any person or member state suffering damage as a result of an unlawful processing operation or an act incompatible with the Regulation is entitled to receive compensation so each member state must ensure that fingerprints taken are lawful, as well as all operations involving the use, transmission, conservation or erasure of the data themselves.[18]

The first evaluation report on the functioning of Eurodac after its first operational year revealed that in 17,287 cases (7 per cent of the total number of cases), the same person had already made at least one asylum application in another country (multiple application).[19] Operational since 15 January 2003, Eurodac processed in one year 246,902 fingerprints of asylum seekers, 7,857 fingerprints of people crossing the borders illegally and 16,814 fingerprints of people apprehended on the territory of a member state in an illegal situation. The report also claimed highly satisfactory results in terms of efficiency, quality, and cost-effectiveness, with no data protection

---

18 See   http://www.europaworld.org/DEVPOLAWAR/Eng/Refugees/ Refugees_DocD_eng.htm.

19 See http://europa.eu.int/scadplus/leg/en/lvb/l33081.htm.

problems reported, and it is assisting greatly with the development of the Common European Asylum System called for by the European Council in October 1999.[20] The total European Community budget allocated for Eurodac is 11.6 million euro; the total expenditure on all externalised activities specific to Eurodac, after one year of operations, totals 7.5 million euro.[21]

Interpol

Forensic DNA profiling is now in use by all the members of Interpol,[22] with many countries also holding a DNA database. However, domestic success has not been replicated across borders, with legislation or data protection rules often prohibiting international cooperation in DNA matters. In addition, many countries do not use compatible technologies that would enable the sharing of DNA profiles. Thus, in 1998, the Interpol General Assembly established the DNA Monitoring Expert Group, to provide direction for the harmonisation of international use of forensic DNA methods. The DNA MEG, a group of international experts, has advised Interpol member countries and produced a handbook on DNA data exchange and practice, as well as hosting a biennial International DNA Users Conference.

In June 2003 Interpol introduced an international DNA database with all major marker systems used, based upon the Interpol Standard Set of Loci (ISSOL), with the database already storing 6,300 profiles from 19 separate countries. This database is intended to overcome the difficulties of cross-border data transfer, and also to enable international 'cold hits'. The system is still being improved, with the intention of providing an online secure system for all Interpol's members and for member states to increase their submission of samples to the database. Interpol do not retain samples, and only the submitting police agency retain the identity data for the profiles, thus protecting data protection rules (Fisher 2004).

The first 'hit' recorded on Interpol's database occurred in 2004, after police from Slovenia submitted three DNA profiles to the international database, which were matched to a profile submitted

---

20 EC Press Release of 5 May 2004 available at:
    http://europa.eu.int/rapid/pressReleasesAction.do?reference=IP/04/
    581&format=HTML&aged=0&language=en&guiLanguage=en.
21 *Ibid.*
22 See http://www.interpol.int/Public/News/dna20040505.asp.

by Croatia. The DNA matched an individual wanted for thefts in Croatia. The two police forces then communicated directly after being alerted by Interpol, able to share their information with each other.

USA

As detailed in previous chapters, fingerprints have recently been challenged on several occasions in the USA, with the case of *US* v. *Byron Mitchell*[23] now described as 'the first shot across the bow for fingerprint evidence' (Wise 2004: 427). In this case, Judge Joyner ruled inadmissible testimony from witnesses who were to challenge the credibility of fingerprint evidence. Since the Mitchell trial, there have been a further 40 challenges to fingerprint evidence, but the case of *Llera-Plaza*[24] appears to have now stemmed the flow of challenges.[25] DNA evidence has also gone from being regularly challenged in the courts, to being accepted: in *US* v. *Bonds*, Bond attempted to have DNA evidence suppressed, but the Court of Appeal accepted that the DNA evidence met *Daubert* standards, with the method having gained 'general acceptance' (Wise 2004: 430). However, the case of *State* v. *Traylor*[26] did stress the importance of following established FBI National Guidelines on DNA.

The challenging of fingerprints and DNA in the courts has not been the primary problem facing the use of these technologies in the USA however, rather it is simply one of resources. While states have expanded the opportunities to use DNA, the laboratories have struggled to keep up, with the main concerns in the USA surrounding DNA backlogs and also the quality of some laboratories, with poorly qualified analysts working in less than ideal conditions. However, DNA databases and their use continues to grow across the states, including a national DNA database, the Combined DNA Index System (CODIS).

The Californian legislature was the first to pass a law permitting the collection of blood from certain suspects in 1983 (though it didn't mention DNA). Colorado was the first to demand the DNA testing of sex offenders in (1988), followed by the Commonwealth of Virginia;

---

23 Cr. No. 96-407 (1999).
24 Check www.onin.com/fp/index.htm for a summary and update.
25 12 F.3d.540 (CA6, 1993).
26 656 N.W.2d. 885 (Minn, 2003).

the first state in the USA to pass a DNA databasing law in 1989, to include all felons. Virginia lauded their new DNA database in the state's General Assembly as a 'powerful technology for prosecutors and a tremendous investigative tool'.[27] In 1991, the FBI established guidelines on the operation of sex offender DNA database laws, promoting their adoption, and considering the commencement of a national DNA database. States then began enacting their own sex-offender DNA databases (before they were required to by the *Anti-Terror and Effective Death Penalty Act* in 1996), with Congress enacting the *DNA Identification Act* in 1994, enabling the establishment of CODIS.

A number of states then started expanding their sex-offender databases, to include other felons, such as violent offenders and burglars. The California DNA Databank similarly had a limited list of crimes requiring the taking of a sample compared with other states, so Proposition 69 was introduced in 1998 to extend the list (Cameron 2002: 219). Further expansion also mandated the collection of a DNA sample from anyone arrested for a serious crime, whether convicted or not.[28] By 1999, 50 states had sex-offender databases, with 27 including violent offenders, and 14 including burglars. Just six DNA databases included all convicted felons, a development that prompted a short-lived opposition campaign by the American Civil Liberties Union (ACLU).

In 2000, Congress began to take seriously the very large backlogs that had developed across the nation, appropriating $140 million for states in the *DNA Backlog Elimination Act*. Within a couple of years, the number of all-felon databases had increased to 31 in 2003, with Virginia in 2002 and Louisiana in 2003 extending their DNA sampling in line with California to include some arrestees, developments that added to the strain on the national backlog problem. By 2002, 27 states required samples from those convicted of robbery, while 24 required samples of burglars, with seven states requiring DNA from individuals convicted of any felony (Cameron 2002: 223). Such

---

27 Anon. (1999) *Profiles in DNA* p. 3. The Virginian public are kept updated of 'hits' by the media, so that they can be assured of the 'success' of the program, including: 'tremendous savings in terms of police investigative time and prevention of future crimes ... savings in terms of lives.' (Information on the database is published by the public relations company of the private custodians so may require caution.)

28 Bieber, F. (2004) 'Guilt by association' *New Scientist*, 23 October.

expansion prompted further money from Congress to be appropriated, under a Presidential DNA Initiative.

The FBI National DNA Index System (NDIS), permits state, federal and local law enforcement agencies to add DNA samples to a national database and 'enhance the investigation of violent crime'.[29] The FBIs Combined DNA Index System, CODIS, was established as a pilot project in 1990 serving 14 state and local laboratories, until the *DNA Identification Act* 1994 (Public Law 103 322) formalised the FBI's authority to establish a national DNA databank system (NDIS), becoming fully operational in 1998.[30] As at 2000, the FBI have two DNA analysis units and also operate the CODIS, which includes the Convicted Offender Index (offender profiles) and the Forensic Index (crime scene stains). By 2000, the NDIS contained more than 370,000 profiles but there remained a backlog of 500,000 samples to be loaded.

The FBI laboratory is one of the largest in the world. It contains the DNA Analysis Units I and II. Unit I provides serological and nuclear DNA testing to all federal agencies, US attorneys, military tribunals, and state, county and municipal law enforcement agencies. Unit II does mitochondrial testing, working on missing persons cases and the Federal Convicted Offender Program. To December 1999, there were 600 'hits' assisting in more than 1,100 investigations. In July 1999, CODIS had its first 'cold hit', when six sexual assault cases from Washington DC were linked to three sexual assault cases being investigated in Florida. A deceased man was then identified as the perpetrator of all of these offences.[31] As at September 2004, CODIS had more than 1,700,000 STR profiles, with the FBI reporting over 17,200 'hits' in 20,300 investigations.[32] In Texas, use of CODIS assisted with 'resolving' 145 crimes in 2004, including 183 'cold hits'. The local Texas database entered 16,000 DNA profiles in 2004, taking the Texas database total to 182,130.[33]

29 FBI Press Release, 'The National DNA Index System', 13 October 1998: www.fbi.gov/pressrm/pressrel/pressre198/dna.htm.

30 US Department of Justice (2002) 'The FBI's DNA and Databasing Initiatives', see http://www.fbi.gov/hq/lab/codis/fbidna.pdf.

31 FBI Press Release, 21 July 1999, available at www.fbi/gov/pressrel/pressrel99/coldhit.htm.

32 See www.fbi.gov/hq/lab/codis/.

33 Tinsley, B. (2005) 'Nationwide database helps solve Texas crimes', *The Star-Telegram, Texas*, 8 May, p. 2.

In October 2004, the *Justice For All Act* allowed an expansion of CODIS so that states can now upload profiles of almost anyone charged with a crime, not just those convicted. The ACLU responded that: 'If your DNA is on the database it means that you are forever an automatic suspect for any crime in the future. It undermines the principle of presumptive innocence'.[34] Objections have also arisen in response to other consequences arising from the *Justice For All Act*, which has seen the development of a list of military offences comparable to civilian felonies for inclusion on CODIS. This list has incorporated any court martial sentence attracting a sentence of a year or more, which includes: 'refusal to take the anthrax vaccine, fraternization, faking an illness to get out of work, showing disrespect to a superior officer or making a false statement when enlisting'.[35]

Canada

Canada's national DNA database (the NDDB) was created in 2000, after government assent of the *DNA Identification Act* in December 1998. This came after the Canadian Association of Chiefs of Police (CACP) joined hundreds of other organisations in urging the government to create a national DNA databank to assist in investigations (they had previously used DNA in investigations, with the first DNA conviction being obtained in 1989). The legislation also amended the Criminal Code to permit judges to order persons convicted of designated offences to provide samples, the law becoming operational on 30 June 2000. The NDDB has two principal indices: the Convicted Offender Index (COI) and the Crime Scene Index (CSI). As at 12 December 2005 there had been 4,371 'matches' from crime scenes to offenders, and 650 'matches' of crime scene to crime scene. There have been 87,593 samples entered onto the COI and 25,575 entered into the CSI.[36]

The databases continue to suffer from significant delays in processing however, with turnaround times for analysis increasing in recent years, with urgent criminal cases taking 102 days for analysis. A Federal Bill *C-13* was passed in 2005, massively expanding Canada's

---

34 Tania Simoncelli, quoted in Gosline, A. (2005) 'Will DNA profiling fuel prejudice?' *New Scientist*, 8 April.

35 'Military Anthrax Vaccinations.' *Daily Press* (Newport News, VA), 8 October 2005.

36 From Canadian DNA Database website, see www.http://www.nddb-bndg.org/main_e.htm.

national DNA database, adding 28 criminal code offences to the list of those that permit for DNA sampling. The Bill was controversial in that it proposed to allow for the automatic DNA sampling of mentally ill persons found not guilty of offences because of their mental disorder.[37]

New Zealand and Australia

In 1995, the New Zealand Police and the Institute of Environmental Science and Research combined to create a national DNA database, prompting the enactment of the *Criminal Investigations (Blood Samples) Act* 1995. Coming into force in August 1996, the Act put strict rules in place regarding the obtaining of blood samples, forcing the police to apply to the High Court to compel a suspect to give a sample, provided specific criteria were met (reasonable cause for suspicion and an indictable offence). A 'hit' on the database is not permitted as evidence in court, and can only lead to further police inquiries. Due to the small population of New Zealand (less than 4 million), accurate information regarding the individuals submitting samples is easily obtained, so that 40 pairs of duplicate samples were identified quickly (usually from people using aliases but also from brothers and a relative submitting their DNA in place of the suspect).[38]

The New Zealand DNA database commenced with the passing of the *Criminal Investigations (Blood Samples) Act* 1995. The database initially used SLP (Single Locus Profiling) more commonly known as Restriction Fragment Length Polymorphism (RFLP) testing, but was later upgraded to STR (PCR) testing. This change enabled the conviction of a rapist, whose DNA sample was submitted when suspected for the rape of a teenager in 1996 and resulted in a 'no match' report. However in 1999, when arrested again, Peter Howse's sample did match the crime scene stains, and those of the rape in 1996. An inquiry ordered by the New Zealand government found that the first test should have been reported as a 'no result' rather than a 'no match', but that the conservative approach in reporting matches

---

37 Schmitz, C. (2005) 'CBA criticises DNA Bank expansion', *The Lawyers Weekly*, 18 February.
38 Harbison, S., Hamilton, J. and Walsh, S. (2002) 'The New Zealand DNA Databank'. Paper presented at the *First International Conference on Human Identification in the Millennium*.

was correct and the case demonstrated the benefit in upgrading the database and testing technologies.

There were now over 53,000 DNA samples on the New Zealand national database and 12,000 samples on the unsolved crime database, with a match rate of 55 per cent. This was further enhanced by legislation passed in 2003 that allowed DNA to be taken from burglary suspects and those facing at least seven years in jail.[39] Controversies over DNA testing in New Zealand continued however, with a further inquiry ordered into the investigation of a Christchurch man for murder after his DNA had been sampled after being the victim of an assault in 1998. Police had taken his blood sample to exclude his DNA from samples taken at the scene of the assault. His profile was then 'matched' to a sample taken from a murder scene, leading the police to subject the man to 'extensive police enquiries' for over three months, including the seizing of his financial records. It was subsequently proven that the man had never been to Wellington, where the murders had occurred.

The Sharman inquiry which ensued suggested that the assault victim may have had a brother who had been at the crime scene, until it was established that he had no brothers, which was countered by the rather preposterous sounding-argument that he may have had 'an unknown half-brother', but a subsequent inquiry in 1999, conducted by Sir Thomas Eichelbaum and Prof. John Scott and an array of forensic experts, found that there was accidental contamination of samples in the laboratory during an early stage of processing.[40]

Similar controversies have beset the adoption and development of DNA use in criminal investigations in Australia. Charges in the infamous 1997 Arnott's biscuit extortion case were dropped as a result of flawed DNA testing procedures at Queensland's DNA testing laboratory. Joy Thomas had been charged with sending letters to Arnott executives threatening to poison their biscuits, linking her DNA to one of the stamps on a letter. The charges were dropped after potential contamination was found, along with a number of laboratory errors, reportedly due to poor funding and bad management (Edwards 2005: 71). Again, in Queensland in April

---

39 http://www.stuff.co.nz/stuff/0,2106,3304887a11,00.html.

40 Author Unknown, 'Legally Scientific: A brief history of DNA evidence in the criminal justice system', 9 June 2001, available at www.home. iprimus.com.au/dna_info/dan/JA_DNA_LegSci_top.html, accessed 24 November 2003.

2001, Frank Button, 32, was released from prison after serving almost a year of a seven-year sentence for the rape of a young intellectually impaired girl. Independent DNA testing established that the DNA evidence relied upon had been seriously flawed and he was in fact innocent.

The building of a DNA database in Queensland did not commence until 2000, with arrestees becoming eligible for sampling in 2001. By 2003, more than 30,000 samples had been collected, yet the DNA laws of Queensland came under serious fire for being too vague, and not making clear when police should be taking samples from suspects. The criticisms, prompting the ordering of a review of the law by the Premier, followed controversy over police demands for a DNA sample from the Deputy Chairman of ATSIC (Aboriginal and Torres Strait Islander Commission) when facing forgery charges.[41] More recently, a report in 2005 has again criticised the Queensland DNA testing centre in Brisbane, finding it to be under-resourced and badly managed. The John Tonge Centre has a DNA backlog that requires an investment of millions of dollars to address, with an overhaul of the centre estimated to cost AU$63 million with further improvements required costing an additional AU$2.4 million. The backlogs identified include 12,056 samples from property crimes; more than 100 unidentified skeletons; and hundreds of autopsy specimens being stored in a shipping container in the car park.[42]

Conclusion: England and Wales – leading the way?

The expansion of DNA databanks has become a modern trend, with all the countries sampled making legal provision for the continued growth of their DNA databases. Most countries, like England and Wales, have, fairly soon after commencing the use of DNA in criminal investigations, recognised that changes could improve the efficiency of the database. This has included expanding the list of those who can undergo sampling (often permitting non-consensual sampling), and the retroactive testing of convicted offenders. However, no countries have yet gone as far as the legislature in England and Wales,

---

41 'Beattie orders review of DNA test rules' (2003) *Courier Mail*, 22 January.
42 'Final analysis damns forensic science centre' (2005) *The Courier-Mail* (Queensland, Australia), 12 October.

permitting the non-consensual sampling, and indefinite retention of all samples, of all people arrested for any recordable offence.

Attempts to bring about international harmonisation have to date, only met with partial success. Further international cooperation will only be achieved when there are uniform quality standards, and adherence to clearly defined quality requirements. Information needs to be standardised to ensure compatibility, so that data can be shared and can travel across borders. Such developments are essential if advances in DNA technology are able to reap benefits in international and cross-border crime. Such challenges for the law enforcement and forensic community are now demanding that countries bring their DNA databases into line with international standards (Fereday 2004). However, these challenges appear as insurmountable as ever, with countries such as England and Wales rapidly developing their DNA technologies, and benefiting from generous private and public investment, as well as legislative licence to develop an unrivalled database. Other countries have invested greater time in public and political debate over the acceptable boundaries of DNA sampling, and have insisted upon greater safeguards for citizens. However, it looks increasingly like the lead shown by England and Wales is being followed by more and more countries. Such emulation requires that England and Wales retains the highest standards of quality and integrity, as a scandal hitting the domestic DNA database could have international ripples.

Chapter 6

The future of forensic identification: issues and prospects

Fingerprints and DNA in the 'fight against crime'

The ongoing development of forensic identification technologies and the increase in their utilisation may not represent a major break with policing tradition, but further examination of the potential impact that greater reliance on fingerprints and DNA may be having on police activity, and social control more generally, is clearly now required. As historical accounts and text books detail,[1] fingerprints were originally developed for purposes other than crime detection. However, since the first cases utilising the new 'science' in the early twentieth century (one of the first recorded convictions attributed to fingerprinting was in Argentina in 1892), fingerprints have been closely associated with the detection and prosecution of crime. More recently, there have been changes to investigative practices, which have seen fingerprinting and other forensic technologies taking a more prominent role in policing, particularly since the advent of databases: 'There has been strategic shift in the use of forensics that's happened since the introduction of databases. We've moved forensics up the investigative chain'.[2] Such developments are not novel, with new methods to detect crime always having been sought, even when the crimes committed may have changed little through the years:

---

1 See Beavan (2003) or Deutch, Y. (1982) *Science Against Crime*. London: Marshall Cavendish.
2 Interviewee 1/L/P.

> If you look at the history of the police service, it shows that there is always a search for new ways to detect crime … New technology gives new opportunities for detection. When officers are looking for new lines of inquiry for crimes that wouldn't be detected, they look to new technologies.[3]

Some interviewees however, indicated that they believed there were new reasons for the growth in reliance upon forensic sciences. Such reasons included the closing down of other avenues of investigation and other changes posited by one interviewee:

> If you think of the structure of the *PACE* interview, a seasoned criminal will do a no comment interview. You haven't got the opportunities that were there 20 years ago to actually question and interrogate, using some of the more traditional detective methods, they are just not options anymore. Therefore there is a greater reliance on this technology to identify offenders. That's to do with all sorts of other things, like lack of local knowledge and the movement of people. If you look at these database matches you get this travelling criminal community round the country so the local criminal community who were known to the police, and so could more easily find evidence and mount cases against them, are now broken up …[4]

A breakdown in police-community relations presents a major policing problem, and some interviewees saw the development of forensic science as a means to circumvent lack of public cooperation: 'there are huge pockets of the community where there is a huge distrust of the police and they won't help so DNA can overcome that'.[5] Another interviewee also indicated political and financial driving forces behind the growth of forensic science:

> Crime over the last 40 years or so, has become a lot more of a political issue, and as this has happened, it has become more of a political imperative to be seen to be doing something about crime. As that has come along in tandem with new technologies, the money has been found to drive forward the new technologies in a form of sufficient scale to be able to impact on crime. That's

---

3 Interviewee 2/L/P.
4 Interviewee 1/L/P.
5 Interviewee 6/P/C.

one of the major driving forces behind the expansion of DNA, as the government has seen the potential of DNA as a detection tool ... In terms of volume crime, because the cost per process has lessened, the government has started to say that surely DNA can be effective against volume crime, but they have had to put the money into it to make sure that the police use it.[6]

That science had made the breakthrough into 'normal' policing was attested to by all interviewees, though the contribution that science made to criminal detection was reported as not always fully appreciated by officers, with science working to overcome years of 'marginalisation' and mismanagement:

Scientific support has not been very well managed ... [and] has traditionally been seen as a little bit stand-alone – even marginal. Science was seen as a marginal thing, well it's not anymore. We've reached a crossover point where the contribution to volume crime is there ... So, the conceptual thinking of a lot of officers is behind the reality and there is a lot of work to be done in marketing those figures, operationally. If you ask officers what contribution science makes to detections, they have no idea.[7]

There were differences highlighted however in the uses made of fingerprints and DNA samples, as well as limitations in their use. Fingerprints are now used primarily to identify those who come into contact with the police, only being used to detect unknown perpetrators as a secondary, subsidiary role. Identifying perpetrators from stains left at crime scenes is the primary task of DNA, not yet being routinely used for identifying individuals in custody.[8] The time involved in DNA analysis also impacts upon its use with police indicating that often a 'hit' on the DNA database could provide the evidence with which to support an arrest and charge, so the time taken to perform the analysis did not impact upon the process post-arrest but could speed up the actual arrest: 'The arrest can come as a result of the hit, the scientific hit usually provides the evidence to

6 Interviewee 2/L/P.
7 Interviewee 9/L/P.
8 Interviewee 1/L/P.

lock up'.[9] Whether DNA has actually made a significant impact on the time taken to make an arrest and on detection rates was a source of dissent however, with one interviewee explaining a possible reason for conflicting views on the impact of DNA:

> [DNA] has impacted significantly on crime investigation. It provides a means of solving crimes, and solving them very quickly. A homicide incident room in London costs about £15,000 a day. If you get a quick fingerprint or DNA mark then the case is over quick. Where perhaps there is a downside is if you get into volume crime, there was a theory – hence the huge investment by the government – that as you scale this [DNA profiling] up, you would actually make a real impact on crime. I think that is still unproven and for a lot of 'bottom end' crime, you may not have sufficiently robust processes to prosecute. You have got a situation where the impact on volume crime – and it was shown in the Pathfinder Project, where the Home Office expected to find crime reduction – well life's just not that simple.[10]

Both police officers and forensic scientists indicated that there needed to be proper processes and procedures in place for forensic science to be useful:

> If you want scientific evidence to be effective, you have got to look at it from cradle to grave. You've got to have scene attendance policies, not just SOCOs but officers, how they deal with scenes and what they do when the public ring in, right through the other end of the scale through to interviews and file preparation, and if you don't do that, you fail. All the bits have to work.[11]

Indeed, it has been the police application and interpretation of forensic science that interviewees identified as causing the greatest difficulties, with police processes having to account for the demands of scientific investigation. Training of constables as well as senior officers was highlighted by many interviewees as an essential requirement of

---

9 Interviewee 9/L/P.
10 Interviewee 1/L/P.
11 Interviewee 3/F/S.

developing the effectiveness of forensic science in investigations. Again, both police officers and forensic scientists highlighted problems encountered when insufficiently trained officers relied upon forensic evidence, including the continuation of a thorough investigation after a 'hit'. Abbreviated, or skewed investigations were seen by many interviewees as a real risk, indeed one interviewee expressed a fear that this was probably already occurring and represented a particular 'problem' with DNA 'matches':

> It's almost like the police getting a confession or a fingerprint, they tend to be so sure that that is enough that they close their mind to all other avenues that could be explored. There is a danger that people are thinking that DNA evidence is the be all and end all. Everything needs to be looked at in detail. Probably too much reliance is already placed on DNA and that has repercussions at every stage in the chain.[12]

Such dangers should be protected against by the duty imposed on the police by s. 23 of the *Criminal Procedure and Investigations Act* 1996, which states that: 'where a criminal investigation is conducted all reasonable steps are taken for the purposes of the investigation and, in particular, all reasonable lines of inquiry are pursued'.

There were also implications for investigations when not only were the police poorly informed, but offenders were 'forensically aware', with such awareness influencing criminal behaviour:

> when the suspect is arrested they will probably know that they have been arrested on the basis of [a forensic] 'hit'. There are high levels of forensic awareness, the offenders clearly know the power of this technology. They change their MO [*modus operandi*] to avoid leaving DNA or fingerprints. So the fact that they are developing strategies to do that suggests that they know that if DNA or fingerprints are found, then a) they will be identified and b) they will be brought before the courts with a reasonable chance of success. Stolen cars are now more often burnt out to try and make sure they don't leave any clues.[13]

---

12 Interviewee 6/P/C.
13 Interviewee 1/L/P.

Statistics collated by the police demonstrate that at least a third of cases that proceed to trial have some forensic evidence, though DNA is only pivotal in relatively few cases.[14] Forensic identification databases have, however, impacted upon the conduct of investigations, and are used not simply at trial but to identify suspects at the outset:

> What we have seen as a consequence of the introduction of these forensic databases is a shift from [forensic identification] being seen as something about the courts and evidence to being about information, intelligence and identifying suspects. So the traditional role of forensic services, someone was arrested and gave a no comment interview or denied the offence, changed when people thought of using forensic science as a means of generating evidence for the courts. What the intelligence databases has allowed us to do is to identify a suspect from a cold search ... That's why now forensics is more important to the police as it's one of the main means ... for identifying offenders.[15]

There were also doubts that the use of forensic identification techniques by the police would result in a discernible impact upon crime:

> DNA will never affect crime figures. It could mean that more guilty people are convicted, but it will have absolutely no impact whatsoever on the amount of crime. DNA could improve detection rates but it's really about improving police resources, not detecting more crime. It's about the police having another tool at their disposal and more intelligence. It only aids investigations in a small amount of crime ... I can't see how the creation of the NDNAD stops crime. Getting caught doesn't matter to someone whose addicted to crack cocaine, and they certainly won't care if their DNA is on a national database. There might be situations where people may think twice about committing a crime because of the database but I don't think it will make much of an impact on the 5 million crimes committed a year.[16]

---

14 Interviewee 1/L/P.
15 Interviewee 1/L/P.
16 Interviewee 1/P/C.

Such 'hype' around DNA was also in spite of the fact that fingerprints were probably still the more important forensic tool:

> If you asked them [the public] what the most important forensic tool was they would probably say DNA whereas in reality it is probably still fingerprints and will remain so for the foreseeable future. That is probably a consequence of the media and hype around DNA where fingerprints are seen as being 'old fashioned'...[17]

There were clear problems presented by forensic identification evidence for defendants, with concerns over the funding of DNA tests for example, by the Legal Aid Commission.[18] Legal professionals explained that many suspects will plead guilty in the face of forensic evidence, impacting upon their subsequent appeal opportunities, and in particular, their chances of a referral from the Criminal Cases Review Commission (CCRC) back to the appeal courts:

> Because of the very restricted way the Court of Appeal defines the categories of person who can plead guilty and then appeal, we couldn't justify getting a DNA test done ... I just wonder how many people have pleaded guilty on the basis of not-very reliable DNA evidence from a few years ago before techniques improved. Legal advice back then would have been different because DNA was being hailed as better than fingerprints, so most people faced with DNA evidence would be under a lot of pressure to plead guilty. A lot of requests come in for re-testing of DNA tests done in early years. Cases that do have strong DNA evidence though don't come to us as I am sure they don't appeal it, or they just plead guilty so don't even go to trial. If they don't go to trial, they won't get to us. Relatively few of CCRC cases involve DNA – about 5 per cent, if that.[19]

Interviewees did not present a consensus then, over whether the use of forensic identification technology and DNA in particular, was a positive development in policing, with many feeling that critical debate had been stifled by official enthusiasm for the new technologies:

---

17 Interviewee 1/L/P.
18 Interviewee 6/P/C.
19 Interviewee 6/P/C.

The current benefits to DNA in investigations are outweighed by the concerns. In individual cases, the impact of a positive DNA match is huge – it will essentially convict on its own. But DNA is not a perfect science … if you are going to use it to secure a conviction, then because it is so overwhelming … then the concerns about it outweigh the benefits.[20]

There was conflicting opinion on the benefits of getting 'hits' on fingerprint or DNA databases which could link a suspect to crimes perhaps committed years previously. Police officers were enthusiastic about such 'cold hits', using examples to demonstrate the power of forensic identity databases:

to arrest someone for a minor offence and then get a hit for a major offence is just brilliant. There might be a rape or murder unsolved, then the perpetrator is caught by his fingerprints years later. A very dangerous individual was not caught after a huge investigation, we had his DNA but he wasn't on database but then we caught him years later by fingerprint.[21]

But others had reservations about such 'fortuitous' detections with lawyers arguing that raising a defence to a case from years prior would be difficult: 'It would be an abuse of process if the case was too old – a defendant can't raise a defence if murder was 30 years ago.'[22] Despite this, cases are prosecuted that can be considerably more than 30 years old, and in the USA, the use of 'John Doe' warrants, using DNA profiles in place of the suspect's details are being used to circumvent time-restrictions on bringing prosecutions.

Future applications for forensic identification technologies

Forensic DNA technology has led to the establishment of Innocence Projects across the US which have utilised DNA evidence to exonerate almost 200 inmates, many from death row. Further, DNA analysis has undoubtedly prevented the conviction of many more, statistics showing that approximately up to 30 per cent of samples

---

20 Interviewee 1/P/C.
21 Interviewee 9/L/P.
22 Interviewee 8/L/P.

submitted by the police exclude prime suspects (Lee and Tirnady 2003: xviii). The CCRC of England and Wales fulfils a different role to that of Innocence Projects, but still utilises DNA during post-appeal investigations of alleged miscarriages of justice. With time now elapsed since the advent of DNA testing, most of the CCRC work is re-testing, which can often strengthen the case against the applicant.[23] Since *Hanratty*[24] new scientific evidence that supports a conviction can be used during appeal by the Crown, to strengthen their case, a ruling that 'shifted the goalposts' and may prevent the almost 'automatic' request for DNA testing in applications to the CCRC.[25] Further, an unexpected budget cut of 17 per cent for the year 2004–05 will now mean a requirement for greater justification when requesting expensive forensic tests.[26]

One of the strategic objectives stated for the NDNAD is to: 'pursue opportunities to derive more intelligence from the data (for example, by more sophisticated searching of the Database)'.[27] Further to their direct use in criminal investigations, forensic identity databases are now increasingly viewed as vital 'intelligence' tools, with added potential to impact upon crime through research on criminal behaviour. Indeed, the NDNAD has already been made available to researchers working on 'crime patterns' and tracing criminal careers. Such research has shown a series of 'crime-to-crime' links, for example, there are approximately 30–40 crimes that have been committed over a wide geographic area by the same offender who is not coming to the attention of police, a realisation that impacts upon policing:

> We have an offender who for whatever reason is not coming under suspicion and these people can seemingly commit crime at will. Such 'unknown prolifics' challenge preconceptions of the police. For example, a series of burglaries in Reading were linked by DNA to shoplifters in Woking. The police had never expected that. It was almost as if the criminals knew what they were doing was against the police expectations so they wouldn't get caught. So the early cases of DNA linking did shatter some

---

23 Interviewee 6/P/C.

24 *R v. Hanratty* [2002] EWCA Crim 1141.

25 Interviewee 6/P/C.

26 Personal communication with Mark Emerton, CCRC Commissioner, 7 July 2004.

27 *NDNAD Annual Report 2003/4*, available at www.forensic.gov.uk, p. 3.

myths about who was committing crime in different parts of the country. You can clearly see people committing burglaries on a small scale, but not across the whole country via rail or road links, now we can.[28]

Such developments dovetail nicely with ambitions of 'intelligence-led policing':[29]

If you are looking at intelligence-led policing, which is about understanding your criminal problem, and devising strategies to deal with it, that's going beyond just simply measuring detections and counting crimes. Forensic intelligence databases give you an insight into the problem; you put this together with a strategic analysis and information, you can analyse for example, drugs, and then map out the distribution. What forensics gives you is a perspective on criminality, which provides intelligence, which gives you a strategy to reduce it. This is the future use of forensic databases, giving an insight into criminality combined with other information.[30]

The police increasingly purport to be 'intelligence led',[31] requiring powers to detain citizens to obtain information. Crime control has been replaced by 'the efficient production of knowledge useful in the administration of suspect populations' (Ericson and Haggerty 1997: 504). As Maguire (2000: 316) documents, changes in police practices in recent years have in common 'a *strategic, future-oriented and targeted* approach to crime control, focusing upon the *identification, analysis and 'management' of persisting and developing 'problems' or 'risks'* ... rather than on reactive investigation and detection of individual crimes' [author's emphasis]. The drive to expand the NDNAD is then underpinned by the hope that such a wealth of information, will improve our ability to tackle crime:

In the long run, when it reaches critical mass, you could use it to understand criminal careers, from a research perspective.

---

28 Interviewee 1/L/P.
29 See the *National Policing Plan 2004–08*, available at www.policereform. gov.uk/natpoliceplan.
30 Interviewee 1/L/P.
31 See the *National Policing Plan 2004–08*, available at www.policereform. gov.uk/natpoliceplan.

That may reveal some very valuable insights into patterns of crime. If you understand the criminal career, you can perhaps do something about it.[32]

Problems with large databases however can compound problems previously outlined. Yet it is the ability to store DNA profiles as digital records in databases that has prompted the huge investment in forensic identification technology, and innovation in biometrics, although the reliability of biometrics at present is questioned. For example, a study commissioned by the UK Passport Service, DVLA and Home Office, points out that approximately one in every 10,000 individuals do not have an iris that can be 'read' by available technology, while one person in 1,000 causes problems for fingerprint readers.[33] Biometrics have false 'rejection', or 'match', rates with a feasibility study undertaken by the National Physical Laboratory finding a false match rate in fingerprints of one in 100,000, and one in 1,000,000 with iris recognition.[34] A study by the US General Accounting Office demonstrated higher error levels, and highlighted the high levels of training required for personnel.[35] The future of biometric technologies then, 'remains to be seen' (Wise 2004: 433). While investment in improving biometric technologies is significant, there is considerable research ongoing to develop the utility of DNA analysis, with new techniques and technologies increasing the potential uses of DNA profiling.

Developments in forensic DNA analysis

In addition to continual developments in the analysis of DNA, such as the production of DNA profiles from mixed, single-cell, or degraded samples, for many years there has been much technological research into DNA profiling automation and miniaturisation. Automated processes have been introduced and are proving successful. However, prototype 'lab-on-a-chip' systems have been trialled but are proving

---

32 Interviewee 1/L/P.

33 HC Home Affairs Committee (2004) *Identity Cards*, Fourth Report of Session 2003–04 Volume I HC 130-I. London: HMSO 30 July, p. 44. para. 169.

34 Mansfield T. and Rejman-Greene M. (2003), *Feasibility Study on the Use of Biometrics in an Entitlement Scheme*, National Physical Laboratory, available at www.homeoffice.gov.uk/comrace/identitycards/publications. html, p. 3.

more problematic (Home Office Science Policy Unit 2004: 8). Although mobile fingerprint systems have now been trialled in Project Lantern, DNA mobile or hand-held analysis may yet take longer, with efforts ongoing as part of the police science and technology strategy.

Familial searching

Familial searching is used when a full profile has been obtained from the scene of a serious crime, but there are no matches on the NDNAD. The profile can then be searched looking for 'close' matches, profiles where donors could be related. Identity can then be established through a familial match, for example the suspect could be a parent, child or sibling of someone whose profile is on the NDNAD. The technique had first been used in 2002 to identify a rapist and murderer, with a search of the NDNAD providing a list of 100 possible 'close' matches which led the police to a previously named suspect who had since died. After taking samples from surviving relatives, Joe Kappen was exhumed and his DNA matched samples obtained from the bodies of his three victims.[36]

Familial searching has now been successfully used in a criminal prosecution, with Craig Harman convicted of manslaughter in April 2004 after a close relative's DNA was found on the NDNAD. In small village in Italy, the murder of an elderly lady was solved using familial searching techniques (Pizzamiglio *et al.* 2004). Having taken 400 saliva samples from men of the village (the first reported intelligence screening in an Italian crime investigation), one sample suggested a potential parental link (father–son). The donor of this sample had a 19 year old son who was away on military service. When located, the son confessed to the murder and subsequent DNA testing confirmed his identity as the perpetrator. There may yet be broader ethical and civil liberties implications of familial searching that have yet to be fully explored, for example: 'it brings with it the indirect lifelong surveillance of citizens simply because they are related to someone whose DNA profile is on the record'.[37]

---

35 US General Accounting Office (2002), *Technology Assessment: Using Biometrics for Border Security*, GAO-03-174, November, www.gao.gov.

36 Forensic Science Service, *'Fact Sheet – Familial Searching'*, available at www.forensic.gov.uk.

37 Bieber, F. (2004) 'Guilt by association' (2004) *New Scientist*, 23 October.

DNA 'identikits'

Additionally, ongoing scientific research is seeking to produce 'DNA identikits': a description of a suspect's physical appearance from their DNA, so that police can focus their search on those matching the appearance detailed by the forensic scientist in lieu of eyewitnesses. At present, the FSS offer an 'ethnic inference' service where an individual's ethnicity can be calculated, giving the results of: white-skinned European; Afro-Caribbean; Indian Subcontinent; South East Asian; and Middle Eastern. In addition, there is a 'red hair' test which can detect approximately 84 per cent of redheads, which can be used to supplement the ethnic profiling. Ongoing research on the human genome is promoting further advances in this type of research, with expectations that in the future, other characteristics may be identified from DNA samples.[38]

Mitochondrial DNA analysis

Mitochondrial DNA (MtDNA) is obtained from hair, teeth, blood, or other tissues which contain low concentrations of DNA, or where DNA is degraded, making it unsuitable for nuclear DNA testing. Mitochondrial DNA testing permits the analysis of samples from evidence from old cases or material containing little biological material. It can also assist in the tracing of maternally-related persons (mitochondria being inherited from the mother), although because mitochondria is inherited, it cannot be used to positively identity an individual. This technology of profiling mitochondrial DNA was demonstrated in 1994 when members of a forensic team used MtDNA analysis to identify the remains of the Romanov family (Gill *et al.* 1996).

Mitochondrial DNA can be chosen for its specific characteristics, which include its maternal inheritance, the absence of recombination and its high divergence rate, as well as its high copy number per cell (Yao *et al.* 2004). There have been challenges however to MtDNA technology, in the case of *US* v. *Coleman*,[39] which ruled that MtDNA testing did constitute a scientific knowledge that was based upon reliable methods. There have been a number of academic articles that have called for quality controls in MtDNA testing, outlining five different errors that tend to occur: base shifts; reference bias;

---

38 Forensic Science Service, '*Fact Sheet – Commonplace Characteristics*', available at www.forensic.gov.uk.
39 *US* v. *Coleman* 202 F.Supp.2d. 962 (E.D.Mo., 2002).

phantom mutations; base mis-scoring; and artificial recombination (Yao *et al.* 2004). Such errors have led to calls for greater scrutiny of the technique and the quality of MtDNA data published.[40]

Low Copy Number DNA analysis (LCN)

Low Copy Number DNA analysis is a particular technique that can be used on samples that are too small for conventional DNA testing. The FSS in the UK began using LCN DNA testing in forensic casework in 1999, subsequently reporting a number of 'successes' in finding a DNA profile on 'cold cases' where a DNA profile had previously been unobtainable. However, the method remains controversial because by increasing the PCR cycles (from 28 to 34) to multiply the amount of DNA to be worked with, there is an increased risk in contamination, with any contamination present having a substantial effect on the results. The use of such small samples sizes also makes replication and thorough peer review near impossible (Wise 2004: 432). The method has led to the successful analysis of DNA from fingerprints however, with researchers reporting that DNA can now be detected after transfer to an object for nearly 3 months in some cases, and in one case for two years (van Oorschot and Jones 1997). While this technology is being perfected and utilised in the UK, the FBI in the USA remain sceptical of its application and do not at present use this DNA technique (Wise 2004: 432).

Y chromosome analysis

The analysis of DNA on a single Y chromosome (which is paternally inherited) can target Y chromosome STRs, which then separate mixtures of male and female DNA, particular usefully in sexual assault cases where previously male and female DNA could not be isolated (Wise 2004: 432). As only males carry the Y chromosome, this successfully isolates the male DNA, a method which is less discriminating than normal DNA analysis, so it should only be used to include or exclude suspects rather than for positive identification. However, in a high profile case in the USA, a man was sentenced to death for the murder, kidnap and sexual assault of five year old Samantha Runnion in California with the use of Y-STR DNA analysis. The judge in *People* v. *Avila*[41] admitted the forensic DNA

---

40 See Yao *et al.* (2004) for summary of arguments, p. 1–6.
41 *People* v. *Avila*, No, 02CF1862 (Orange Co., Calif., Super. Ct.).

evidence against the strong objections of the defence who argued that Y-STR analysis is not very discriminating and can be unreliable in degraded samples. It has however, also been successfully used in the USA to exonerate wrongfully convicted offenders, including the case of Wilton Dedge, released in 2004 after Y-chromosome analysis excluded him as a suspect for the rape for which he had been in prison since 1982.[42]

Single Nucleotide Polymorphisms (SNPs)

SNPs (referred to as 'SNIPS') are the latest development in DNA analysis, but are still most commonly used in the diagnosis of genetic disorders (such as sickle-cell anaemia). This DNA analysis is best used to offer additional information when identifying an individual (and can produce results in minutes), but despite early hopes it is unlikely that they will supplant the existing database methods used, particularly because of the huge costs involved in re-analysing the 3 million samples already on the NDNAD (Wise 2004: 433). The technology of SNIPS is still under development however, and may result in changes to forensic DNA methods in the future.

Forensic identification: human rights and civil liberties[43]

These few highlighted developments in DNA analysis continue to raise expectations that IDENT1 and the NDNAD will increase their powers to assist in the fight against crime whilst saving police resources and aiding 'intelligence' efforts, fuelling the drive to expand forensic identification databases by retaining fingerprints and DNA samples. However, while the technology is still undergoing development, the sophistication of ethical and normative debates have not advanced at a similar pace, leaving issues of human rights and civil liberties still to be properly accounted for.

---

42 *Florida* v. *Dedge*, 873 So. 2d 338 (Fla. 5th Dist.Ct.App.2004).

43 It is noted that there is scholarly debate surrounding the parameters of human rights and civil liberties, a debate that brevity dictates this book cannot engage with. For the purposes of this section, as per Feldman (2002: 4), 'human rights' are taken to be those rights legally defined in international human rights treaties and the *Human Rights Act* 1998, while 'civil liberties' are those liberties which impact upon the relationship of the citizen to the state in civil society.

Populist demands for the efficient arrest and conviction of offenders, as a consequence of the pre-eminent desire for managing the risk of victimisation, is fuelling the use of forensic science and technologies of surveillance. This trend, with forensic science hailed as the guarantor of certainty, reflects 'the general revolution of rising expectations as to the possibilities of fact determination and its power to settle intractable issues that the general culture of scientism has induced in all of us'.[44] However, technology brings both 'benefits and problems for society as well as for the legal system' (Redmayne 1998: 453).

The collection and retention of personal identity data raises issues of human rights and civil liberties of individuals most obviously, but also has wider consequences for society. The government has legislated to keep up with technology, with developments in fingerprint and DNA technologies dictating new police powers. The police have also stimulated innovation in forensic technologies, and lobbied for powers to take advantage of new technologies, even to combat 'problems' to which only they can attest to anecdotally. Fiscal or normative constraints on policy are significantly weakened in the face of the prioritisation of risk aversion. Pragmatism and populism replace principled Parliamentary and public debate, with the situation now urgently requiring the formation of informed normative positions on forensic sampling, its evidential use, and the construction and reliance upon large scale identity databases. Each of the three different sites of concern have differing impacts and implications, and need to be considered in depth, each on micro- and macro-levels.

Forensic sampling and individual rights

The 1992 Council Of Europe Recommendation on sampling stated that it was evident: 'that use of the technique itself carried risks, not only in the technical application but also, and in particular, as regards fundamental rights such as the rights to respect for the private and family life, the right to a fair trial and the respect of the human body'.[45] Yet the most recent changes to the law in the *Criminal Justice Act* 2003 accelerate the routinisation of sampling, permitting the fingerprinting and DNA sampling of arrestees, regardless of the arrest outcome. Latest government announcements propose further 'clarification, simplification and modernisation' (Home Office 2004b),

---

44 Gertz 1983: 171–2 quoted in Ericson and Haggerty (1997: 34).
45 Council of Europe Recommendation R (92) 1, 11.

permitting arrest where there is reasonable suspicion a citizen has, or is going to commit an offence, as long as arrest is 'necessary' (by a list of 'arrest criteria'), bringing 'a wider range of offences within the orbit of the trigger powers currently only available at the "serious" end of the offence range'.[46] These changes – so that now all offences are 'arrestable' – became law in January 2006. However, the law remains that DNA sampling can occur upon arrest for a *recordable* offence, so it remains to be seen whether the sampling regime will expand to all arrestees (so you could be DNA sampled after having been arrested for dropping litter), making the changes to the arrest laws a far more serious potential infringement on civil rights.

The consultation paper also proposed allowing fingerprinting *in situ*, now possible with the latest fingerprint technology, and covert DNA sampling powers. This is justified on the basis that undercover police may need to take DNA from a suspect without revealing how or when a sample was obtained. It is stated that samples obtained covertly will be for intelligence only, and not for evidential use (although speculative searches of the NDNAD are permitted) (Home Office 2004b), but such statements were made at the inception of the NDNAD, and its remit soon expanded.

At present, the sampling regime in England and Wales has been ruled compatible with human rights law. Contravention of Article 3, covering extreme interference with physical or psychological integrity of the person is unlikely, 'because the authorities would stop before that point was reached but also because most people would submit' (Alldridge *et al.* 1995: 276). With technological developments now only requiring a cotton swab from the inside of the cheek, this becomes a more remote possibility, though getting cells from a person without their consent could still require force – perhaps prompting the latest proposals to permit the police powers to covertly seize samples. In respect of Articles 6 and 8 cases in Europe, and the House of Lords decision in *Marper*, make clear that challenges to police powers are to be decided upon grounds of 'proportionality', inevitably invoking popular and persuasive 'community safety' and 'security' arguments favoured by the government: 'Everyone in the community has the right to live in a safe and secure environment and it is essential that we provide the police and other investigative agencies with the right level of powers to prevent, disrupt and investigate crime'.[47] The 'right level' is clearly not yet reached, despite expanding police powers.

---

46 See Home Office 2004b at p. 6, para. 2.18.
47 See Foreword in Home Office (2004b).

Human rights legislation offers the individual little protection: the judiciary assisting government policy by permitting derogation; the prevention and prosecution of crime providing the requisite excuse for the exercise of sampling powers. The protection of the public in risk-averse society will always trump individual rights. Such rulings exemplify: 'modern utilitarianism in which the majority who never expect even to be suspected of a crime are protected against the minority criminal element ...'.[48] Individual civil liberties, such as 'the freedom from arbitrary or discriminatory treatment' (Feldman 2002: 4), are then sidelined, with even reluctant critics admitting that 'some new police powers ... do appear to be difficult to justify' (Redmayne 1998: 443) (a reservation expressed prior to the *Criminal Justice Act 2003*). With arrests permitted where there is 'reasonable suspicion', this is the only criteria required for the fingerprint and sampling regime to be triggered. As such, the category of the 'innocent' diminishes, with almost every citizen capable of arousing suspicion in a society lacking in trust. Critics warn however:

> the acceptance and use of DNA evidence should rest on more than scientific accuracy. Care needs to be taken to balance the rights of the accused with the interests of justice, particularly in an era when 'scientific' is generally equated with 'correct'. In the face of increasing reliance on, and the reliability of such evidence, human rights issues need to be considered, and measures need to be put in place at the relative genesis of this form of evidence, rather than trying to redress human rights breaches when they happen. (Hocking *et al.* 1997: 75)

Charges that fingerprinting or DNA sampling breaches individual rights are then difficult to sustain (despite reservations about proportionality in some instances), particularly when it is clear that if innocent of a crime, most suspects would welcome the opportunity to rely upon DNA or fingerprints if it were to exculpate them during investigation, or lead to their acquittal at trial. The power of forensic identification technologies to exonerate the innocent is then not denied. Yet despite the desire to have technologies assisting with the detection of crime and police investigations, there is still cause for caution. The faith placed in the accuracy of forensic science and

---

48 Adrian Waterman. 'Whose DNA is it anyway?' Case Comment (*R* v. *Chief Constable of South Yorkshire ex parte Marper (2002)*), 2 May 2002.

technology is now supporting and driving a shift in the underlying ideology of the criminal process. While the police have always had wide investigative powers in cases of serious crimes, these powers now incorporate not just 'suspects' of serious crime, but almost all those who come into any contact with the police. Further, personal identity information gathered in the course of even minor investigations is retained. It is the retention of data that causes the most concern, with the proliferation and rapid growth of databases in society and increasing compulsion and inclusiveness causing more widespread concern about the impact on society of sampling and the retention of identity data.

Comprehension and compulsion in the 'database nation'[49]

Legislation enacted in response to particular threats (such as terrorism) has been 'normalised' so that powers to deal with terrorists have become applied to 'normal' criminals, then 'suspects', then social 'others' such as asylum seekers, immigrants etc. Technological weapons in the armoury against terrorism or serious crime have also spread to areas concerned with 'anti-social' behaviour, and the pursuit of 'security', or just bureaucracy, until England and Wales faces the possibility of becoming a 'database nation'. Medical databases are proposed, with a white paper on the NHS and genetics heralding a 'BioBank' of genetic profiles taken at birth, while there are also plans for a database detailing treatments and social care for all patients (the 'modernising' of medical records). *The Children Act* 2004 has also established a database of all children from birth until adulthood, including school achievements, medical and social services records, and records of 'anti-social behaviour'. There is also a planned 'Missing Person's DNA Database' (Home Office 2004b: 22), as well as a database of 'population data' to be held by the Office of National Statistics. These databases will add to the many already in operation in both the forensic arena, and the public and private sectors. Taken en masse, these databases will represent the retention of information on almost all citizens, with the avoidance of being on a database becoming as difficult as avoiding being caught on a CCTV camera whilst shopping. Non-inclusion will also come with drawbacks and may result in the withdrawal of essential services (such as welfare

---

49 See Garfinkel 2000.

benefits or medical treatment), or exclusion from places, activities, or employment opportunities, exacerbating social exclusion (Young 1999).

The latest and most obvious example of a specific threat being generalised to incorporate the population is the introduction of ID cards (although the government appear to no longer justify ID cards as essential for combating terrorism), supported by a National Identity Register. The Home Affairs Select Committee Report on the draft *Identity Cards Bill* was critical of several aspects of the plans including the scale and complexity of the proposed scheme and the lack of clarity about its aims and operation, as well as the procurement process.[50] ACPO claim that an ID card would assist efforts to combat organised crime, people trafficking, the sex trade and money laundering; while the Metropolitan Police argue that 'a society built around an individual's true identity and their ability to prove it would significantly reduce the opportunity for crime in a number of areas'.[51] The ID card legislation will permit disclosure of information on the register in the interests of national security, or for the prevention and investigation of crime (Clause 20(3)), if there is no other way of obtaining the information. The legislation will also effectively establish a national fingerprint database, with 80 per cent of the economically active population included within five years, rising to total inclusion when the ID scheme becomes compulsory. As the Committee point out, Parliament may not presently sanction the construction of a comprehensive forensic fingerprint database for the police, yet are proposing to do so under the ID card scheme.[52]

There is also the possibility that face recognition technology will continue to improve, enabling individuals captured on CCTV to be identified via the National Identity Register, the Committee stating that they doubted whether the pressure to use the system in such a way could be resisted in future.[53] The Committee concluded that the ID card plans are significantly wider than is necessary to introduce a simple system to establish and demonstrate identity, with the government gaining wide powers to require and register a wide range

---

50 HC Home Affairs Committee (2004) *Identity Cards*. Fourth Report of Session 2003–04, vol. I HC 130-I. London: HMSO, 30 July, p. 23, para. 64.
51 As above at p. 28.
52 As above at p. 42, para. 155.
53 As above at p. 42.

of information, with access available to a myriad of organisations.[54] They do not base objections on grounds of principle however, but on cost, and question whether the scheme is proportionate to achieve the supposed aims.[55] The Information Commissioner also expresses concern about widening access to personal information: 'My anxiety is that we don't sleepwalk into a surveillance society where much more information is collected about people, accessible to far more people, shared across many more boundaries than British society would feel comfortable with.'[56]

The desirability of comprehensive forensic identity databases has been commented upon favourably by judges, scientists and police, claiming them to be 'non-discriminatory,' and a 'real and worthwhile gain in the endeavour to ensure that the guilty, and only the guilty, are convicted of crimes'.[57] This does not allow for discriminatory practice in their application, and has led to criticisms that a compulsory national DNA database 'solves the discrimination problem because it makes us all suspects'.[58] While police-targeted mass screens may be of use on occasion (a judgement which should remain a matter of police policy and subject to consent), 'area or national testing on a compulsory basis should be rejected ...' (Walker and Cram 1990: 489). Policing by consent remains essential: 'a society that does not ultimately rest for its lawfulness on the voluntary, willing adhesion of the vast majority of citizens to its policing and court system is a failing society ...'.[59]

Examination of the role of identification databases in society and in the criminal justice system must then proceed on a theoretical, as well as pragmatic basis. An ideological framework is necessary to facilitate ethical, philosophical debate, addressing 'major questions about the likely short and long term implications for human rights, the shape and tenor of social control, and the future of criminal justice:

---

54 As above at p. 56, para. 222.
55 As above at p. 56, para. 219.
56 Richard Thomas (2004) 'Beware rise of Big Brother state, warns data watchdog', *The Times*, 16 August.
57 *R. (on the application of S)* v. *Chief Constable of South Yorkshire* [2002] EWCA Civ 1275; [2003] Crim LR.
58 (CA) Sedley LJ at para. 87.
59 John Wadham, 'Databasing of innocent people – why it offers problems not solutions', Liberty Press Release 13 September 2002, available at www.liberty-human-rights.org.uk/.

in effect, about the new risks created by the expansion of the "risk business"'.[60] As detailed, the establishment of identity databases is not without risk; risk that cannot be justified on a law enforcement basis alone (Mooki 1997: 565, 578). A US court expressed such sentiment when stating that: 'if we choose to violate the rights of the innocent in order to discover and act against the guilty, then we will have transformed our country into a police state and abandoned one of the fundamental tenets of our free society'.[61]

Forensic identity databases: issues and prospects

Over the course of the century in which fingerprints have been taken and retained by the police any initial reservations have been overshadowed by overwhelming support for the creation of fingerprint databases. The existence of a police national fingerprint database meets with little resistance, and retains its primary function as a forensic tool. However, the use of fingerprints in other situations is increasing, with 'biometrics' being almost single-handedly sought as the new guarantor of security and safety (in passports, ID cards, credit cards and so on, to tackle anything from benefit fraud to international terrorism). The creation of large fingerprint databases such as EURODAC, or small 'private' fingerprint databases in school libraries, escape critical attention that may question the proliferation of such databases, their desirability, and potential (ab)uses. It remains to be seen whether the public will remain so compliant, or warm to fingerprinting in the street.

In contrast, forensic DNA retention does attract some, if largely uncritical, attention. In limited debate surrounding the large-scale retention of DNA, the first rebuttal to objections is that the information is in the custody of the FSS, a public sector agency, with no interest in profiteering from the database, thus ensuring integrity. However, the FSS is currently undergoing significant organisational change after the statement in Parliament in July 2003 that the FSS was to be privatised. After much inquiry, the situation presently stands that the FSS has become a Government Owned Company (GovCo) with the aim of becoming a PPP (Public Private Partnership) for now, delayed indefinitely. However, privatising an integral part of the criminal

---

60 Lord Phillips of Sudbury, HL Deb, col. 962 (8 May 2001).
61 *Capua* v. *City of Plainfield* (1986) 643 F Supp 1507 DNJ.

justice system must be carefully considered and the practical and ethical issues addressed. Privatisation is far from a clear solution to investment problems (although the FSS pays for itself, according to National Audit Office reports). Whilst it could be beneficial in bringing about further independence from the police (which has historically been sorely lacking), the police would remain the primary consumers of forensic services so a private company would need to ensure that they maintained a close relationship, possibly leading to greater company efforts to please their primary customer.

The NDNAD itself is to be retained by the public sector, with new governance arrangements being put in place, and custodianship remaining in the hands of the Home Office, ACPO and the Association of Police Authorities (APA). Current protections will then hopefully be enshrined, as these would be largely negated if the database were to be given over to a private, profit-seeking company. The DNA samples were taken solely for the purposes of detecting and prosecuting crime, which precludes a company from profiting from a database which is expensive to maintain and utilise. This raises the question of where the motivation is to own something so expensive without the ability to profit from it. Despite such concerns, one interviewee did not view privatisation, or ownership of the NDNAD, a particular problem:

> The ownership of the DNA database is an esoteric question, an answer to which of course has to be found. But I don't think it is a very difficult question, there will be a limited number of choices and you just choose the safest one. I myself wouldn't be happy to hand over the stock of DNA samples to a public limited company however reputable. It is the responsibility of the state – including the FSS as a government agency, to retain such items. If the FSS becomes privatised, then I would remove the DNA stock and take it and put it into the hands of another state organisation.[62]

Questions also still surround regulation. The Council for the Registration of Forensic Practitioners (CRFP) is attempting to address problems, but is far from being a regulatory body. If the FSS dominated an open 'forensic science' market (it currently has an 83 per cent share of the 'market'), it would create a monopoly with the potential to manifest all the associated problems of monopolies.

---

62 Interviewee 3/L/P.

To protect its market position, commercial pressures would entail a reluctance to leave themselves open to scrutiny, raising several questions:

- Who would be responsible for taking on a inspection role to ensure standards?
- Would there be a contingency plan if standards dropped?
- Would a person wrongly convicted on flawed scientific evidence be able to sue the company?
- Can the government ensure profits are re-invested into resources and training?

Whilst laboratory upgrading is required now, there must be a long-term commitment to resources, research, and training; yet shareholders may not be happy to see profits spent on training and research, with little if any financial return on their investment. Privatisation could have a negative impact on forensic science standards; tighter controls on forensic science are required to prevent miscarriages of justice, and the introduction of a profit motive is rarely helpful in such situations.

There are also problems with charging for forensic tests. Individual police forces budget for forensic services and if charges were raised, they may be forced to limit forensic testing. Additionally, the Legal Aid Commission would have to pay for more expensive tests, so the government will pay more through police and legal aid budgets. A worrying scenario then arises: forensic testing would be pursued less often by the police, or permitted less often for defendants seeking to challenge evidence, raising questions over whether crimes are being investigated thoroughly, and whether indigent defendants are afforded a proper defence.

Of course, practical problems could be overcome by clever contract writing and built-in penalty clauses and so on, yet there remain serious ethical questions. The prosecution of criminals is a state task which should not be derogated from (and the government must meet the cost), although they increasingly encourage private prosecutions to be brought by the private sector for offences such as shoplifting and so on. Indeed, it remains deeply controversial whether the government, or any private body, should seek to make money from the pursuit and conviction of criminals. Currently there are ongoing debates about the fining of motoring offenders to pay for victim compensation schemes, and indeed the use of speed cameras as a means of raising revenue for police forces. The introduction of fiscal considerations to policing and prosecution does little but introduce another contentious variable to the debate.

The future of the NDNAD will not be predicated upon profitability however, leaving the measure of cost-effectiveness unclarified. As Freiberg (2001: 273) suggests, 'success' may be more about 'capturing the public imagination rather than success in controlling crime'. Political rhetoric, and the use of 'hits' or conviction statistics by partial agencies, indicate that the utility of forensic identity databases is measured by reference to their ability to aid detection and provide evidence with which a conviction can be pursued and secured. However, there may be other implicit aims of investment in forensic identity databases. They may lend the criminal process the aura of objectivity and impartiality, with the ability to establish 'facts' beyond doubt; scientific reliability and validity enabling certainty about the veracity of convictions or exculpations.

Investigating the role of forensic identity databases gives insight into their true purposes and potential outcomes for society. In common with a general growth in 'forensics', and increased resort by society to science to resolve problems or alleviate uncertainty, forensic science is considered a neutral, objective 'arbiter of truth' (Dreyfuss and Nelkin 1992: 339). However, forensic science has previously, and continues to be, implicated in miscarriages of justice, demonstrating that uncritical faith in forensic science can be misplaced. This will continue, despite scientific progress and technological innovation, while there is a lack of proper regulation. Indeed, regulation of forensic science, and of expert witnesses more generally, is an urgent challenge. The British Medical Association has recently investigated the involvement of doctors in 'cot death' trials, however, there is no regulatory body to which errant forensic scientists can be referred to be 'struck off'. The CRFP is a welcome development, and can investigate individuals to a degree, but stops far short of bringing necessary rigorous scientific scrutiny to bear upon forensic science.

If criminal justice reform is to be founded upon a belief that forensic science can reconstruct the 'truth' of a criminal event, that belief needs to be based upon more solid ground than at present. It will not always be the case that forensic science can bring the certainty and accuracy required; sometimes it can obfuscate matters, making the criminal justice reform agenda not only ill advised but likely to result in greater incidence of wrongful convictions, which may prove near impossible to overturn. Yet, to placate those that may wish to preserve their remaining civil liberties and retain some control over personal data, the establishment of national identity databases are preceded by assertions of the accuracy, and infallibility of the science behind the technology, and the security of the technology. Such assertions themselves would be non-scientific, for: 'science, by definition, can only ever offer provisional answers. Scientific statements must be falsifiable and therefore remain open to the possibility that they may be revised or even replaced in due course' (Paterson 2003: 531). As with all human endeavour, infallibility may be an unattainable goal.

The 'infallibility' of forensic identification

It is undeniable that forensic identification technology has substantial benefits: in linking crimes; identifying or eliminating suspects; enabling convictions; and perhaps most importantly, reducing reliance upon notoriously unreliable and partial evidence – human testimony. The 'science', while complex, has developed and to a significant degree been 'perfected' since the nascence of DNA profiling. However, the complexity of the science and the strict controls required for the processes undertaken still present problems, largely because of the involvement of non-scientists in the process (such as police officers), although scientists themselves retain their human fallibility. The involvement of humans is normally at the root of problems with both fingerprinting and DNA; while it is not always the evidence itself that is problematic, it can also be related issues such as disclosure, and presentation in court.

A consequence of reliance on forensic identification and categorisation has been the removal or diminution of protections in place to avert miscarriages of justice or wrongful convictions. The focus of the criminal process has increasingly become the use of forensic techniques to reconstruct 'scientifically' (in other words, objectively) the crime event and identify those involved. People are arrested without any judicial proceedings ever taking place, with trials reserved for the few, more serious cases. The criminal process is therefore undertaken swiftly, often within the confines of the police station (with limited oversight), with minimal judicial intervention (leaving courts free) other than sentencing decisions for those cases that do reach court: 'ritual and tradition in public have given way to informality in private, legal formalism to professional judgement, and public justice to performance indicators' (Hillyard and Gordon 1999: 522).

Criminal appeals have illuminated problems that can occur with fingerprint evidence, including the non-disclosure of exculpatory fingerprint evidence,[63] as well as the prejudicial use of fingerprint evidence that did not indicate guilt.[64] However, in cases where there is fingerprint evidence, defendants may be advised to plead guilty, which makes an appeal or challenge to fingerprint evidence difficult.[65] Training, and internal verification procedures within fingerprinting continue to cause concern, while challenges to fingerprint evidence in the US since *Daubert* continue, with examiners under pressure to prove the 'scientific' basis of their evidence. Accusations of subjectivity look set to increase with the removal of a numerical standard in England and Wales, and continued lack of stringent testing of personnel, with experts warning that the fingerprint examination system is 'riddled with flaws', with the number of known misidentifications 'the tip of the iceberg'.[66]

Likewise, DNA evidence can be flawed, through human error, contamination, or misinterpretation; as DNA scientists Penacino *et al.* (2003: 877) conclude: 'No amount of care can eliminate the possibility of error'. There may be problems with collection, storage, analysis, or interpretation of samples. HMIC (2002: 21) found 'procedural laxity' in both DNA and fingerprint processes, while inept interviewing and inappropriate disclosure of evidence was enabling suspects to form 'spurious explanations for the presence of marks and stains and thus avoid prosecution' (HMIC 2002: viii), a problem to which interviewees attested. There is also the potential for deliberate tampering with evidence, a concern raised by scientists during and since the O.J.Simpson trial,[67] and more recently in the case of Shirley McKie. The quality of forensic evidence continues then to be an issue, as well as the presentation of forensic identifications in court. Most clearly, there remains a 'grave danger' that juries are 'seduced by the purity of the science without fully considering the impurity of its application' (Walker and Stockdale 1999: 149).

DNA evidence remains problematic although is now less likely to be routinely challenged, and can often be taken as conclusive proof of guilt. The reluctance of criminal justice professionals to

---

63 *R* v. *Stephen Craven* (2001) 2 Cr App R 12.
64 *R* v. *McNamee* [1998] LTL 18/12/98 (Unreported elsewhere).
65 Interviewee 6/P/C.
66 James Starrs, quoted in 'Expert warns fingerprinting system is riddled with flaws', *Sunday Herald*, 30 May 2004: 9.
67 'Shadows of Doubt', *The Weekend Australian Magazine*, 27–28 September 2003: 15–18.

critically engage with the science of forensic DNA identification 'has given this evidence form a degree of legitimacy that enhances its attractiveness as a crucial evidentiary element in the prosecution case' (Findlay and Grix 2003: 270). In a culture where DNA is compelling, probability ratios presented to juries may be sufficient to overcome doubts, making DNA evidence especially relevant for circumstantial cases, with DNA 'the centrepiece of a circumstantial case and only require corroboration of the slightest form to confirm its significance' (Findlay and Grix 2003: 272). It is questionable whether lay triers of fact are not vulnerable 'when faced with evidence which they may not be competent to evaluate' (Roberts 1994b: 470). Decision-makers at each point in the criminal process require careful instruction and direction, which has not often been forthcoming (Findlay and Grix 2003: 271). This could lead also to a *lack* of DNA evidence being a problem; with no DNA evidence to confirm mistaken identification, proving innocence may become difficult with juries expecting forensic evidence to support alibis (Hocking *et al.* 1997).

In society the proliferation of databases continues unabated, supporting the growth of surveillance to enable the management of 'risk'. The priority of risk aversion, has given forensic identification databases a significant role in the criminal justice process, with their impact felt not simply in terms of their direct utilisation, but also in altering perceptions of the aims of criminal justice and faith in the ability of the criminal process to achieve accuracy and certainty. These constituents are then replacing 'fairness' as the crucial factor in legitimacy, with the 'integrity' of the system predicated upon rectitude, rather than a 'moral' basis, influencing modernisation of the system as well as the society of which it is a part. Solid conclusions upon reforms, in particular the *Criminal Justice Act* 2003, and the implications for justice may be premature or remain problematic if the reality is that:

> there can be no justice in criminal justice, … The debate between those who are committed to the present procedures and practices (or a reformed version of them) as a commitment to truth, and those seeking to defend the existing values of due process, including rights, is one between hopeless idealists. (Nobles and Schiff 2000: 35)

The modernisation programme, in promoting 'truth' as the basis for all decision-making, is creating a climate where 'fairness' is a subsidiary concern. Yet, fairness of procedure and the establishment of the truth, 'must be seen as distinct but related aspects of criminal justice, which, at their most abstract, share no necessary relationship; they are neither complementary nor contradictory' (Jorg *et al.* 1995: 53). While accuracy is a necessary prerequisite to legitimacy, is not the only value to be upheld. Treating 'truth' as pre-eminent risks making other values 'appear irrational and often subjective' (Nobles and Schiff 1994: 49). Yet it was the integrity of the criminal process and the denial of due process that led to the famous miscarriages of justice that prompted a Royal Commission. There is no stable correlation between truth and fairness, though they both intersect with 'justice'. There must necessarily then be choices as to which is to take priority; although as Hunt (1993) points out, a final agreement may never be reached. An example of one possible choice is advanced by Maclean (2001: 600): 'fairness must come first. Considerations of speed and cost follow on'. However, this may simply be another 'balancing act', with attendant problems.

At present, reforms reflect the prioritising of the efficient, and speedy securing of convictions, with 'public interest' in community safety and the aversion of risk pre-eminent within an actuarial regime of risk management. In line with this prioritising are reforms that eschew concern with fairness, evidenced by 'the absence of substantial opposition to altering the implications for maintaining silence in police interviewing, and to altering the rules of disclosure of evidence because it is thought that too many guilty people are being acquitted' (Hudson 2001: 144). While searching for the zenith of efficiency and effectiveness 'the criminal justice system cannot avoid being referenced to some set of values, however problematic the connection may be between these and the way it operates' (Greer 1994: 74).

The philosophical gaps left by managerialism, and the ideological consequences of professionalisation, populism, and pragmatism, then need addressing. If rights are to be upheld, fairness and probity need to be entrenched throughout the criminal process, and any deviation from procedural rules and ethical standards needs to be accounted for and rectified, particularly during the vital stages of evidence gathering and case construction (Ashworth 1998). It is hoped that exculpation of innocent suspects; exoneration of the wrongly convicted; and the prevention of miscarriages of justice through the use of forensic science continues, and that those wrongful convictions brought to light will provoke consideration of the operation of the criminal justice system, both domestically and internationally. However, whilst forensic science can be an invaluable tool, its capabilities must not be permitted to drive unprincipled reform, and its limitations must be recognised and protected against, if miscarriages of justice are to be avoided, and wider injustice prevented.

The information society: heading for 'information overload'?

Evidence that the value of information has risen exponentially in late-modern society is not difficult to amass. It could also be relatively easily argued that post-9/11, the onus on the collation and storing of information of all kinds has gained public and political support. Efforts to collate yet more information continue with the growth of private surveillance continuing unabated. The government, while reserving the power to utilise private surveillance data for their purposes, have also stepped up their own information-gathering efforts. Legislation presently facilitates the collection of communications data, requires the reporting of 'suspicions' by financial and legal personnel, and the sharing of 'risk' reports on citizens between multiple agencies.

Examples also abound of situations where securing 'information' has become the *raison d'etre* of action, Guantanamo Bay is just one high-profile example. Yet, the US congressional investigation into 9/11 has claimed that many of the failings amongst the intelligence community stemmed from the possession of 'too much' information, as opposed to too little. This phenomenon, the over-efficient collection of information without the ability to decipher its meaning or the required response, led to the cancellation of several flights bound for Washington, and America was accused of 'jumping at shadows' when insisting that the passenger manifests were checked with 22 agencies before clearance. The proliferation of information could also be to blame for the size and cost of many public inquiries, while the Bichard Inquiry reported that during the immediate police investigation into the Soham murders there was 'too much' information for the police to deal with. This problem has been highlighted in previous major police inquiries; and yet the Bichard Inquiry concluded that it was a lack of information that led to Ian Huntley's evasion from suspicion, thus leading to recommendations for the creation of a national database recording all allegations, suspicions, and dropped charges against individuals.

The creation of identity databases therefore occurs within global efforts to pursue the information with which to guarantee 'security'. Yet the growth in 'intelligence' services, and the retention and utilisation of information, does not spell the end of insecurity or the attainment of 'safety', despite official faith in the preventative capabilities created by the very act of intelligence gathering and retention. Identification technologies, and biometrics in particular, are therefore benefiting from increased investment; but should investment in forensic technologies be at the expense of investment in the pursuit of other values such as fairness, equality of treatment, privacy, or freedom? Indeed, it could be posited that investment in making society and the global environment 'fairer', more inclusive, and more equal, could pay greater dividends in the 'war against terror' currently being waged with little success.

Conclusion: cause for optimism, pessimism or scepticism?

As stated by the Chairman of the NDNAD Board: 'If DNA technology is to continue to be an important tool in the drive to reduce crime and detect offenders, it is vitally important that those charged with the responsibility of managing and operating the Database do so in an environment of integrity, probity and independent scrutiny'.[68] Forensic identification technologies do make a vital contribution to crime detection and it would be wrong to portray the significant advances made in forensic identification in a wholly negative light. Indeed, the potential for the administration of justice to proceed free of the blight of miscarriages of justice where innocent defendants are convicted in error, is undoubtedly brought a step closer by reliance upon scientific techniques of identification rather than notoriously flawed and unreliable human testimony. Scientific advances then, treated with caution and respect, are to be welcomed. Measured caution should accompany claims, with investment in future developments to take place within a strong normative framework. However, questionable science (or 'junk science') as well as misinterpreted or misrepresented scientific testimony has been, and will continue to be, responsible for injustices.

Technological innovation and scientific progress demand that vigilance is maintained, and strong regulatory controls put in place. Stricter inspection regimes for forensic scientists and their laboratories have increased since recognition of the role that forensic science has played in many miscarriages of justice. Similarly, pro-prosecution

---

68 *NDNAD Annual Report 2003–4*, available at www.forensic.gov.uk, p. 4.

bias in scientific evidence and fraud has been partly recognised. The 'cot-death' cases in the UK have publicised the problem of expert evidence in both the civil and criminal courts. It is hoped that in light of the potential magnitude of problems in these cases, further steps will be taken to address the hallowed status of experts and their evidence. If scientific dispute were to be seen as going to the reliability of the evidence, the great reliance placed on expert evidence may be adjusted to indicate to the jury that such evidence should not be accepted unquestioningly, with controversial claims to truth deemed inadmissible.

Whilst accepting risks attendant with scientific and technological advance, it is not automatically the case that it is the science that is to blame, just as it should not be assumed that whilst the police have an array of scientific technologies available for use, these dictate what the police actually do (Ericson and Shearing 1986). Splitting the atom was a scientific breakthrough; the invention of the atom bomb was a human application decision. Though it may be partially true that technology drives uses ('where there is a way there is a will'), (Ericson and Haggerty 1997: 34) it is the manipulation of technologies which requires vigilance:

> technology is itself shaped by social and organisational conditions. The impact of a specific technology on social life is often determined by a range of factors beyond its technical capacity ... Hence, technology may be constraining or enabling, but people have the ability to adapt, bend, shape, develop, subvert, misuse and otherwise manipulate technological specifications ... (Chan 2001: 143)

The portrayal of surveillance technologies as representing a repressive and controlling 'Big Brother' often verge on the hysterical. As surveillance has proliferated, there have been benefits in terms of crime detection and prevention. However, modern analyses of surveillance demonstrate that the 'panopticon' vision has been revived, albeit under a variety of proprietors, and in computerised form. While the consequences may not be rightly portrayed as apocalyptic, potentially undesirable implications of radical change to the criminal process, including the diminution of suspect's rights and changes to the rules of evidence to facilitate 'truth seeking' (concerned primarily with 'wrongful acquittals'), can be protected against by recourse to a strong human rights commitment, and a normative criminal justice model based upon fairness and the enhancement of freedom.

However, there is little confidence that the state, or agencies and agents of social control are motivated to be constrained by normative principles such as 'fairness' or 'freedom'. More cynically, the greatest constraining force may be fiscal, with cost–benefit analyses ultimately leading to a reconfiguration of the role of forensic science. Society however, appears to be prepared to pay for 'security', via either personal payment for security technologies (alarms, lighting, home CCTV), or a community paying for its own security force, or via the public purse, paying through taxes for increased deployment of 'risk technologies' including CCTV, ID cards and identity databases.

During the last quarter of a century, a myriad of reports, white papers, and Acts of Parliament, as well as two Royal Commissions have attempted to identify the foundational principles and aims of the England and Wales criminal justice system. For example, in 2001 the Law Commission identified the twin aims of *accuracy of outcome*; 'to ensure, as far as possible, that those who are guilty are convicted and those who are not guilty are acquitted' and also a *process aim*; 'ensuring that the system shows respect for the fundamental rights and freedoms of the individual'. Such process aims 'arise out of the relationship between the citizen and the state, and regulate what the state can properly do to the citizen. They reflect society's valuation of the citizen's autonomy and entitlement to be treated with dignity and respect'.[69] The question is whether the present operation of the criminal justice system, in utilising the forensic identification methods of fingerprinting and DNA profiling, achieves or attempts to achieve, both of these aims, or are they treated unequally?

A focus upon the potential for injustice caused by reliance upon scientific identification techniques and the extension of powers to take and retain bodily samples from citizens, can rightly lead to accusations of 'playing to the grandstand of alarmed public opinion' (Rule 1974: 32). As Maguire (2000: 334) exhorts, debate on vital issues will be much more productive if commentators refrain from lapsing 'into unhelpful gross exaggerations and apocalyptic visions of the future...'. Retained DNA samples have the power to exonerate the wrongly convicted, a power which has saved many innocent inmates on death in the USA.[70] Forensic DNA technology can be used as

---

69 Law Commission (2001) Final Report: *Double Jeopardy and Prosecution Appeals* (CM 5048) London: TSO. Part III., para. 7.1256.

70 At least 149 post-conviction exonerations have been secured by DNA; see www.innocenceproject.org/.

a definitive test of guilt, and 'given that eyewitnesses can make mistakes, and that police officers can be misled, the Forensic Science Service clearly has an intermittent but vital role to play in protecting the innocent, as well as strengthening the case against those who commit offences' (Ramsay 1987: 20).

The culture of scientism however, has resulted in heightened expectations in the ability of science to provide solutions to problems, with forensic science increasingly asked to answer 'whodunnit?' (along with 'howdunnit?') questions posed by the criminal justice system. The ability to answer such questions with greater ease and accuracy has in turn increased trust in forensic sciences, with the expectation that turning to scientists will increasingly be a first, and not last, resort. In light of a perceived inability on the part of the police, or other law enforcement agencies, to catch criminals or convict them using traditional policing (or detective) methods, hopes are raised that scientists will be able to tip the justice scales back in favour of the police and prosecution.[71] These developments have taken place almost in a vacuum of academic critical interest in the UK, with minimal research undertaken on the impacts of the wholesale implementation of a novel 'crime science' discipline into the legal system. This is despite the increasing acknowledgement that 'all scientific knowledge exists in a state of flux. Dogmatic assertions have no place' (Mahendra 2004: 269).

The use of forensic science raises at least three discrete policy issues:

- How can new technology be utilised whilst insuring against error or abuse?
- Are the technological advances necessary?
- Do they produce appreciable benefits at reasonable cost?

It is with an objective and critical lens then with which the use of forensic evidence in criminal investigation, in particular the use of information derived from bodily samples, must be examined, for 'forensic science makes an important and ever expanding contribution to the investigation of crime and the successful prosecution of offenders, but at the same time, miscarriages of justice' (Hocking *et al.* 1997: 469). While the present research has been restricted, ongoing research is clearly required into the issues raised, as well as many of

---

71 'Police: We're not good enough to catch crooks', *The Independent*, 1 July 2002.

those only touched upon, including the use of biometric technology; the continued growth of identity databases; and the widening of the social control net in the risk society, which in turn increases the risk of miscarriages of justice and social injustice. The specific utilisation of forensic fingerprint and DNA technology also requires greater scholarly attention, accompanied by high-quality quantitative and qualitative research in police stations (or on the street with mobile technology), legal practitioners offices, CPS offices and courts across the UK.

To prevent forensic identity techniques, and databases, from becoming a 'technological tyranny' (Blake 1989), it is incumbent upon legal practitioners, criminal justice agencies, and legal reformers to end the 'culture clash' between the law and science. Adapting the legal process to utilise scientific evidence and aid its correct application and interpretation is essential. This will take research, education of practitioners, and considered legal reform, undertaken with underlying principles of fairness strengthened, with science an *aid* to justice, not as arbiter. In the risk society, reliant on science but suspicious of its motives, the role of forensic science in the criminal process and wider social control processes needs to be far more open to critical examination, and received in a more sceptical manner.

There needs to be quantitative and qualitative standards imposed on practitioners, technologies and techniques, with strict oversight and regulation. Forensic scientists need to take responsibility for professionalisation and accountability, although it may require government intervention to instigate an independent body to undertake oversight, regulation, and importantly, policy formation and future planning (a recommendation made in April 2005 by the Science and Technology Select Committee). Such oversight and regulation needs to be independent, maintaining institutional separation between those prosecuting offences, those defending, those providing forensic evidence, and policy development, standard setting, and regulation. Similarly, during the criminal process, the standards required of forensic evidence need to be high to minimise the risks of wrongful conviction based upon flawed or weak scientific evidence. There needs to be greater scepticism in the power of forensic science to avert risk, bring certainty to the criminal process and provide security for society, and less reference to new technologies to justify the removal of safeguards and protections for individuals and society. Finally, recognition that: 'There's a difference between what one can do, scientifically or otherwise, and what one ought to do' (Dinerstein 2001: 430).

References

Aas, K.F. (2004) 'The body does not lie: biometrics, trust and identification in technoculture', paper presented to the British Society of Criminology Conference, Portsmouth, July.

ACPO (2003) *DNA Good Practice Manual* (http//www.forensic.gov.uk/forensic_t/inside/news/docs/DNA_Good.pdf).

Akdeniz, Y., Taylor, N. and Walker, C., (2001) 'Regulation of Investigatory Powers Act 2000: BigBrother.co.uk: State surveillance in the age of information and rights' *Criminal Law Review*, 73–90.

Alderson, J. (1992) 'The police', in E. Stockdale and S. Casale (eds) *Criminal Justice Under Stress*. London: Blackstone Press, 10–33.

Allan, T. (1998) 'Procedural fairness and the duty of respect', *Oxford Journal of Legal Studies*, 18(3): 497.

Alldridge, P., Berkhout-Van Poelgeest S. and Williams K. (1995) 'DNA profiling and the use of expert scientific witnesses in criminal proceedings', in P. Fennell, C. Harding, N. Jorg and B. Swart (eds) *Criminal Justice in Europe: A Comparative Study*. Oxford: Clarendon Press, 265–82.

Annas, G. (1993) 'Privacy rules of DNA databanks: protecting coded future diaries', *Journal of the American Medical Association*, 270: 2346–7.

Armer, M. (2001) 'Fingerprint evidence', *New Law Journal*, 151: 1660.

Ashworth, A. (1979) 'Concepts of criminal justice', *Criminal Law Review*, June: 412.

Ashworth, A. (1996) 'Crime, community and creeping consequentialism', *Criminal Law Review*, April: 220.

Ashworth, J. (1997a) 'Science in society', in *Science, Policy and Risk*. Papers from meeting held at the Royal Society on 18 March 1997. London: Royal Society.

Ashworth, J. (1997b) 'Science, policy and risk: an introduction', in *Science, Policy and Risk*. Papers from meeting held at the Royal Society on 18 March 1997. London: Royal Society.

Ashworth, A. (1998) *The Criminal Process: An Evaluative Study* (2nd edn). Oxford: Clarendon Press.

Ashworth, A. (2001) 'Criminal proceedings after the human rights act: the first year', *Criminal Law Review*, November: 855.

Ashworth, A. (2002) *Human Rights, Serious Crime and Criminal Procedure*. London: Sweet and Maxwell.

Ashworth, A. and Blake, M. (1996) 'The presumption of innocence in English criminal law', *Criminal Law Review*, May: 306.

Audit Commission (1993) *Helping With Enquiries: Tackling Crime Effectively*. London: HMSO.

Auld, L.J. (2001) *Review of the Criminal Courts* (http://www.lcd.gov.uk).

Austin, L. (2003) 'Privacy and the question of technology', *Law and Philosophy*, 22: 119–66.

Baird, J. (1992) 'Forensic DNA in the trial court 1990–1992: a brief history' in P. Billings (ed) *DNA On Trial: Genetic Identification and Criminal Justice*. Cold Spring Harbor, NY: Cold Spring Harbor Laboratory Press, 61–108.

Ball, K. and Webster, F. (2003) 'The intensification of surveillance' in K. Ball and F. Webster (eds) *The Intensification of Surveillance*. London: Pluto Press, 1–15.

Bar, W. (2003) 'DNA profiling: evaluation of the evidentiary value', *Legal Medicine*, 5: 541–544.

Barsby, C. and Ormerod, D. (2003) 'Retention by police of fingerprint and DNA samples of persons subject to a criminal investigation but not subsequently convicted', *Criminal Law Review*, January: 39.

Beavan, C. (2003) *Fingerprints*. London: Fourth Estate.

Beck, U. (1992) *Risk Society: Towards A New Modernity*. London: Sage.

Beck, U. (2003) 'Politics of risk society' in J. Franklin (ed.) *The Politics of Risk Society*. Cambridge: Polity Press.

van der Beck, K. and Tullener, F. (2004) 'The use of DNA for the investigation of high volume crime in the Netherlands', in M. Townsley and G. Laycock (eds) *Beyond DNA – Integration and Harmonisation*. London: Home Office Science Policy Unit.

Belloni, F. and Hodgson, J. (2000) *Criminal Injustice*. Hampshire: Macmillan.

Bentham, J. (1827) *Rationale of Judicial Evidence*. London: Hunt and Clarke.

Bereano, P. (1992) 'The impact of DNA-based identification systems on civil liberties', in P. Billings (ed.) *DNA On Trial: Genetic Identification and Criminal Justice*. Cold Spring Harbor, NY: Cold Spring Harbor Laboratory Press, 119–28.

Beulke, W. (2005) 'Germany', in D. Chambers (ed.) *Genetic Testing and the Criminal Law*. London: UCL Press.

Blake, C. (2001) 'Judging asylum and immigration claims: The Human Rights Act and the Refugee Convention', *Public Money and Management*, July–September: 25.

Blake, E. (1989) 'Scientific and legal issues raised by DNA analysis' in J. Ballantyne, G. Sensabaugh and J. Wirkowski. Banbury Report No. 32: *DNA Technology and Forensic Science*. Cold Spring Harbor, NY: Cold Spring Harbor Laboratory Press.

Blakey, D. (2002) Foreword to *Under the Microscope – Refocused*, Report of Her Majesty's Inspectorate of Constabulary. London: Home Office.

Bogard, W. (1996) *The Simulation of Surveillance*. Cambridge: Cambridge University Press.

Bohme, G. and Stehr, N. (1986) 'The growing impact of scientific knowledge on social relations' in G. Bohme and N. Stehr (eds) *The Knowledge Society*. Dordrecht: Kluwer Publishing.

Bottoms, A. and McClean, J. (1976) *Defendants in the Criminal Process*. London: Routledge.

Bourne, C. (2002) 'Retaining fingerprints and DNA samples', *New Law Journal*, 152(7055): 1693.

Boyes, M. (1999) 'Whose DNA? Genetic surveillance, ownership of information and newborn screening', *New Genetics and Society*, 18(2/3): 145–55.

Boyne, R. (2000) 'Post-panopticism', *Economy and Society*, 29(2): 285–307.

Bradley, C.M. and Hoffman, J.L. (1996) 'Public perception, justice, and the "search for truth" in criminal cases', *Southern California Law Review*, 69: 1267.

Bramley, B. (2004) 'Civil rights, public accountability and quality assurance in forensic science evidence', in M. Townsley and G. Laycock (eds) *Beyond DNA – Integration and Harmonisation*. London: Home Office Science Policy Unit.

Bratby, L. (2003) 'DNA secrets', *Police Review*, June: 24.

Bridges, L. and McConville, M. (1994) 'Keeping faith with their own convictions', in M. McConville and L. Bridges (eds) *Criminal Justice in Crisis*. Aldershot: Edward Elgar.

Briody, M. (2002) 'The effects of DNA evidence on sexual offence cases in court', *Current Issues in Criminal Justice*, 14(2): 159–81.

Briody, M. (2004) 'The effects of DNA evidence on homicide cases in court', *Australian and New Zealand Journal of Criminology*, 37(2): 231–52.

Brownlee, I. (1998) 'New Labour – new penology? Punitive rhetoric and the limits of managerialism in criminal justice policy', *Journal of Law and Society*, 25(3): 313.

Bucke, Y. and Brown, D. (1997) 'In Police Custody: police powers and suspect's rights under the revised PACE codes of practice.' Home Office Research Study 174. London: Home Office.

Callan, K. (1997) *Kevin Callan's Story*. London: Little, Brown and Company.

Cameron, S. (2002) 'California's DNA databank joins the modern trend of expansion', *McGeorge Law Review*, 33: 219.

Campbell-Tiech, A. (2001) 'Woolf, the adversarial system and the concept of blame', *British Journal of Haemotology*, 113: 261.

Carson, D. (2003) 'Therapeutic jurisprudence and adversarial injustice: questioning limits', *Western Criminology Review*, 4(2): 124–33.

Casey, D. (1999) 'Genes, dreams and reality: the promises and risks of the new genetics', *Judicature*, 83(3): 105.

Castells, M. (2001) *The Rise of the Network Society*. Vol. I (2nd edn). Oxford: Blackwell.

Chan, J. (2001) 'The technological game: how information technology is transforming police practice', *Criminal Justice*, 1(2): 139–59.

Choo, A. (1993) *Abuse of Process and Judicial Stays of Criminal Proceedings*. Oxford: Clarendon Press.

Choongh, S. (1998) 'Policing the dross: a social disciplinary model of policing', *British Journal of Criminology*, 38: 623.

Christie, N. (1993) *Crime Control as Industry: Towards GULAGS Western Style?* London: Routledge.

Clarke, R. (1994) 'Dataveillance: delivering "1984"' in L. Green and R. Guinery (eds) *Framing Technology: Society, Choice and Change*. Sydney: Allen and Unwin.

Clarke, R. (2001) 'While you were sleeping … Surveillance technologies arrived', *Australia Quarterly*, 73: 1.

Cohen, S. (1979) 'The punitive city: notes on the dispersal of social control', *Contemporary Crises*, 3(4): 341–63.

Cole, S. (2001) *Suspect Identities*. Cambridge, MA: Harvard University Press.

Coleman, D. (2004) 'Beyond DNA in the UK – the police perspective', in M. Townsley and G. Laycock (eds) *Beyond DNA – Integration and Harmonisation*. London: Home Office Science Policy Unit.

Colvin, M. (1998) *Under Surveillance, Covert Policing and Human Rights*. London: Justice.

Comptroller and Auditor General (2003) *The FSS: Improving Service Delivery*. London: HMSO.

Cooper, S. (2003) 'Human rights and legal burdens of proof', *Web Journal of Current Legal Issues*, 3 (http://www.webjcli.ncl.ac.uk).

Corns, C. (1992) 'The science of justice and the justice in science', *Law in Context*, 10(2): 7.

Corte-Real, F. (2004) 'Forensic DNA database', *Forensic Science International*, 1465: 143–4.

Creaton, J. (1994) 'DNA profiling and the law: a critique of the Royal Commission's recommendations', in M. McConville and L. Bridges (eds) *Criminal Justice in Crisis*. Aldershot: Edward Elgar.

Cretney, A., Davies, G., Clarkson, C. and Shepherd, J., 'Crimininalising assault: the failure of the offence against society model', *British Journal of Criminology*, 34: 16.

Crown Prosecution Service Inspectorate (2000) *Thematic Review of the Disclosure of Undisclosed Material*. London: HMSO.

Damaska, M. (1986) *The Faces of Justice and State Authority*. New Haven, CT: Yale University Press.

DeCew, J. (1997) *In Pursuit of Privacy: Law, Ethics and the Rise of Technology*. Ithaca, NY: Cornell University Press.

Dennis, C. (2003) 'Error reports threaten to unravel databases of mitochondrial DNA', *Nature*, 20 February: 773.

Dennis, I. (1989) 'Reconstructing the law of criminal evidence', *Current Legal Problems*, 42: 21.

Dennis, I. (2000) 'Rethinking double jeopardy: justice and finality in the criminal process', *Criminal Law Review*, December: 933.

Dennis, I. (2002) *The Law of Evidence* (2nd edn) London: Sweet and Maxwell.

Devlin, Lord (1960) *The Criminal Prosecution in England*. London: Oxford University Press.

Dinerstein, D. (2001) 'Criminal law and DNA science', *American University Law Review*, 51: 401.

Dingwall, G. (2002) 'Statutory exceptions, burdens of proof and the Human Rights Act 1998', *Modern Law Review*, 65: 450.

Dixon. D. (1997) *Law in Policing: Legal Regulation and Police Practices*. Oxford: Clarendon Press.

Douglas, M. (1992) *Risk and Blame*. Oxford: Routledge.

Douzinas, C. and Warrington, C. (1994) 'The faces of justice: a jurisprudence of alterity', *Social and Legal Studies*, 3: 405.

Dreyfuss, R. and Nelkin, D. (1992) 'The jurisprudence of genetics' *Vanderbilt Law Review*, 45(2): 313–48.

Duff, P. (1986) *Trials and Punishments*. Cambridge: Cambridge University Press.

Durant, J. (2003) 'Once the men in white coats held the promise ...' in J. Franklin (ed.) *The Politics of Risk Society*. Cambridge: Polity Press.

Dworkin, R. (1977) *Taking Rights Seriously*. London: Duckworth.

Dworkin, R. (1981) 'Principle, policy and procedure', in C. Tapper (ed.), *Crime, Proof and Punishment: Essays in Memory of Sir Rupert Cross*. London: Butterworths.

Dworkin, R. (1986) *Law's Empire*. London: Fontana.

Easton, S. (1991) 'Bodily samples and the privilege against self-incrimination', *Criminal Law Review*, 18.

Eddy, J.P. (1955) 'The infallibility of fingerprints', *Criminal Law Review*, April: 34.

Edwards, K. (2005) 'Ten things about DNA contamination that lawyers should know', *Criminal Law Journal*, 29: 71–93.

Elias, R. (1990) 'Which victim movement? The politics of victim policy,' in A.J. Lurigio, W.G. Skogan and R.C. Davis (eds) *Victims of Crime: Problems, Policies and Programs*. London: Sage.

Elkins, L. (2003) 'Five foot two with eyes of blue: physical profiling and the prospect of a genetics-based criminal justice system', *Notre Dame Journal of Law, Ethics and Public Policy*, 17: 269–305.

Ericson, R. (1994) 'The division of expert knowledge in policing and security', *British Journal of Sociology*, 45(2): 149–75.

Ericson, R. and Haggerty, D. (1997) *Policing the Risk Society*. Oxford: Oxford University Press.

Ericson, R. and Shearing, C. (1986) 'The scientification of police work' in G. Bohme and N. Stehr, *The Knowledge Society*. Dordrecht: Kluwer Publishing.

Etzioni, A. (1999) *The Limits of Privacy*. New York: Basic Books.

Evans, J. (1973) 'Police powers and road traffic offences', *Modern Law Review*, 36: 260.

Evett, I.W. and Williams, R.L. (1995) *A Review of the Sixteen Point Fingerprint Standard In England and Wales*. London: Home Office.

Evison, M. (2002) 'DNA database could end problem of identity fraud', *Nature*, 420: 359.

Farrington, D. (1993) 'Unacceptable evidence Pt. I', *New Law Journal*, 4 June: 806.

Fay, S.J. (1998) 'Tough on crime, tough on civil liberties: some negative aspects of Britain's wholesale adoption of CCTV surveillance during the 1990s', *International Review of Law, Computers and Technology*, 12(2): 315–47.

Feeley, M. and Simon, J. (1992) 'The new penology: notes on the emerging strategy of corrections and its implications', *Criminology*, 30(4): 452.

Feeley, M. and Levine, K. (2001) 'Assaults on the adversarial process', *Punishment and Society*, 3(4): 537.

Feldman, D. (2002) *Civil Liberties and Human Rights in England and Wales*. Oxford: Oxford University Press.

Fereday, L. (2004) 'Transforming the use of forensics through the DNA Expansion Programme', in M. Townsley and G. Laycock (eds) *Beyond DNA – Integration and Harmonisation*. London: Home Office Science Policy Unit, 11–13.

Field, S. and Thomas, P. (1994) 'Justice and efficiency? The Royal Commission on criminal justice', *Journal of Law and Society*, 74.

Findlay, M. and Grix, J. (2003) 'Challenging forensic evidence? Observations on the use of DNA in certain criminal trials.' *Current Issues in Criminal Justice*, 14(3): 269–82.

Fisher, T. (2004) 'International charter DNA gateway', in M. Townsley and G. Laycock (eds) *Beyond DNA – Integration and Harmonisation*. London: Home Office Science Policy Unit, 31–2.

Fitzpatrick, T. (2002) 'Critical theory, information society and surveillance technologies', *Information, Communication and Society*, 5(3): 357–78.

Fitzpatrick, B. and Taylor, N. (2001) 'Human Rights and the discretionary exclusion of evidence', *Journal of Criminal Law*, 65(4): 349–59.

Forbes, T. (1985) *Surgeons at the Bailey: English Forensic Medicine to 1978*. London: Yale University Press.

FSS (2001) *Annual Report* (http://www.forensic.gov.uk/forensic_t/inside/about/docs/001-01.pdf).

FSS (2004) *NDNAD Fact Sheet* (http://www.forensic.gov.uk/forensic_t/inside/news/docs/NDNAD.doc).

Forster, S. (2002) 'Retention of DNA/fingerprint samples: a fair and proportionate response', *Justice of the Peace*, 166: 968–71.

Forster, S. (2001) 'The taking and subsequent retention of DNA/fingerprint samples: striking a difficult balance', *Justice of the Peace*, 165: 556–61.

Foucault, M. (1978) *Discipline and Punish: The Birth of the Prison*. New York: Vintage Books.

Fox, R. (2001) 'Someone to watch over us: back to the panopticon?', *Criminal Justice*, 1(3): 251–76.

Freckleton, I. (1992a) 'DNA profiling: forensic science under the microscope' in J. Vernon and B. Selinger (eds) *DNA and Criminal Justice*. Canberra: AIC.

Freckleton, I. (1992b) 'Problems posed by DNA evidence: of blood, babies and bathwater', *Alternative Law Journal*, 17(1): 10.

Freckleton, I. (1996) 'Wizards in the crucible: making the boffins accountable' in J.F. Nijboer and J.M. Reijntjes (eds) *Proceedings of the First World Conference on Criminal Investigation and Evidence*. The Hague: Kroninklijke Vermande.

Freckleton, I. (2000) *Monitoring Error in Forensic Science: Lessons to be Learned from the Reviews of the FBI Laboratory*. Second World Conference on New Trends in Criminal Investigation and Evidence, 255–66.

Freeman, M. and Reece, H. (1998) *Science in Court*. Dartmouth: Ashgate.

Freiberg, A. (2001) 'Guerilla's in our midst? Judicial response to governing the dangerous', in M. Brown and J. Pratt (eds) *Dangerous Offenders: Punishment and Social Order*. London: Routledge.

Gains, F. (1999) 'Implementing privatisation policies in Next Steps agencies, *Public Administration*, 4: 77.

Galligan, D. (1988a) 'More scepticism about scepticism', *Oxford Journal of Legal Studies*, 8: 249.

Galligan, D.J. (1988b) 'The right to silence reconsidered', *Current Legal Problems*, 69.

Galligan, D. (1996) *Due Process and Fair Procedures: A Study of Administrative Procedures*. Oxford: Clarendon Press.

Gamero, J.J, Romero, J.L., Peralta, J.L., Carvalho, M., Vide, M.C. and Corte-Real, F. (2003) 'Study of Spanish public awareness regarding DNA databases in forensic genetics', *International Congress Series*, 1239: 773.

Gans, J. (2001) 'Something to hide: DNA, surveillance and self-incrimination', *Current Issues in Criminal Justice*, 13(2): 168–84.

Gans, J. and Ubas, G. (2002) 'DNA identification in the criminal justice system', *Trends and Issues in Crime and Criminal Justice*, 226.

Garland, D. (2001) *The Culture of Control*. Oxford: Oxford University Press.

Garfinkel, S. (2000) *Database Nation: The Death of Privacy in the 21st Century*. Cambridge: O'Reilly.

Gavison, R. (1980) 'Privacy and the limits of law', *Yale Law Journal*, 89: 421.

Gianelli, P. (1998) 'The DNA story: an alternative view', *Journal of Criminal Law and Criminology*, 88(1): 380–422.

Giddens, A. (1987) *The Nation State and Violence*. Berkeley, CA: University of California Press.

Giddens, A. (1990) *The Consequences of Modernity*. Stanford, CA: Stanford University Press.

Giddens, A. (2003) 'Risk society: the context of British politics', in J. Franklin (ed) *The Politics of Risk Society*. Cambridge: Polity Press.

Gill, P., Ivanov, P., Kimpton, C., Piercy, R., Benson, N., Tully, G., Evett, I., Hagelberg, E. and Sullivan, K. (1994) 'Identification of the remains of the Romanov family by DNA analysis', *Nature Genetics*, 6: 130–5.

Gordon, D. (1986) 'The electronic panopticon: a case study of the development of the National Criminal Records System', *Politics and Society*, 15(4): 483.

Grabosky, P. (1998) 'Technology and crime control', *Trends and Issues in Crime and Criminal Justice*, (available at http://www.aic.gov.au).

Greer, S. (1994) 'Miscarriages of justice reconsidered', *Modern Law Review*, 57: 58.

Grevling, K. (1997) 'Fairness and the exclusion of evidence under section 78(1) of PACE' *Law Quarterly Review*, 113: 667.

Grove-White, R. (1997) 'Science, trust and social change', in *Science, Policy and Risk*. Papers from meeting held at the Royal Society on 18 March 1997. London: Royal Society.

Haggerty, K. and Ericson, R. (2000) 'The surveillant assemblage', *British Journal of Sociology*, 51(4): 605–22.

Hall, A. (1994) 'It couldn't happen today?', in M. McConville and L. Bridges (eds) *Criminal Justice in Crisis*. Aldershot: Edward Elgar.

Havard, J. (1967) 'The Road Safety Bill Part 1 – a medical view', *Criminal Law Review*, December: 151.

Henham, R. (1998) 'Human rights, due process and sentencing', *British Journal of Criminology*, 38: 592.

Her Majesty's Inspectorate of Constabulary (HMIC) (1999) *Police Integrity: Securing and Maintaining Public Confidence*. London: HMSO.

HMIC (2000) *Under The Microscope: An HMIC Thematic Inspection Report on Scientific and Technical Support*. London: Home Office.

HMIC (2002) *Under the Microscope – Refocused*. London: Home Office.

Herrera, R.J. and Tracey, M. (1992) 'DNA fingerprinting: basic techniques, problems and solutions', *Journal of Criminal Justice*, 20: 237–48.

Hibbert, M. (1999) 'DNA databanks: law enforcement's greatest surveillance Tool?', *Wake Forest Law Review*, 34(3): 767–825.

Hibbs, M. (1989) 'Applications of DNA fingerprinting – the truth will out', *New Law Journal*, 5 May: 619–21.

Higgs, E. (2001) 'The rise of the information state: the development of central state surveillance of the citizen in England, 1500–2000', *Journal of Historical Sociology*, 14(2): 175–97.

Hillyard, P. and Gordon, D. (1999) 'Arresting statistics: the drift to informal justice in England and Wales', *Journal of Law and Society*, 26: 502.

Hocking, B., McCallum, H., Smith, A. and Butler, C. (1997) 'DNA, human rights and the criminal justice system', *Australian Human Rights Journal*, 3(2): 72.

Home Office (2001) *Policing a New Century: A Blueprint for Reform* (CM 5326). London: HMSO.

Home Office (2002) *Justice for All* (CM 5563). London: HMSO.

Home Office (2003) *Access To Communications Data: Respecting Privacy and Protecting the Public from Crime*. Consultation paper. London: HMSO.

Home Office (2004a) *One Step Ahead: A 21st Century Strategy to Defeat Organised Crime* (CM 6167). London: HMSO.

Home Office (2004b) *Policing: Modernising Police Powers to Meet Community Needs*. Consultation paper. London: Home Office Communications Directorate.

Home Office (2004c) *Cutting Crime, Delivering Justice* (CM 6288). London: HMSO.

Home Office (2004d) *Crime in England and Wales 2003/04*. London: HMSO.

Home Office Science and Pathology Unit (2006) *DNA Expansion Programme 2000–2005: Reporting Achievement*. London: HMSO.

Home Office Science Policy Unit (2004) *Police Science and Technology Strategy 2004–09*. London: HMSO.

House of Lords Select Committee on Science and Technology (1992–3) *Forensic Science*. 5th Report [HL 24, 24-1].

House of Commons, Home Affairs Committee. *Criminal Records Bureau*. Second Report (2000–1) HC227.

Hudson, B. (1996) *Understanding Justice*. Buckingham: Open University Press.

Hudson, B. (2001) 'Punishment, rights and difference: defending justice in the risk society', in K. Stenson and R. Sullivan (eds) *Crime, Risk and Justice* Cullompton: Willan Publishing.

Hudson, B. (2003) *Justice in the Risk Society*, London: Sage.

Hudson, R. (1997) 'DNA profiling', *New Law Journal Practitioner*, January 127.

Hughes, G. (2000) 'Community safety in the age of risk society', in J. Ballantyne, K. Pease and V. McClaren (eds) *Secure Foundations: Key Issues in Crime Prevention, Crime Reduction and Community Safety*. London: IPPR.

Human Genetics Commission (2002) *Inside Information: Balancing Interests in the Use of Personal Genetic Data.* London: Human Genetics Commission.

Hunt, A. (1993) *Explorations in Law and Society: Toward a Constitutive Theory of Law.* London: Routledge.

Imwinkelreid, E. and Kaye, D. (2001) 'DNA typing: emerging or neglected issues', *Washington Law Review*, 76: 443.

Irish Law Reform Commission, *The Establishment of a DNA Database* (LRC CP 29-2004) Consultation Paper, March 2004, Dublin.

James, A. and Raine, J. (1998) *The New Politics of Criminal Justice.* London: Longman.

James, A., Taylor, N. and Walker, C. (2000) 'The reform of double jeopardy', Web *Journal of Current Legal Issues*, 5 (available at http://www.webjcli.ncl.ac.uk).

Jeffreys, A.J., Brookfield, J.F.Y. and Semeonff, R. (1985) 'Positive identification of an immigration test case using human DNA fingerprints', *Nature*, 317: 818.

Jobling, M. and Gill, P. (2004) 'Encoded evidence: DNA in forensic analysis', *Nature Review Genetics*, 5: 739–51.

Johnson, P., Martin, P. and Williams, R. (2003) 'Genetics and forensics: making the National DNA Database', *Science Studies*, 2(16): 25.

Jones, C. (1993) 'Auditing Criminal Justice', *British Journal of Criminology*, 33: 187.

Jones, R. (2001) 'Digital rule: punishment control and technology', *Punishment and Society*, 2(1): 5–22.

Jones, T. and Newburn, T. (2002) 'The transformation of policing? Understanding current trends in policing systems, *British Journal of Criminology*, 42: 129–46.

Jorg, N., Field, S. and Brants, C. (1995) 'Are inquisitorial and adversarial systems converging?' in P. Fennell, C. Harding, N. Jorg and B. Swart (eds) *Criminal Justice in Europe: A Comparative Study.* Oxford: Clarendon Press.

Kaiser, M., Kury, H. and Albrecht, H.J. (eds) (1991) *Victims and Criminal Justice: Victimological Research: Stocktaking and Prospects.* Freiburg-im-Breisgau: Max-Planck-Institut für Ausländisches und Internationales Strafrecht.

Kellie, D. (2001) 'Justice in the age of technology: DNA and the criminal trial', *Alternative Law Journal*, 26(4) 173–95.

Kelsen, H. (1996) 'What is justice?' in J. Westphal (ed.) *Justice.* Indianapolis: Hackett Publishing Co.

Kemshall, H. (2003) *Understanding Risk in Criminal Justice.* Open University Press.

Kimmelman, J. (2000) 'Risking ethical insolvency: a survey of trends in criminal DNA databanking', *Journal of Law, Medicine and Ethics*, 28: 209–21.

King, M. (1981) *The Framework of Criminal Justice*. London: Croom Helm.

Kingston, M. (2000) 'Case closed by "Dead Man Walking"?', *New Law Journal*, 150: 705.

Kloosterman, A. and Janssen, H. (1997) 'Forensic DNA testing and its legislation in the Netherlands', *Forensic Science International*, 88: 55–8.

Koehler, J., Chia, A. and Lindsey, S. (2001) 'The random match probability in DNA evidence: irrelevant and prejudicial?, *Jurimetrics*, 35: 201.

KPMG LLP (2003) *Review of Regime for Handling Suspicious Activity Reports: Report of Recommendations*. July (available at http://www.kporg.co.uk).

Krebs, J. and Kacelnik, A. (1997) 'Risk: a scientific view', in *Science, Policy and Risk*. Papers from meeting held at the Royal Society on 18 March 1997, London: The Royal Society.

Krucken, G. (2002) 'Panta rei – re-thinking science, re-thinking society', *Science as Culture*, 11(1): 125–30.

Lacey, N. (1994a) 'Government as manager, citizen as consumer: the case of the Criminal Justice Act 1991', *Modern Law Review*, 57: 534.

Lacey, N. (1994b) 'Missing the wood ... pragmatism versus theory in the Royal Commission', in M. McConville and L. Bridges, *Criminal Justice in Crisis*. Aldershot: Edward Elgar.

Law Commission (2001) *Double Jeopardy and Prosecution Appeals* (CM 5048). London: TSO.

Leary, D. and Pease, K. (2002) 'DNA and the active criminal population'. Briefing paper. London: Jill Dando Institute of Crime Science.

Lee, H.C and Tirnady, F. (2003) *Blood Evidence*. Cambridge: Perseus Publishing.

Leigh, L.H. (1985) *Police Powers in England and Wales* (2nd edn). London: Butterworths.

Levenson, H. (1980) 'The fingerprinting of children' *Criminal Law Review*, May: 698.

Lianos, M. and Douglas, M. (2000) 'Dangerization and the end of deviance', *British Journal of Criminology*, 40: 261–78.

Lidstone, K. and Palmer, C. (1996) *The Investigation of Crime: A Guide to Police Powers*. London: Butterworths.

Lingerfelt, J. (1997) 'The challenge of emerging technologies: balancing the needs of law enforcement against the duty to protect individual rights', *Proceedings of the International Society for Optical Engineering* (SPIE), 2939: 20.

Loveday, B. (1997) *Current Issues in Criminal Justice*. University of Portsmouth: Institute of Criminal Justice Studies.

Lucas, D.M. (1989) 'The ethical responsibilities of the forensic scientist: exploring the limits', *Journal of Forensic Science*, 34: 710–29.

Lund, S. (2003) 'Mistakes made submitting DNA samples', *Police Review*, 29 August: 6.

Lynch, M. (2003) 'God's signature: DNA profiling, the new gold standard in forensic science', *Endeavour*, 27(2): 93.

Lyon, D. (1991) 'Bentham's panopticon: from moral architecture to electronic surveillance', *Queens Quarterly*, 98(3): 606.

Lyon, D. (2001) *Surveillance Society: Monitoring Everyday Life.* Buckingham: Open University Press.

Lyon, D. (2002) 'Everyday surveillance, personal data and social classifications', *Journal of Information, Communication and Society*, 5(2): 242–57.

Lyon, D. (2003a) 'Introduction' in D. Lyon (ed) *Surveillance as Social Sorting: Privacy, Risk and Digital Discrimination.* London: Routledge.

Lyon, D. (2003b) 'Surveillance technology and surveillance society', in T. Misa, P. Brey and A. Feenberg. (eds) *Modernity and Technology.* London: MIT Press.

Maclean, M. (2001) 'How does an inquiry inquire? A brief note on the working methods of the Bristol Royal Infirmary inquiry', *Law and Society Review*, 28(4): 590.

MacPherson, Sir William (1999) *The Stephen Lawrence Inquiry – Report* (CM 4262-I). London: TSO.

Maguire, M. (2000) 'Policing by risks and targets: some dimensions and implications of intelligence-led crime control', *Policing and Society*, 9: 315.

Maguire, M and Norris, C. (1993) *The Conduct and Supervision of Criminal Investigations.* Royal Commission on Criminal Justice Research Study No. 5. London: HMSO.

Maguire-Shultz, M. (1992) 'Reasons for doubt: legal issues in the use of DNA identification techniques' in P. Billings (ed.) *DNA On Trial: Genetic Identification and Criminal Justice.* Cold Spring Harbor, NY: Cold Spring Harbor Laboratory Press.

Mahendra, B. (2002) 'Citizens, DNA and civil liberties', *New Law Journal*, 27 September: 1405.

Mahendra, B. (2004) 'Expertise Miscarried' *New Law Journal*, 27 February: 269.

Mangin, P. (1997) 'Ethical and legal issues raised by DNA fingerprinting in France', *Forensic Science International*, 88: 67–9.

Manning, P.K. (2001) 'Technology's ways: information technology, crime analysis and the rationalizing of policing', *Criminal Justice*, 1(1): 83–103.

Mansfield, T. and Rejman-Greene, M. (2003) *Feasibility Study on the Use of Biometrics in an Entitlement Scheme.* National Physical Laboratory (available at http://www.homeoffice.gov.uk/comrace/identitycards/publications.html).

Margulis, S. (2003) 'Privacy as a social issue and a behavioural concept', *Journal of Social Issues*, 59(2): 249.

Martin, P.D., Schmitter, H. and Schneider, P. (2001) 'A brief history of the formation of DNA databases within Europe', *Forensic Science International*, 119: 225–31.

Marx, G. (1988) *Undercover: Police Surveillance in America.* Berkeley: University of California Press.

Marx, G. (1998) 'An ethics for the new surveillance', *The Information Society*, 14(3): 1.

Marx, G. (2001) 'Technology and social control: the search for the elusive silver bullet', *International Encyclopedia of the Social and Behavioural Sciences*: 1.

Marx, G. (2002) 'What's new about the "new surveillance"?', *Surveillance and Society*, 1(1): 9–29,

Matthews, R. (2002) 'Crime and control in late modernity', *Theoretical Criminology*, 6(2): 222.

McBarnet, D. (1981) *Conviction, Law, the State, and the Construction of Justice*. London: MacMillan.

McCartney, C. (2006) 'Forensic DNA sampling and the England and Wales National DNA Database: a sceptical approach', *Critical Criminology*, 12(2): 157–78.

McCartney, C. (2006) 'The DNA expansion programme and criminal investigation', *British Journal of Criminology*, 46: 175–192.

McClaughlin, E., Muncie, J. and Hughes, G. (2001) 'The permanent revolution: New Labour, new public management and the modernization of criminal justice', *Criminal Justice*, 1(3): 301.

McConville, M., Hodgson, J., Bridges, L. and Pavlovic, A. (1994) *Standing Accused*. Oxford: Oxford University Press.

McConville, M., Sanders, A. and Leng, R. (1997) 'Descriptive or critical sociology: the choice is yours', *British Journal of Criminology*, 37: 347.

McConville, M., Sanders, A. and Leng, R. (1991) *The Case for the Prosecution*. London: Routledge.

McMullan, J. (1998) 'Social surveillance and the rise of the "police machine"' *Theoretical Criminology*, 2(1): 93–117.

Michael, M. (2002) 'Between science and the public', *Science as Culture*, 11(1): 115.

Mnookin, J. (2001) 'Fingerprint evidence in an age of DNA profiling', *Brooklyn Law Review*, 67(1): 13–70.

Mooki, O. (1997) 'DNA typing as a forensic tool: applications and implications for civil liberties', *African Journal on Human Rights*, 13(4): 565.

Morris, N. (1994) 'Dangerousness and incapacitation' in A. Duff and D. Garland (eds) *A Reader on Punishment*. Oxford: Oxford University Press.

Motulsky, A. (1989) 'Societal problems of forensic use of DNA technology' in J. Ballantyne, G. Sensabaugh and J. Wirkowski, *DNA Technology and Forensic Science*, Banbury Report No. 32. Cold Spring Harbor, NY: Cold Spring Harbor Laboratory Press, 3–9.

National Institute of Justice (NIJ) (1998) 'The Unrealised Potential of DNA Testing', *NIJ Research in Action*, June. Washington, DC: US Department of Justice.

NIJ (2000) *National Commission on the Future of Forensic DNA Evidence (Report)*. Washington, DC: US Department of Justice.

NIJ (2004) *Education and Training in Forensic Science*. Special Report, June. Washington, DC: US Department of Justice (http://www.aafs.org/pdf/ NIJReport.pdf).

National Research Council of the US National Academy of Sciences (2002) 'A national ID scheme? No easy answers', *Card Technology Today*, 14(6): 11.

Nelkin, D. (1989) 'The social meaning of biological tests' in J. Ballantyne, G. Sensabaugh and J. Wirkowski, *DNA Technology and Forensic Science*, Banbury Report No. 32. Cold Spring Harbor, NY: Cold Spring Harbor Laboratory Press.

Nelkin, D. and Lindee, M.S. (1995) *The DNA Mystique: The Gene as a Cultural Icon*. New York: W.H. Freeman.

Neville-Rolfe, L. (1997) 'Good regulation: weighing up the risks', in *Science, Policy and Risk*. Papers from meeting held at the Royal Society on 18 March 1997. London: The Royal Society.

Newburn, T. (2001) 'The commodification of policing: security networks in the late-modern city', *Urban Studies*, 38(5–6): 842.

Nguyen, A. (2002) 'Here's looking at you, kid: has face-recognition technology completely outflanked the Fourth Amendment?', *Virginia Journal of Law and Technology* Part VI, 7(2): B36.

Nobles, R. and Schiff. D. (1994) 'Optimism writ large: a critique of the Royal Commission on Criminal Justice', in M. McConville and L. Bridges, *Criminal Justice in Crisis*, Aldershot: Edward Elgar.

Nobles, R. and Schiff, D. (1996) 'Miscarriages of justice: a systems approach', *Modern Law Review*, 59: 299.

Nobles, R. and Schiff, D. (2000) *Understanding Miscarriage of Justice*. New York: Oxford University Press.

Nobles, R. and Schiff, D. (2001a) 'Due process and Dirty Harry dilemmas: criminal appeals and the Human Rights Act', *Modern Law Review*, 64(6): 912.

Nobles, R. and Schiff, D. (2001b) 'The Criminal Cases Review Commission: reporting success?', *Modern Law Review*, 64(2): 280.

Norris, C. and Armstrong, G. (1999) *The Maximum Surveillance Society: The Rise of CCTV*. Oxford: Berg.

Nowotny, H., Scott, P. and Gibbons, M. (2002) *Re-Thinking Science: Knowledge and the Public in an Age of Uncertainty*. Cambridge: Polity.

Nuffield Council on Bioethics (2002) *Genetics and Human Behaviour: The Ethical Context*. London: Nuffield Council.

O'Donnell, G. (1997) 'Legal situation of forensic DNA analysis in the Republic of Ireland', *Forensic Science International*, 88: 63–5.

van Oorschot, R. and Jones, M. (1997) 'DNA fingerprints from fingerprints', *Nature*, 387: 767.

O'Riordan, T., Marris, C. and Langford, I. (1997) 'Images of science underlying public perceptions of risk', in *Science, Policy and Risk*. Papers from meeting held at the Royal Society on 18 March 1997. London: Royal Society.

Paciocco, D. (2001) 'Evidence about guilt: balancing the rights of the individual and society in matters of truth and proof', *Canadian Bar Review*, 80: 442.

Packer, H. (1968) *The Limits of the Criminal Sanction*. Stanford, CA: Stanford University Press.

Paterson, J. (2003) 'Trans-science, trans-law and proceduralization', *Social and Legal Studies*, 12(4): 531.

Patton, J. (2000) 'Protecting privacy in public? Surveillance technologies and the value of public places', *Ethics and Information Technology*, 2: 181–87.

Peck, R. (2001) 'The adversarial system: a qualified search for the truth', *Canadian Bar Review*, 80: 450–80.

Peissl, W. (2003) 'Surveillance and security: a dodgy relationship', *Journal of Contingencies and Crisis Management*, 11(1): 22.

Penacino, G., Sala, A. and Corach, D. (2003) 'Are DNA tests infallible?', *International Congress Series*, 1239: 873–77.

Peterson, R.S. (2000) 'DNA databases: when fear goes too far', *American Criminal Law Review*, 37(3): 1219–38.

Pizzamiglio, M., Mameli, A., Denari, D. and Garofono, L. (2004) 'Forensic identification of a murderer by typing volunteers of a small village in Northern Italy', *International Congress Series*, 1261: 440–2.

Pizzi, W.T. (1999) *Trials Without Truth*. New York: New York University Press.

Plaxton, M. (2002) 'Are wrongful convictions wrong? The reasonable doubt standard and the role of innocence in criminal procedure', *Criminal Law Quarterly*, 46: 407–46.

van der Ploeg, I. (1999) 'The illegal body: Eurodac and the politics of biometric identification', *Ethics and Information Technology*, 5(4): 295–302.

Popper, K. (1992) *In Search of a Better World: Lectures and Essays from Thirty Years*. London: Routledge.

Pratt, J. (1995) 'Dangerouness, risk and technologies of power', *ANZ Journal of Criminology*, 28(2): 3–31.

Pugilese, J. (1999) 'Identity in question: a grammatology of DNA and forensic genetics', *International Journal for the Semiotics of Law*, 12: 419–44.

Purcell, N., Thomas-Winfree, L. and Mays, G. (1994) 'DNA evidence and criminal trials: an exploratory survey of factors associated with the use of "genetic fingerprinting" in felony prosecutions', *Journal of Criminal Justice*, 22(2): 145–57.

Raab, C.D. (2003) 'Joined-up surveillance: the challenge to privacy' in K. Ball and F. Webster (eds) *The Intensification of Surveillance*. London: Pluto Press.

Raine, J. (2001) 'Modernizing courts or courting modernization?', *Criminal Justice*, 1(1): 105.

Raine, J. and Willson, M. (1993) *Managing Criminal Justice*. London: Harvester Wheatsheaf.

Raine, J. and Willson, M. (1997) 'Beyond managerialism in criminal justice', *Howard Journal*, 36: 80.

Ramsay, M. (1987) *The Effectiveness of the FSS*. Home Office Research Study No. 92. London: HMSO.

Randerson, J. and Coghlan, A. (2003) 'Forensic evidence stands accused', *New Scientist*, 181: 6.

Rawls, J. (1973) *A Theory of Justice*. London: Oxford University Press.

Redmayne, M. (1995) 'Doubts and burdens: DNA evidence, probability and the courts', *Criminal Law Review*, June: 464.

Redmayne, M. (1998) 'The DNA Database: civil liberty and evidentiary issues', *Criminal Law Review*, July: 437.

Redmayne, M. (2001) *Expert Evidence and Criminal Justice*. Oxford: Oxford University Press.

Redmayne, M. (2002a) 'Appeals to reason', *Modern Law Review*, 65(1): 25.

Redmayne, M. (2002b) 'Review of "Suspect Identities"' by S. Cole, *Modern Law Review*, 65(1): 147.

Reiman, J. (1995) 'Driving to the panopticon: a philosophical exploration of the risks to privacy posed by the highway technology of the future', *Computer and High Technology Law Journal*, 11: 27–44.

Roberts, H. (1998) 'Interpretation of DNA evidence in courts of law: a survey of the issues', *Australian Journal of Forensic Sciences*, 30: 29–40.

Roberts, P. (1994a) 'Forensic science after Runciman', *Criminal Law Review*, November: 780.

Roberts, P. (1994b) 'Science in the criminal process', *Oxford Journal of Legal Studies*, 14: 496–506.

Roberts, P. (2002) 'Double jeopardy law reform: A criminal justice commentary', *Modern Law Review*, 65(3): 393–424.

Roberts, P. and Willmore, C. (1993) *The Role of Forensic Science Evidence in Criminal Proceedings*. (Runciman Report, CM 2263). Research Study No. 11. London: Royal Commission on Criminal Justice.

Roberts. S. (2003) '"Unsafe" convictions: defining and compensating for miscarriages of justice', *Modern Law Review*, 66: 445.

Robertson, B. and Vignaux, G.A. (1995) *Interpreting Evidence: Evaluating Forensic Evidence in the Courtroom*. Chichester: John Wiley & Sons.

Rock, P. (1991) 'The victim in court project at the Crown Court at Wood Green', *The Howard Journal*, 30(4): 251.

Rose, N. (2000a) 'Government and control', *British Journal of Criminology*, 40: 321–39.

Rose, N. (2000b) 'The biology of culpability: pathological identity and crime control in a biological culture', *Theoretical Criminology*, 4(1): 5.

Royal Commission on Criminal Justice (Runciman Commission) (1993) Report (CM 2263). London: HMSO.

Royal Commission on Criminal Procedure (The Phillips Commission) (1981) Report (CM 8092). London: HMSO.

Rule, J. (1974) *Private Lives and Public Surveillance*. New York: Schocken Books.

Rutherford, A. (1993) *Criminal Justice and the Pursuit of Decency*. Oxford: Oxford University Press.

Rutherford, A. (2001) *Criminal Justice Choices*. London: IPPR.

Saks, M. (2003) 'The legal and scientific evaluation of forensic science (especially fingerprint expert testimony)', *Seton Hall Law Review*, 33: 1166–87.

Samuels, A. (1994) 'Forensic science and miscarriages of justice', *Medicine, Science and the Law*, 34(2): 148–54.

Sanders, A. (1993) 'What principles underlie criminal justice policy in the 1990s?', *Oxford Journal of Legal Studies*, 18: 533.

Sanders, A. (1994) 'Thinking about criminal justice', in M. McConville and L. Bridges, *Criminal Justice in Crisis*. Aldershot: Edward Elgar.

Sanders, A. and Young, R. (2000) *Criminal Justice* (2nd edn). London: Butterworths.

Sanders, J. (1998) 'Scientifically complex cases, trial by jury, and the erosion of the adversarial processes', *DePaul Law Review*, 48: 355–88.

Saul, B. (2001) 'Genetic policing: forensic DNA testing in New South Wales', *Current Issues in Criminal Justice*, 13(1): 74–109.

Schiermeier, Q. (1988) 'German sex killings prompt decision to create DNA database', *Nature*, 392: 749.

Schklar, J. and Diamond, S. (1999) 'Juror reactions to DNA evidence: errors and expectancies', *Law & Human Behaviour*, 23(2): 159–84.

Schneider, P. and Martin, P. (2001) 'Criminal DNA databases: the european situation', *Forensic Science International*, 119: 232–38.

Scutt, J. (1990) 'Beware of new technologies', *Legal Services Bulletin*, 15: 9–12.

Shearing, C. and Stenning, P. (1985) 'From the panopticon to Disney World: the development of discipline', in A. Doob and E. Greenspan (eds) *Perspectives in Criminal Law*. Ontario: Canada Law Book Inc.

Simon, J. (1988) 'The ideological effects of actuarial practice', *Law and Society Review*, 22: 772.

Smith, A. (2004) 'Programme delivery and the impact on combating crime', in M. Townsley and G. Laycock (eds) *Beyond DNA – Integration and Harmonisation*. London: Home Office Science Policy Unit.

Smith, K. and Imwinkelried, E. (2001) 'DNA data from everyone would combat crime and racism'. 26 July. *USA Today*, p. 15A.

Stalder, F. (2002) 'Privacy is not the antidote to surveillance', *Surveillance and Society*, 11(1): 121.

Starmer, K. and Woolf, M. (1999) 'The right to silence' in C.P. Walker and K. Starmer (eds) *Miscarriages of Justice*. London: Blackstone.

Starmer, K., Strange, M. and Whitaker, Q. (2001) *Criminal Justice, Police Powers and Human Rights*. London: Blackstone.

Steer, D. (1980) *Uncovering Crime: The Police Role*. Royal Commission on Criminal Procedure Research Study No.7. London: HMSO.

Stenning, P. (2004) 'Two modes of governance – is there a viable third way?'. Opening Plenary at *British Society of Criminology Annual Conference*, Portsmouth, 6 July.

Stevens, A. (2001) 'Arresting crime: expanding the scope of DNA databases in America', *Texas Law Review*, 931.

Steventon, B. (1993) *'The Ability to Challenge DNA Evidence'*, Royal Commission on Criminal Justice (Runciman) Report, Research Study No. 9. London: HMSO.

Steventon, B. (1995) 'Creating a DNA database', *Journal of Criminal Law*, 59(4): 411–19.

Steyn, Lord (2000) 'The new legal landscape', *European Human Rights Law Review*, 6: 549.

Stoney, D.A. (1991) 'What made us ever think we could individualise using statistics?', *Journal Forensic Science*, 31(2): 197.

Strehler, M., Kratzer, A. and Bar, W. (2003) 'Swiss federal DNA profile information system', *International Congress Series*, 1239: 777–81.

Sullivan, J. (2002) 'Human rights and criminal justice' by Emmerson, B. (Book review). *Criminal Law Review*, February: 156.

Summers, R. (1999) 'Formal legal truth and substantive truth in judicial fact-finding – their justified divergence in some particular cases', *Law and Philosophy*, 18: 497–511.

Sykes, C. (2000) *The End of Privacy*. New York: St Martin's Press.

Taylor, N. (2002) 'State surveillance and the right to privacy', *Surveillance and Society*, 1(1): 66–85.

Taylor, N. (2003) 'Policing, privacy, and proportionality', *European Human Rights Law Review: Special Issue on Privacy*, 2: 85–102.

Telling, D. (1978) 'Storm in a teacup – and the fingerprinting issue', *Justice of the Peace*, 15 April: 219.

Thomas, T. (2001) 'The national collection of criminal records: a question of data quality', *Criminal Law Review*, November: 886.

Thompson, W. (1997) 'A sociological perspective on the science of forensic DNA testing', *UC Davis Law Review*, 30: 1113–36.

Thornton, J. (1983) 'Uses and abuses of forensic science', *American Bar Association Journal*, 69: 288.

Tilley, N. and Ford, A. (1996) *Forensic Science and Crime Investigation*. Home Office Police Research Series Paper No. 73. London: Home Office.

Tonry, M. (2001) 'Unthought thoughts: the influence of changing sensibilities on penal policies', *Punishment and Society*, 3(1): 167–82.

Townsley, M. and Laycock, G. (eds) *Beyond DNA – Integration and Harmonisation*. London: Home Office Science Policy Unit.

Tracy, P. and Morgan, V. (2000) 'Big Brother and his science kit: DNA databases for 21st century crime control?', *Journal of Criminal Law and Criminology*, 90(2): 635–90.

Travers, M. (1997) *The Reality of Law*. Aldershot: Ashgate.

Twining, W.L. (1990) *Rethinking Evidence*. Oxford: Basil Blackwell.

Urs, L. (1999) '*Commonwealth* v. *Joseph O'Dell*: truth and justice or confuse the courts? The DNA controversy', *New England Journal on Criminal and Civil Confinement*, 25(1): 311–31.

US General Accounting Office (2002) *Technology Assessment: Using Biometrics for Border Security* (GAO-03-174), November (http://www.gao.gov).

Valier, C. (2001) 'Criminal detection and the weight of the past: critical notes on Foucault, subjectivity and preventative control', *Theoretical Criminology*, 5(4): 425–43.

Walker, C. (1999) 'Miscarriage of justice in principle and practice', in C. Walker and K. Starmer, *Miscarriages of Justice*, London: Blackstone.

Walker, C. and Cram, I. (1990) 'DNA profiling and police powers', *Criminal Law Review*, July: 478.

Walker, C. and Starmer, K. (1999) *Miscarriages of Justice*. London: Blackstone.

Walker, C. and Stockdale, R. (1999) 'Forensic evidence' in C. Walker and K. Starmer, *Miscarriages of Justice*. London: Blackstone.

Walsh, S. (2004) 'Legal perceptions of forensic DNA profiling Part I: a review of the legal literature', *Forensic Science International*, 155(1): 51.

Wambaugh, J. (1989) *The Blooding*. New York: Bantam.

Warburton, D. (2004) 'A critical review of English law in respect of criminalising blameworthy behaviour in HIV+ individuals', *Journal of Criminal Law*, 68(55): 32.

Warner, J. (1978) 'Fingerprinting, some aspects of law and practice', *New Law Journal*, 29 June: 639.

Wells, C. (1994) 'The Royal Commission on criminal justice: a room without a view', in M. McConville and L. Bridges, *Criminal Justice in Crisis*, Aldershot: Edward Elgar.

Westin, A. (1967) *Privacy and Freedom*. New York: Bodley Head.

Whitaker, R. (1999) *The End of Privacy*. New York: The New Press.

White, P. (1999) *From Crime Scene to Court*. Cambridge: The Royal Society of Chemistry.

Wikeley, N. (2000) 'Burying Bell: managing the judicialisation of social security tribunals', *Modern Law Review*, 63(4): 475.

Wilcock, P. and Bennathan, J. (2004) 'New disclosure rules for 2005', *New Law Journal*, 154(7133): 918.

Williams, K.S. and Johnstone, C. (2000) 'The politics of the selective gaze: CCTV and the policing of public space', *Crime, Law and Social Change*, 34(2): 183–210.

Williams, R., Johnson, P. and Martin, P. (2004) *Genetic Information and Crime Investigation*. Wellcome Trust (http://www.dur.ac.uk/p.j.johnson).

Wise, J. (2004 'Under the microscope: legal challenges to fingerprints and DNA as methods of forensic identification', *International Review of Law, Computers and Technology*, 18(3): 425–34.

Wrench, P. (1995) 'National DNA Database: Home Office Circular No. 16/95', *Justice of the Peace and Local Government Law*, 159: 270–73.

Yao, Y., Bravi, C.M. and Bandelt, H.J. (2004) 'A call for MtDNA data quality control in forensic science', *Forensic Science International*, 141: 1–6.

Young, J. (1999) *The Exclusive Society*. London: Sage.

Zander. M. (1996) *Cases and Materials on the English Legal System*. London: Butterworths.

Zander, M. and Henderson, P. (1993) 'The Crown Court study', Research Study No. 19. *Royal Commission on Criminal Justice*, London: HMSO.

Zedner, L. (2000) 'The pursuit of security', in T. Hope and R. Sparks (eds) *Crime, Risk and Insecurity*. London: Routledge.

Zuckerman, A. (1992) 'Miscarriage of justice – a root treatment', *Criminal Law Review*, May: 323–45.

Index

—